The Motor Neurone Disease Association is extremely grateful to Peter Gilbert for the donation of his royalties from the sale of this book. The proceeds will be used by the Association to support its work.

The Motor Neurone Disease (MND) Association is the only national organisation in England, Wales and Northern Ireland dedicated to the support of people with MND and those who care for them. The Association funds and promotes research to understand what causes MND, how to diagnose it and, most importantly, how to effectively treat it so that it no longer devastates lives.

MND is a rapidly progressive and fatal disease. It can affect any adult at any time and attacks the motor neurones that send messages from the brain to the muscles, leaving people unable to walk, talk or feed themselves. The cause of the disease is unknown and there is no known cure. Around 5,000 people in the UK have MND at any one time, with half of people with the disease dying within 14 months of diagnosis. It kills five people every day in the UK.

For more information please visit www.mndassociation.org

motor neurone disease
association

St Richard's Hospice offers our sincerest thanks to Peter Gilbert for his generous donation of royalties from the sale of this book.

St Richard's provides free specialist palliative care for patients living with cancer and other life-threatening illnesses, and supports their families. Each year the hospice team supports over 2,300 patients and family members in Worcestershire. Patients are cared for in the day hospice, the 16-bed inpatient unit, or in their own homes by a specialist professional team, as well as many trained volunteers.

In the inpatient unit, specialist staff are on hand 24 hours a day to manage patients' symptoms and where, if they so choose, patients may spend the last few days of life in comfort and dignity. St Richard's is grateful for all donations towards the £6.7m required each year to continue their work.

St. Richard's
Hospice
CARING FOR LIFE
Reg. Charity No. 515668

For more information please visit www.strichards.org.uk

Contents

Acknowledgements

I am deeply grateful to all 27 authors for their excellent contributions to the chapters in this book and for being so helpful in working with me as the editor. A warm thank you also to those who kindly gave their personal stories, especially the late Christopher Jones for the moving description of his final journey.

A special thank you to Professor John Swinton for his foreword; John has been something of a mentor to me since his seminal work on spirituality as a 'forgotten dimension' in his 2001 publication. Thanks also go to Dr Neil Deuchar, whose vision embraces the spiritual dimension of care, for his generous epilogue.

Kerry Boettcher, Catherine Ansell-Jones and their colleagues at Pavilion have been most supportive, and my thanks to them also for asking me to edit this new work following the publication of *Spirituality and Mental Health* in 2011.

It has been important to ground this publication in child care and adult care, and in values-based practice, and so it has been most helpful to have strong partnerships with Professor Bill Fulford at the University of Warwick, Rev Andrew Goodhead, St Christopher's Hospice, Rev Paul Nash, Birmingham Children's Hospital, Mark Jackson, St Richard's Hospice, members of the National Spirituality and Mental Health Forum and the British Association for the Study of Spirituality, and professors Paul Kingston, Bernard Moss and colleagues at Staffordshire University. My warm thanks to them.

Editing a book is a complex task and I'm indebted to my wife, Sue, for her support and patience, and proofreading skills.

My thanks also to members of Black Pear Joggers of Worcester for their comradeship.

Half way through editing this book I discovered that, ironically, I had developed the life-limiting condition motor neurone disease. I would like to thank my GP and the care teams at Worcestershire Community Trust, QE Hospital, Birmingham, the University Hospital North Staffordshire and St Richard's Hospice for their excellent care and support at this challenging time. I hope that readers will find this text helpful in their work in compassionate and dignified end of life care.

Peter Gilbert

March 2013

Contributors

Ben Bano has been a social worker for 38 years and was director of older people's services in East Kent Mental Health Partnership Trust from 2002 to 2005. In 2007 he founded Telos Training and he has delivered a range of training workshops across a range of subjects in mental health care and dementia across the statutory and non-statutory sector. Ben's interests include social inclusion and the spiritual and holistic dimension to mental health and dementia care. Ben is particularly interested in spiritual accompaniment at the end of life in dementia care. He is a member of the chaplaincy team at two local hospitals.

Ben produced the DVD 'It's still ME, Lord' for Caritas Social Action Network, as well as an online learning resource. Recent publications include the article 'Positive approaches to the fourth age' with Professor Susan Benbow. He has also co-authored a chapter on spirituality and dementia for *Spirituality and Mental Health* (2011). His book for people whose lives have been touched by dementia will be published by McCrimmons Publishers in February 2013.

Ben has delivered workshops on spirituality and dementia across England and Wales to more than 500 people, including faith communities and those involved in pastoral work. Following feedback that a more concerted approach is needed to providing a welcome for people with mental health problems and dementia in faith communities, in April 2012 he launched a new, not-for-profit community interest company – www.welcomemeasiam.org.uk.

Alison Bennett qualified as a physiotherapist at the Queen Elizabeth School of Physiotherapy, Birmingham, in 1981 and has worked at Acorns children's hospice in Worcester since its opening in February 2005. It was a few years after her arrival at Acorns that Alison requested permission to bring together a group of staff and volunteers who were interested in further developing the spiritual care on offer to the children, young people and their families at Acorns. At present, she still continues to chair the spiritual care interest group there and now co-leads the in-house training on spiritual care for staff.

Alison has been involved in children's ministry, church leadership and pastoral care. After the death of her youngest daughter she began training as a counsellor and has recently completed her foundation degree in counselling at Worcester University. In addition to working as a physiotherapist at the children's hospice, Alison also works as a voluntary counsellor at an adult hospice and a counselling centre.

Jen Close is a retired social worker and a volunteer carer's group facilitator at St Richard's Hospice, Worcester. Originally a generic social worker, Jen later specialised in children and family work and then, during the latter 10 years of her 30-year social work career, became a lecturer and course leader for the BA degree validated by the University of Worcester. She feels the most important aspects of this work was the involvement of service users and carers in the training of new social workers and helping students to understand an holistic approach to their profession, with recognition of the creativity necessary to work with vulnerable, damaged and disadvantaged people.

Jan Cooper is currently a principal teaching fellow, deputy director of masters programmes and continuing professional development and co-course director of the MA in health sciences (palliative care) at Warwick Medical School, University of Warwick. Jan has over 20 years' experience of lecturing to a diverse range of students at both undergraduate and post-graduate level and her previous educational posts include Macmillan tutor at St Richard's Hospice, Worcester, and Macmillan senior lecturer at Coventry University. Prior to working in education, Jan's clinical professional background was as a registered general nurse working primarily in palliative care, both in an inpatient hospice and as a community-based clinical nurse specialist. It was through her experience of providing emotional support to patients, families and staff that she developed her interest in the spiritual dimensions of end of life care. Her research into aspects of caring for dying patients which cause anxiety to first year student nurses identified some important issues related to spirituality for professional care-givers, which she integrates into her teaching on this topic. Jan is particularly interested in values-based practice and applies this in her teaching of palliative care, particularly in relation to interprofessional teamwork.

Neil Deuchar was born and bred in South London and studied medicine at Guy's Hospital, graduating in 1984. After periods of time as a GP, journalist and freelance communications consultant in London, Neil undertook specialist training in psychiatry in the Midlands, becoming a consultant psychiatrist in 1997 and medical director of Birmingham's Mental Health Trust in 2003. He then went on to become medical director at West Midlands Strategic Health Authority and currently provides specialist advice on commissioning to the Royal College of Psychiatrists.

KWM (Bill) Fulford is a member of the philosophy faculty and fellow of St Cross College, University of Oxford. He is emeritus professor of philosophy and mental health at the University of Warwick Medical School. His previous posts include honorary consultant psychiatrist, University of Oxford, co-director, Institute for Philosophy, Diversity and Mental Health, University of Central Lancashire; and special adviser for values-based practice in the Department of Health, London. Bill has published very widely and influentially on the philosophy of psychiatry, including co-authoring *The Oxford Textbook of Philosophy and Psychiatry*. He is lead editor for the Oxford book series International Perspectives in Philosophy and Psychiatry, and founder and co-editor with John Sadler of the international journal *Philosophy, Psychiatry & Psychology*, which he founded in 1993. His most recent book is the launch volume for a new book series from Cambridge University Press on values-based practice – *Essential Values-based Practice: Clinical stories linking science with people* (2012).

Cristina Gangemi holds a master's degree in pastoral theology with a special focus on disability theology. She is a co-director, with Professor John Swinton, of The Kairos Forum, which focuses on enabling communities to be places of belonging for people with a disability. Cristina is a national adviser to the Catholic Bishops' Conference and many other national Christian organisations. She has had extensive experience in special education, issues concerning bereavement for people with intellectual disabilities, specialised ministry formation and parent support. She was the co-ordinator of disability access and provision during the recent visit of Pope Benedict XVI and was a national press spokesperson for the Christian community during the 2012 Olympic Games.

Andrew Goodhead joined St Christopher's Hospice as chaplain in January 2005. He was ordained as a Methodist minister in 1993. In his role at St Christopher's, Andrew is concerned to ensure that all end of life care professionals have the skills and confidence to offer spiritual assessment and ongoing support to all patients and their families. He has a particular interest in the concept of spiritual pain as a way of understanding spiritual need.

Andrew has published his PhD thesis with Wipf & Stock (USA) under the title 'A Crown and a Cross: The origins, development and decline of the Methodist class meeting in eighteenth century England'. In November 2010, *Mortality* published the results of Andrew's research into memorialisation: 'A Textual Analysis of Memorials Written by Bereaved Individuals and Families in a Hospice Context'. In July 2011, *The European Journal of Palliative Care* published 'Physiotherapy in Palliative Care: The interface between function and meaning', which is a philosophical examination of how physical ability affects the way in which meaning can be made. Andrew is a co-facilitator for the Spirituality Education Group on the European Association of Palliative Care and a member of the Spirituality Taskforce of the EAPC.

Peter Gilbert is emeritus professor of social work and spirituality at Staffordshire University, and honorary research associate with the University of Sussex. Peter was the National Institute for Mental Health in England (NIMHE) project lead on spirituality from its inception in 2001 to 2008, and then with the National Spirituality and Mental Health Forum; he is now a trustee of the forum. From 2008–2010 he was chair of the National Development Team for Inclusion and visiting professor at the Birmingham and Solihull Foundation NHS Trust, leading their spirituality research programme. He is now an adviser to Birmingham Children's Hospital on spiritual care. A former director of social services for Worcestershire, Peter had 13 years of direct practice as a social worker. Between 2003 and 2006 he was NIMHE/SCIE fellow in social care with Professor Nick Gould; and he has been on advisory groups for a number of government departments. He is on the executive of the British Association for the Study of Spirituality (BASS).

Peter was principal social worker in one of the old institutions; and has worked with, and managed services for, all user groups. He was involved in leading partnership working in both Staffordshire as director of operations, and Worcestershire as director of social services, initiating service user, carer and advocacy groups. Having experienced an episode of depression in 2000/2001, Peter is very committed to an holistic and person-centred approach, and the integration of personal experience.

Signed up to ensuring the integration of theory with practice, Peter is an associate member of ADASS, and wrote the national ADSS/NIMHE guidance on the integration of mental health services. In 2008 he published: *Guidelines on Spirituality for Staff in Acute Care Services*. He is national facilitator for the National Social Care Strategic Network.

Peter published *Leadership: Being effective and remaining human* in 2005, and he and his co-editors published *Spirituality, Values and Mental Health: Jewels for the journey* (2007). He is a co-editor of *The International Journal of Leadership in Public Services* and co-executive editor of the *Journal for the Study of Spirituality*. His latest publications are *Social Work and Mental Health: The value of everything* (with colleagues) in 2010; leadership and supervision development packs, with Dr Neil Thompson; and a chapter on his own experience of mental distress in Basset and Stickley's *Voices of Experience: Narratives of survival and mental health (2010)*. The Pavilion handbook *Spirituality and Mental Health* was published in 2011.

Peter was awarded an honorary doctorate by Staffordshire University in May 2013, in recognition of his work on spirituality.

Hifsa Haroon-Iqbal is equality and diversity officer at Staffordshire University. Hifsa worked for a number of years in the faculty of health where she completed her master's in philosophy entitled 'Implementing Peer Review in Nursing: An assessment of its reliability and validity', before taking up her current role. She is a well-known figure across Staffordshire and Muslim communities and uses her position to raise awareness and promote equality and diversity across many community groups and professional forums. A member of the Staffordshire Police Authority, Hifsa also chairs both the Stafford and District Friends of Faith Network and North Staffordshire Forum of Faiths. She is chair of Chase Against Crimes of Hate, a multi-agency partnership for reporting hate crime and vice chair of the Standing Advisory Council for RE in Staffordshire. Hifsa's publications include 'Caring for elderly muslims' in *Oxford Handbook of Nursing Older People* (2010) and the co-authored 'The Absent Minority: Access and use of palliative cancer services by black and minority ethnic groups in Leicester' in *Nursing Research in Cancer Care* (1995). In 2011 Hifsa was appointed a deputy lieutenant of Staffordshire and received an MBE in her Majesty's New Year's Honours List for services to community cohesion.

Richard Hayward has been a senior lecturer at Anglia Ruskin University in Cambridge since August 2009. He is course leader for the MSc in health care management and has extensive experience of leadership and management in health and social care. A critical care nurse by background, specialising in the intensive care of liver disease, Richard moved into hospital management as a site practitioner responsible for care delivery out of hours. He then moved into nurse education and subsequently leadership and management developments initially at Canterbury Christchurch University, Kent. As well as being an experienced academic, Richard is currently undertaking a doctorate exploring the role of spirituality in leadership practice. A key part of this research concerns whether spirituality can be measured, and he is currently undergoing training as a facilitator for assessing spiritual intelligence. As well as his academic roles, Richard has also been the Secretary of the British Computer Society Health Group, a role that allowed him to explore leadership across the care domains and the impact that technology can have on outcomes.

Arthur Hawes is Archdeacon emeritus of Lincoln and Canon of the Cathedral, following his retirement in 2008. He was founder chairman of the North Worcestershire Association Mind, following post-graduate work at Birmingham University. From 1976–1992 he was a chaplain at acute psychiatric units in Norwich and from 1986–1995 he was a mental health act commissioner.

From 1995–2010, Arthur was chair of the Church of England's Mental Health Advisory Group. As a member of the Mission and Public affairs Council, he presented two debates in the General Synod of the Church of England on mental health issues. In 1996 he was made Jubilee Patron of Mind and in 1999 he was a member of Mind's National Reference Group. From 1998–2006 he was non-executive director of the mental health trust in Lincolnshire and he was a member of the NHS Confederation Mental Health Policy Committee from 2003–2007. From 2003–2005 he was chairman of the East Midlands NIMHE Regional Development Centre and member of the criminal justice mental health research group at Lincoln University from 2007–2010. From 2006–2008 he was appointed Mental Health Act advisor to the Lincolnshire Partnership Trust and in 2008 he was appointed as training consultant to the Trust. He became a member of the National Spirituality and Mental Health Forum in 2003 and was a co-chairman of the Forum from 2009–2011; he is now its secretary.

Arthur is a visiting fellow of Staffordshire University and one of two vice chairs of the British Association for the Study of Spirituality. He has published many occasional papers, edited The Anne French Memorial

Lectures and contributed to a number of publications on theology, spirituality and mental health.

Jo Hockley is a consultant nurse for the care home project and research team at St Christopher's Hospice, London. Jo returned to work at the hospice having originally worked as a ward sister at St Christopher's from 1978–1982. Jo has always had an interest in disseminating hospice principles in order to empower generalist staff. She set up two hospital-based palliative care teams – one at St Bartholomew's Hospital, London, and the other at the Western General Hospital, Edinburgh. In 1999, Jo turned her attention to nursing care homes. Her PhD 'Developing High Quality End of Life Care in Nursing Homes: An action research study' highlighted the importance of developing appropriate end of life care 'systems' and 'valuing staff'. She now leads The Care Homes Project and research team using her thesis as a framework. She leads the practice development with the implementation of various end of life care tools and a number of research projects in nursing care homes across five local PCTs. She is published widely.

Mark Jackson was appointed chief executive of St Richard's Hospice, Worcester, in February 2006, following a full career in the army, serving in the Worcestershire and Sherwood Foresters Regiment, which he commanded on operations. His military service varied from the streets of Northern Ireland to United Nations peacekeeping, serving in a multinational NATO headquarters in the Netherlands to a key liaison post in the USA, guarding Rudolph Hess in West Berlin to the Ministry of Defence in Whitehall, interspersed with much travel around the world. Originally an army scholar, he is a graduate of the Royal Military Academy Sandhurst, the Army Staff College, the Open University and most recently was one of the first ever cohort of students to obtain the Masters in Hospice Leadership from Lancaster University. Having learnt, practised and taught leadership throughout his military career, he has found that many of those skills are equally applicable, if all too often sadly missing, in civilian life and healthcare. He is a fellow of the University of Worcester.

Anna Janssen completed her PhD in psychology in 2004. While completing her PhD she volunteered at Otago Community Hospice in Dunedin, New Zealand. This reflected Anna's interest in understanding the experience of incurable illness for patients, loved ones and health professionals. Her hospice experience inspired her to explore what care means to people who are dying, their experiences of care and how patients can inform advances in clinical education. Anna conducted this research in collaboration with Rod MacLeod, professor in palliative care. Anna continued her end of life care research as a senior tutor at Otago Medical School and later as a lecturer in clinical education at University of Auckland. In 2008 she moved to the UK and joined the Institute of Psychiatry, King's College London, where she ran a longitudinal project exploring the experiences of treatment choices for people with motor neurone disease from the perspectives of patients, carers and health professionals. In collaboration with Professor MacLeod, Anna has published a number of papers on her research in end of life care and presented at a number of international conferences. In 2010, Anna began her doctorate in clinical psychology. Anna is currently completing her final year. Her doctoral thesis explores couples' experiences of Parkinson's disease and she works as a clinical psychologist in training in the cancer ward at Guy's Hospital, London.

Rev Christopher Mark Jones was born 1954. He attended St. Peter's College, Oxford, where he gained a BA in 1975 and an MA 1979. He attended Ridley Hall theological college in Cambridge in 1977. He later attended Selwyn College, Cambridge, where he gained an MPhil in 1980. He was made a deacon in 1980 and became an ordained priest in 1981. He was curate of Putney St. Margaret (Southwark) from 1980–1983, curate of Ham St. Andrew from 1983–1986 and chaplain of HM Remand Centre Ham and St John's College, Durham, from 1987–1993. He was a tutor at Cranmer Hall, Durham, from 1987–1993 and a chaplain and fellow of St Peter's College, Oxford, from 1993–2004. He was Home Affairs Policy Adviser for Archbishop's Council Board for Social Responsibility from 2004. Christopher was also vice chairman of the Forum for Spirituality and Mental Health, a member of the Mental Health Alliance and, as an adviser in the Archbishop's Council for Mission and Home Affairs. He regularly provided briefs for bishops and others in the House of Lords on mental health, criminal justice and drug issues. He was co-editor of a collection of essays entitled *The Future of Criminal Justice: Resttlement, chaplaincy and community* (2002) with Dr. Peter Sedgwick. Christopher died in May 2012.

David Albert Jones is director of the Anscombe Bioethics Centre in Oxford. He is a research fellow at Blackfriars Hall, Oxford University, and a visiting professor at St Mary's University College, Twickenham. David read natural sciences and philosophy at Cambridge (1984–1987), and theology at Oxford (1992–2000). He was appointed director of the Linacre Centre for Healthcare Ethics in 2001 and subsequently moved to St Mary's University College, Twickenham, where he helped establish an MA in bioethics and co-founded the Centre for Bioethics and Emerging Technologies. David's doctorate was published as *Approaching the End: A theological exploration of death and dying* (Oxford University Press, 2007). His previous book, *The Soul of the Embryo: An enquiry into the status of the human embryo in the Christian tradition* (Continuum, 2004), was short-listed for the Michael Ramsey Prize. David is vice chair of the Ministry of Defence Research Ethics Committee, is examiner for the Society of Apothecaries Diploma in the Ethics and Philosophy of Healthcare, is on the National Reference Group of the Liverpool Care Pathway for the Dying Patient, and was on a working party of the General Medical Council, which helped draft its 2010 guidance on *Treatment and Care Towards the End of Life*. He has contributed to a number of documents of the Catholic Bishops' Conference of England and Wales, most recently *A Practical Guide to The Spiritual Care of the Dying Person* (CTS, 2010). He was appointed director of the Anscombe Bioethics Centre in 2010.

Peter Kevern was a Franciscan friar for 13 years in the UK and Papua New Guinea before changing course for the life of an academic theologian. After completing his doctorate in 1999, he worked for 10 years training Christian ministers before his field of research (the theological dimensions of dementia) drew him to Staffordshire University. There he has continued to teach – specialising in spirituality in healthcare contexts – as well as researching and publishing on this and a range of related topics through the university's Centre for Ageing and Mental Health. Peter's main research activity is currently focused on the potential role of religious communities as sources of support in dementia care; as providing symbolism and a language to negotiate critical life events such as acute illness; and as a counterbalance to the excessively-individualised discourse on spirituality.

Michaela Morris is a specialist occupational therapist in end of life care. She was trained at the University of Brighton and completed a qualitative masters research project exploring the understanding of spirituality of occupational therapists working in hospice care. She has worked in two hospices as a specialist OT – St. Catherine's Hospice, Crawley, and St Michael's Hospice, Harrogate, and also did an elective placement at Woking and Sam Beare Hospice. She has taught at masters level on the role of the OT in palliative care. Prior to being an OT, she was a teacher of religious studies, and a school chaplain, and also worked for the development agency CAFOD, as schools and youth officer and as a spiritual director. She enjoys walking, baking, singing, a variety of creative activities, including weaving and painting, and also plays the zither. Michaela is a Quaker.

Bernard Moss is emeritus professor of social work education and spirituality at Staffordshire University, where he developed the involvement of service users and carers in communication skills training for social work students. His innovative approach won two national awards for service user involvement. His teaching areas include bereavement and loss, and social work values. As a university teacher his excellence has been recognised by the Higher Education Academy, who awarded him first of all a national teaching fellowship and then a senior fellowship.

Bernard's interest in spirituality was grounded in his own faith-community leadership, but while at Staffordshire University he led the way in demonstrating not only the importance of this topic to social work education and practice, but also how it could be creatively included and explored in the social work curriculum. For this developmental work he was awarded his PhD in 2011.

Bernard has published widely on the theme of spirituality, most notably by co-authoring, with Professor Margaret Holloway, *Spirituality and Social Work* (2010). Currently, he is developing his interest in using labyrinth walks to explore mindfulness, creativity and spirituality, and leads workshops in a wide variety of contexts using his portable labyrinth.

Wilfred McSherry is professor in dignity of care for older people, Staffordshire University and Shrewsbury and Telford Hospital NHS Trust, Stafford and Shropshire. He is also part-time professor at Haraldsplass Deaconess University College, Bergen, Norway. Wilf was appointed professor in dignity of care for older people in August 2008. He has had a career in nursing working as a registered nurse within acute hospital care. His interest in the spiritual dimension developed alongside a realisation that this aspect of care was neglected and forgotten by some healthcare professionals. He has published several books and many articles addressing different aspects of the spiritual dimension such as educational issues and spiritual assessment. He completed his doctoral studies at Leeds Metropolitan University in May 2005 researching 'The Meaning of Spirituality and Spiritual Care: An investigation of healthcare professionals, patients and public's perceptions'.

Prior to being appointed to his current role, Wilf was a senior lecturer in nursing at the University of Hull, where he was also instrumental in creating the Centre for Spirituality Studies, of which he was the director. Wilf is currently one of the vice presidents of the British Association for The

Study of Spirituality. In 2012 Wilf was made a fellow of the Royal College of Nursing for his unique contribution to nursing in the areas of spirituality and dignity.

Rev Paul Nash has worked at Birmingham Children's Hospital since 2002 and has been the senior chaplain since 2004, managing a multi-faith team with a specialism in bereavement care. The team offers over 1,000 episodes of end of life and bereavement care a year. Paul oversaw the publication of the first faith-specific book, which supported Muslim parents who had lost a child, and is managing a project developing virtual rooms to teach faith-specific end of life care to medical and allied health professionals. He is director of Red Balloon Resources, which publishes in the fields of religious and spiritual care in relation to paediatric daily, palliative, end of life and bereavement care. He is the author of *Supporting Dying Children and their Families: A handbook for Christian ministry* (2011), the forthcoming *Exploring Spiritual Care with Sick Children* (JKP, December 2014) and has also published in the fields of chaplaincy and ministry. Paul is the co-founder and co-convenor of the Paediatric Chaplaincy Network for Great Britain and Ireland (www.paediatric-chaplaincy-network.org). Paul also works as a lecturer for Midlands Centre for Youth Ministry and has developed undergraduate and postgraduate modules in paediatric chaplaincy in partnership with Staffordshire University. He secured a Health Foundation Building Networks Award, which included developing a best practice manual for chaplains working with children and young people in healthcare settings. Paul initiated and is convenor of the Grove Youth Series of booklets (www.grovebooks.co.uk).

Brian Nyatanga has been a senior lecturer at the University of Worcester for the last five years. Brian has been working in education and training for over 15 years and in palliative and end of life care for over 23 years. In addition to his teaching role at the University of Worcester, Brian has other activities including being an accredited advanced communication skills facilitator, external examiner to Dundee University, editorial board member with an international journal, and visiting lecturer overseas. Before moving to Worcester, Brian worked at Birmingham City University, where he was jointly employed by Macmillan Cancer Support and instrumental in setting up the Macmillan National Institute of Education (MNIE). His main role with MNIE was to train and develop Macmillan clinical specialists across the West Midlands. Brian is passionate about palliative care, psychological aspects of death and dying, and how different people 'deal' with their own impending death. Because of the multicultural society we now live in, Brian is interested in cultural competence at the end of life. He is well published in nursing press on different topics including death anxiety, assisted dying and cultural competence, which he believes is a noble idea but questions its effectiveness in a changing multicultural society.

Brian's interest in death and dying led to his doctoral research study on death anxiety and burnout among palliative care nurses. He researched the impact of witnessing patients' death and dying experiences on nurses' perception of their own mortality. He also established a relationship between death anxiety and burnout, while highlighting the main aspects/elements of palliative caring seen as responsible for the development of both death anxiety and burnout. From this research study, it became clear that caring can be a double-edged sword.

When not working, Brian can be seen on a squash court playing or coaching beginners. At weekends he is the 'man in black' as he referees adult football matches across the region. A family man with two children, he enjoys holidays abroad. All these social activities tend to help towards a dignified death.

Irene Renzenbrink is a social worker and art therapist currently undertaking doctoral studies in expressive arts therapy at the European Graduate School in Switzerland. Irene is an Australian pioneer in the field of palliative care and grief and bereavement support. She has had extensive experience in hospitals, hospices, aged care settings and funeral services. A member of the prestigious International Work Group on Death, Dying and Bereavement, founded by Dame Cicely Saunders and Elisabeth Kübler-Ross in 1974, Irene gives lectures and conducts workshops throughout the world with a particular interest in training volunteers in hospice care using an intermodal expressive arts approach.

Irene has published several journal articles and book chapters on loss, grief, narrative and story, and her interest in spirituality is directly related to her work with dying and bereaved people who struggle to find meaning in their experiences of brokenness and fragmentation. Irene believes that the expressive arts play a vital role in healing, transformation and resilience in such circumstances. She is an associate editor of the American journal *Illness, Crisis and Loss* and was the editor of *Caregiver Stress and Staff Support in Illness, Dying and Bereavement* (2011). She has also published a collection of her own photographs, stories and inspirational quotations called *Fluttering on Fences: Stories of loss and change* (2010).

John Swinton is professor in practical theology and pastoral care in the School of Divinity, Religious Studies and Philosophy at the University of Aberdeen. He has a background in mental health nursing and healthcare chaplaincy and has researched and published extensively within the areas of practical theology, mental health, spirituality and human well-being and the theology of disability. He is the director of Aberdeen University's Centre for Spirituality, Health and Disability, and Co-Director of the University's Kairos Forum. His publications include: *Dementia: Living in the Memories of God* (2012); *Raging With Compassion: Pastoral responses to the problem of evil* (2007) and *Spirituality in Mental Health Care: Rediscovering a 'forgotten' dimension* (2001).

Dr Neil Thompson is an independent writer, educator and adviser, with 35 years' experience in the people professions. He has held full or honorary professorships at four UK universities and has over 150 publications to his name, including 33 books, many of which are bestsellers. His writings are renowned for their clarity and their success in blending theory and practice and balancing head and heart. He has also been involved in developing a range of multimedia learning resources, training materials and e-learning programmes (see www.avenuelearningcentre.co.uk for details of the full range). He has qualifications in social work; management (MBA); training and development; and mediation and alternative dispute resolution; as well as a first-class honours degree, a doctorate (PhD) and a higher doctorate (DLitt).

In 2011, Neil was presented with a Lifetime Achievement Award by BASW Cymru. He is a fellow of The Chartered Institute of Personnel and Development, the Higher Education Academy and the Royal Society of Arts as well as a life fellow of the Institute of Welsh Affairs; and a board member of the International Work Group on Death, Dying and Bereavement. He has been a speaker at conferences and seminars in the UK, Ireland, Spain, Italy, Norway, the Netherlands, the Czech Republic, Greece, Turkey, India, Hong Kong, Canada, the United States and Australia. He is programme manager for the Avenue Professional Development Programme, a subscription-based online learning community for the people professions (http://tinyurl.co./apdpneilthompson). His personal website is www.neilthompson.info.

Nicola Wilderspin is a consultant in palliative medicine and medical director of St Richard's Hospice in Worcester. Her early training was in hospital medicine, with particular interests in respiratory medicine and infectious diseases. These led to research for her post-graduate thesis exploring the diagnosis and impacts of tuberculosis and HIV in Malawi, Central Africa. Nicola's own spirituality is rooted in the Christian faith following life-changing experiences as a medical student in Oxford. In Malawi she was able to experience the impact of stigma, disease and loss of hope on people affected by the AIDS epidemic. Clinical experience of people living and dying with HIV in this resource-poor setting enabled her to gain insights into the power of a palliative approach to suffering, in particular the impact of simply being alongside the sick and dying. As a result of her research she worked with Malawian colleagues to establish dedicated clinical and grassroots community services for people living with HIV/AIDS, eventually joining the operational research team of the Malawi National TB Control Programme. This led to collaborative work with the World Health Organization, the founding of Malawi's first centre of excellence for HIV care, and a final decision to train as a specialist in palliative medicine.

Alison Wooding is a permanent volunteer in the spiritual care team at a hospice in Hertfordshire. Professionally, she is a coach and development consultant using a 'whole person, whole system' practice in Systemic Constellations. Formerly a marketer specialised in branding, communications and media, Alison's interest in supporting change programmes, creativity and innovation led her to deepen her understanding of transformation processes and capacity to support human potential; from 2004 studying counselling and constellations, while mentoring young people at risk and small business owners.

A longstanding practitioner of meditation and member of a mystical community, Alison works one-to-one and with groups on consciousness and soul development. Her work in the field of death and dying is a natural, meaningful step forwards on the journey to greater awareness of our divine nature and existence beyond physical life. To this end, she is studying the transfer of consciousness at the moment of death and discovering practices that lessen fear and raise consciousness in dying. Drawing on her phenomenological and spiritual training, she is co-creating and sharing ideas with other professionals in the field. Alison is passionately committed to creating spaces and resources for integrated care practices, to help generate more understanding about the transformational nature of death as a process for growth and healing.

Foreword

What might it mean to die well?

John Swinton

What might it mean to die well? The suggestion that we should die well and that death is a positive and meaningful event is somewhat counter-cultural. For many of us today, death is the last enemy; the one thing that threatens to end all of our hopes, dreams and expectations; the dark shadow that reminds us that our self-constructed life goals have limits. But why are we so nervous of death and all of those things in life which seem to remind us of death? One way that we could begin to answer such a question is by observing the apparently obvious fact that death has meaning. By that I don't simply mean that given the correct circumstances the process of dying can be meaningful and indeed fruitful. That is, of course, the case and the writers in this book show this very ably. But our cultural angst about death has deeper roots. We don't just die; we are taught how to die. We are taught how to die by our family, our friends, the media, our culture. All of these things come together to provide us with the parameters that we use to gauge, shape and experience the nature of our lives and our deaths.

A brief and inadequate historical perspective might help to draw the relevance of this point out. In medieval times, Western Europe had a theological view of the world (ie. it had an understanding of the world defined by some concept of God), insofar as belief in God was the prevalent worldview and the way in which both life and death were explained and narrated. Within such a religious worldview there were certain narratives, assumptions and perspectives which gave death a quite specific meaning: life was a place of preparation for the afterlife. That being so, death was perceived as a movement towards or into something that was far superior to the life that we have now. While death was often feared and avoided, ultimately it was deeply meaningful and there was much that was positive in that meaning.

Roll forward several hundred years to that period in the late 17th century that we have come to call the Enlightenment. Here we encounter a cultural shift from a theological understanding of life and death towards a profoundly anthropological view of the world and all that is in it (ie. a movement from God to human beings). With the rise of science and the ascendancy of intellect and reason, combined with a variety of religious wars that had made religion an apparently dangerous cultural perspective, the old stories of religion began to be replaced by the new stories of reason and science. 'Obviously' such intangible things as religion and spirituality were no longer necessary. So, we cast off the old stories of God and an afterlife and bought into some new stories. Now we believed that human beings via science, reason and intellect could progress to a state of perfection wherein all illness would be overcome, peaceful relationships would reign through the sensible use of reason, and all rational people would share in common universal truths that made the idea of battling over the particularity of such things as religion look foolish. In this context, death was perceived simply as the end of life. A good life is enjoying the fruits of human knowledge and dying peacefully, perhaps with a little help from medicine. However, with the rise of triumphalistic medicine, death started to be perceived as a failure of medicine, medicine being that discipline which was now charged with providing a strange form of secular salvation wherein such things as health, peace and healing were removed from a spiritual context into the technological, scientific purview of professional medicine. The idea of death as a failure still permeates some of our thinking today.

But then came the 20th century. More people have killed other people in that century than at any other period in history. Cancer and AIDS have not been cured. The Holocaust has taught us that human beings are not as benign as some may have thought. Science, intellect and reason have proven to be double-edged swords. Poverty has not been overcome and the world is just as violent and unjust as it was when we believed in God! All of which takes us to the present day. For many of us today, there are no stories of the afterlife or of God. The new stories of science and reason leading us to utopia have floundered on the rock of realism. So there is no story to look back on and no story to look forward to other than death as the end. We seem trapped in an eternal present. So what do we do? We seek after health, youth and vitality. If all that we have is what we have just now, then our bodies matter. The parameters of our bodies become the locus of our salvation. Why else would Westerners be quite so obsessed with fitness, youth and intellectual prowess if it wasn't for the fact that we have no stories to tell about death other than our own? Why else would we fear anything that reminds us of death – ageing, illness, disability, madness – if it wasn't for the fact that they remind us that we are moving towards death and that movement is profoundly negative. Death is no longer a movement towards something positive and beautiful. It is now a dreaded end to everything that we desire; the end of all that we think we are. Death has a meaning in contemporary culture but very often that meaning is profoundly negative. But it doesn't have to be that way.

This book offers a challenge to contemporary meanings of death. It doesn't seek to return us to the Middle Ages or demand that we adopt a religious world view! While remaining open to the importance of religion for some people, the book opens up a spiritual and religious window into the meanings of death and the practices of dying that serves as a fascinating and important counter to the death denying culture that we find all around us. Spirituality reminds us that people are meaning seekers, that death is one place where meaning is sought and found, and that that meaning needn't be negative. This book offers a fascinating interdisciplinary approach to death and dying which holds together a critical balance of theoretical and practical perspectives and offers some powerful insights into what it might mean to die well in a culture that is deeply uncertain about dying and what it means to die. If we listen carefully to the voices contained within this book, perhaps we can begin to reclaim a positive meaning for our lives and for our deaths. If the book helps us to do that, then it will have done its job.

Part 1:

Modern society, spirituality and the challenge of life and death

Chapter 1:

Rage against the dying of the light, or a new light shining?

Peter Gilbert

'As a child, be well-behaved; when a young man, self-controlled; in middle age, be just; as an old man, a good counsellor; at the end of your life, free from sorrow.' (Delphic maxim inscribed in a Greek temple, circa 300BCE)

'This individual soul is unbreakable and insoluble, and can be neither burned nor dried. The soul is everlasting; present everywhere, unchangeable, innumerable and eternally the same … Knowing this, you should not grieve for the body.' (Bhagavaga Gita, 2.23–2.25)

'The only thing you know for sure is the present tense, and that nowness becomes so vivid that, in a perverse sort of way, I'm almost serene, you know – I can celebrate life.' (Playwright Dennis Potter, interview with Melvyn Bragg, 1994, shortly before his death from cancer)

Commentators often speak about Western society being 'necrophobic' – having a fear of death. In an individualistic and consumerist society when the value of a human person seems to be measured by what they can purchase, and not who they are and how they relate to others (see Sennett, 2002; Taylor, 2007; Sandel, 2012), we are living in what sociologist, Zygmunt Bauman terms *'liquid life'* (Bauman, 2005). We are like small boats, bobbing on an increasingly turbulent ocean, with no anchor and no port. As Bauman puts it: *'The road to identity is a running battle in an interminable struggle between the desire for freedom and a need for security, haunted by fear of loneliness and a dread of incapacitation'* (Bauman, 2005, p.30).

Recent research by the Mental Health Foundation/Griffen (2010) indicates rising levels of loneliness. Part of this lack of anchor and safe harbour is that we have tended to un-moor life from death. This is commented upon both by those who have no religious faith and those from faith traditions.

Jenni Russell, speaking about the death of her father, talks about not understanding *'how the loss would feel. Perhaps it is something one can never grasp until it has happened, because the imagination refuses to go there. But it is also that death has been so removed from our daily experience that it has become almost embarrassingly private'* (Russell, 2009).

A modern guide to the practice of the Sikh faith quotes the teachings of the Gurus as saying: *'The people in this world fear death and (try to) hide themselves from it lest death's courier should catch and take them away'* (Bakhshi, 2008).

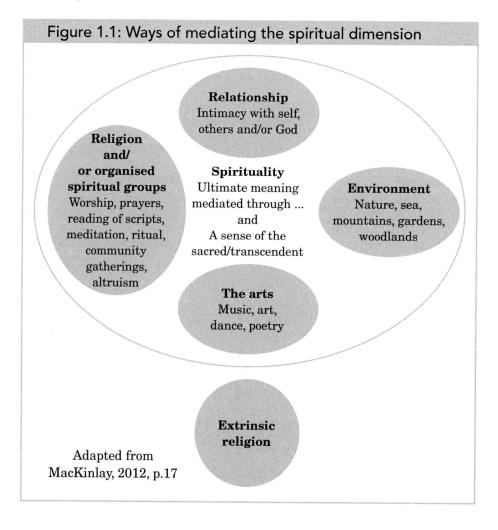

Figure 1.1: Ways of mediating the spiritual dimension

Relationship
Intimacy with self, others and/or God

Religion and/ or organised spiritual groups
Worship, prayers, reading of scripts, meditation, ritual, community gatherings, altruism

Spirituality
Ultimate meaning mediated through ... and
A sense of the sacred/transcendent

Environment
Nature, sea, mountains, gardens, woodlands

The arts
Music, art, dance, poetry

Extrinsic religion

Adapted from MacKinlay, 2012, p.17

Humans as a species have always stretched themselves physically, mentally and spiritually. At the time of writing, Neil Armstrong, the NASA astronaut has just died, aged 82. Famously, Armstrong, when he stepped on to the moon on 20th July 1969, didn't celebrate himself as an individual but human kind in general: *'One small step for man, one giant leap for mankind'*.

Homo sapiens have always grappled with the meanings of life. As Professor Brian Cox in his 2011 BBC2 series *The Wonders of the Universe* put it, standing on a mountain top: 'Where do we come from? What are we doing here?' Professor Cox doesn't ask the other oft posed question: 'Where do we go to when we die?' He sees humans coming from the material of the universe: *'Man (sic) thou art dust, and to dust thou shalt return'* (Genesis, 3:19).

Chief Rabbi, Dr Jonathan Sacks, speaks of humans as 'meaning-seeking creatures', and goes on to say: *'The search for God is the search for meaning … And that is no small thing, for we are meaning-seeking animals. It is what makes us unique. To be human is to ask the question, "why?"'* (Sacks, 2011, p25. See also MacKinlay, 2001; Gilbert, 2011a).

For many people, of course, meaning-seeking does not involve a faith in God and/or an organised religious faith. But it will almost certainly involve a search inwards to the spiritual dimension and outwards to a sense of something which transcends the material world. As 'why-shaped' beings, we are in a continual journey of discovery. Often, human beings have found answers which have promoted progress in health and a range of other disciplines. But even then the answers usually lead on to other questions. As biologist Rupert Sheldrake put it recently: *'The biggest scientific delusion of all is that science already knows the answers'* (Sheldrake, 2012, p6).

Reflection points

What do you see as life's meaning for you?

Anthropologists and archaeologists are clear that at least as far back as the Neolithic Age (4–2,500 BCE) (see **Table 1.1: Civilisation through the ages**), Homo sapiens had elaborate ceremonies, often set in temples such at Gobekli Tebe in southern Turkey, and Skara Brae in the Orkney Islands in Scotland, marking in ritual the transition between this world and the world on 'the other side'. There seems to have been a major contrast between the beliefs and practice of Homo sapiens and Neanderthals, and there is some speculation that this was connected to a development of the brain which propelled Homo sapiens to pre-eminence amongst the human species (see Williams, 2010). As civilisations developed across the world, and at the time that Stonehenge was being erected around 2,500 BC, 80% of the population of Mesopotamia (modern day Turkey, Iran and Iraq) lived in cities with populations of between 15,000–30,000 people. Religion played a vital part in both binding society together in a coherent unit and providing a narrative explanation for and a pathway through the vicissitudes of life (Miles, 2010).

Table 1.1: Civilisation through the ages	
Circa 36,000 BCE (Upper Palaeolithic)	Humans operate as hunter-gatherers.
25,000 BCE (Ice Age)	
8–4,000 BCE (Mesolithic)	The beginnings of settlements.
4–2,500 BCE (Neolithic, new Stone Age)	An agricultural system with domesticated animals. Stone tombs are evident. Increasingly sophisticated artefacts, with religious significance, are evident in the Middle East.
2,500–500 BCE (Bronze Age)	Monuments associated with rituals and death are the most plentiful and enduring relics of this age. In the Bronze Age there is a move to single burial sites, rather than communal burial – pointing to a developing hierarchical social structure.
900–200 BCE (Axial Age)	Ritual remains important, but in demonstrating the importance of compassion and an ethical way of life.

Searching for the meaning of life has had to be in the context of a human being's life being limited, though religious faith may speak of an afterlife or reincarnation. Margaret Holloway (2007) speaks of a change in the 'liminal' or threshold period, from a time when this was seen primarily as the period following death, and is now more often seen in the lead up to an individual's demise, as this is often elongated by dementia, and by improved technological medicine. For the individual and their carers this always produces a very personal challenge, and sometimes we seem to be adding years to life, not life to years.

Box 1.1: Speaking personally

My mother died of breast cancer in the Royal Marsden Hospital in the summer of 1979. Visiting her, I was always struck by the way that all staff combined considerable professional competence with personal and soulful care. The doctors, both senior and junior, were good at communicating with my mother and with us as relatives. They took special care of my father, who was considerably older than my mother and quite frail at the time, and who had to travel from Jersey to visit his wife. Nursing staff always seemed to have time to spend a few minutes making sure that my mother was comfortable, that pain relief was administered properly and appropriately, and that she had water to hand. I often noticed nurses spending a few moments just talking with their patients on a busy ward and that those brief conversations clearly cheered the patients' spirits. My only caveat was that the doctors, quite understandably, were focused on a cure if possible, and perhaps active treatment went on a bit too long. My mother was a devout Roman Catholic, and when her friend, Father Dominic Gaisford, a Benedictine monk, visited her, and gave her the sacraments of the faith, he said to me quietly: 'Your mum has led a very good life. She is fighting hard because she's worried about your Dad, Peter, but she is dying, as we all must do, and perhaps it is time for us to help her to let go?'

I had the privilege of being with my mother when she 'crossed the river'. Following her death, the director of nursing met with my father, who was devastated, and my sister and myself. Thirty-two years later this meeting remains vivid in my mind as an iconic way of treating bereaved relatives. It was clear to me that the care and capability of the nursing staff on the ward was a mirror for the spirit of leadership provided by this director of nursing.

Sadly, recent audits and scandals in the NHS and social care services have demonstrated that the standards of care that my mother and family experienced is not now as we would wish it. In fact, in a conversation with a doctor returning from working at a refuge centre in Bangladesh, following the dire flooding there, she told me that the basic care within the refugee camp was better than it was in the hospital she was now practising in (personal conversation in 2011). The recent National Audit of Dementia (Young *et al*, 2011) found that just 32% of hospital staff in England and Wales said they had received sufficient training in dementia care, while very few demonstrated person-centred care. The audit found that while the majority met basic safety requirements, care was often delivered in an impersonal way, with staff not greeting or talking to patients, explaining what they were doing or responding to patients' requests for assistance.

Striving for immortality

An agnostic such as the playwright Dennis Potter, quoted at the beginning of this chapter, with a positive view on life in the prospect of death, and a person of faith who sees death as part of the journey, can face death with a measure of equanimity. Neolithic graves and burial sites show a value on placing goods in the tomb which would, it was believed, assist the person in the afterlife. The ancient Greeks depicted Hades as a subterranean sphere, where shades (or souls) passed endless days. For the citizens of ancient Egypt the afterlife was an improved version of their day-to-day existence, living a life of bounty on the banks of the Nile. The Vikings appear to have seen Valhalla as a place mainly for the most successful warriors – so only for an elite.

The three Abrahamic faiths: Judaism, Christianity and Islam, envisage a process of judgment and an afterlife; an egalitarian process, where good deeds are recognised, but worldly status is irrelevant. Eastern faiths and philosophies such as Hinduism and Buddhism envisage a process of reincarnation and a move towards a state of perfection for the individual soul through a sloughing off of materialist pretensions.

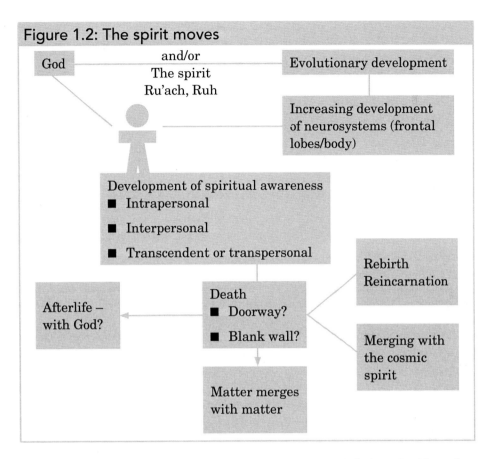

Figure 1.2: The spirit moves

In the 21st century life expectancy in many countries is being significantly extended. But there is also talk of attempting to create a form of immortality through medical advances and cryogenics. But how would human immortality affect the search for meaning? As Brian Appleyard puts it: *'Perhaps medical immortals will simply have to resign themselves through amnesia, to becoming serial, forgetful selves'* (Appleyard, 2007).

Contrasting this is the testimony of the late Christopher Jones (see Chapter 10) who, facing cancer, wrote: *'Finally, I have reviewed the achievements and failures of my life and handed them over to God. My faith in Christ, who passed through death and overcame it, gives me hope not just for the next life but for the life here and now. My conviction that nothing can separate us from the eternal purposes of God for our good has survived the test of living with cancer. It enables me to live each day in thanksgiving and peace, leaving the future in those strong and compassionate divine hands'* (St Helen's Window, 2011).

Spirituality and religion

'What people do every moment of their life is to create meaning… The meanings which people create might be engaged solely in mythos or logos. Usually it is a mixture of the two.' (Rowe, 2009, p.29)

Our thoughts, beliefs and actions are created through a process of engaging both hemispheres of our brain, which neuroscientists are providing more insight into. The left brain has a propensity for linear thought, while the right hemisphere is more to do with making connections in different directions. We sometimes come across people with astonishing intellectual powers but a lack of empathy with other humans. This is also where, in the fields of health and social care, we need to place *scientia* (knowledge) together with *sapientia* (wisdom).

As the philosopher Plato (circa 428–348 BCE) stated: *'As you ought not to cure the eyes without the head, nor the head without the body; so neither ought you to attempt to heal the body without the soul, because the part can never be well unless the whole be well.'* (Phaedo, quoted in Ross, 1997, p.1)

It is sometimes said that spirituality is a 'New Age concept', but this simply isn't true. The ancient Greeks, from whom we gain so much wisdom and knowledge, used four spirit words:

- **Psyche** – the individual soul, providing meaning and purpose. Psyche is the root word for psychiatry, psychology and psychotherapy.

- **Pneuma** – the transpersonal, cosmic soul, connecting to humanity, the universe and, for some people, God or gods.

- **Thumos** – life's vitality, will and feeling.

- **Nous** – a person's intuitive vision and insight (a word still used today to describe somebody who has good common sense).

(See King, 2009; Gilbert, 2011a)

Jewish thought postulates a difference between 'soul', nephesh, and 'spirit', ru'ach. The soul is God-given, but passive; while the spirit is active – not simply 'life', but, hopefully 'invigorated life'. In secular terms we also speak of 'soul' being a deep value-base in a person, while 'spirit' we use in terms of active inspiration.

Historian Keith Thomas points out that Greek and Roman philosophers devoted considerable energy to considering what made for a desirable life, both for the individual and for the person playing a role in society. They called it *eudaimonia: 'the flourishing, well-being, and happiness which came from the realisation of one's daimon or true nature"* (Thomas, 2009, p.10). Philip Pullman's imaginative children's stories capture aspects of this from a non-faith perspective.

It is most important to see the psyche and the pneuma together. A purely 'ME' approach to spirituality can be far too self-centred and ultimately self-defeating. In terms of health and social care research, Dr Harold Koenig and colleagues (2012), say that the purely individual spirituality, 'unmoored' from a religious and/or spiritual tradition, can just make it a proxy indicator for good mental or social health, and therefore makes it difficult to research in terms of its effect on health outcomes. Interestingly the Roman Catholic *Practical Guide to Spiritual Care of the Dying Person* (Gleeson *et al*, 2010) does not push a purely religious approach, but starts by stating that: *'spirituality can be interpreted in a range of ways according to an individual's beliefs'*. It points out what many health and social care workers experience, that people will explore the meaning of life and death in a more profound way when faced with the ultimate challenge and *'there is much a health care worker can do to help support a dying patient and make these moments as valuable as possible'* (Gleeson *et al*, 2010, p.9) with family members and friends also engaged in a journey.

Professor John Swinton lays out the following central features of spirituality.

- **Meaning:** the ontological significance of life; making sense of life situations; deriving purpose of existence.

- **Value:** beliefs and standards that are cherished; having to do with the truth, beauty, worth of a thought, object or behaviour; often discussed as 'ultimate values'.

- **Transcendence:** experience and appreciation of a dimension beyond the self; expanding self-boundaries.

- **Connecting:** relationships with self, others, God/higher power and the environment.

- **Becoming:** an unfolding of life that demands reflection and experience; includes a sense of who one is and how one knows.

(Swinton, 2001, p.25, see also Parkes with Gilbert, 2011, and Figures 1.1 and 1.2)

> ### Reflection points
>
> How do you see both your psyche and your pneuma?
>
> Does your inner spirit assist you in connecting with others and the Other (nature, the cosmos, God or gods)?

Religion is becoming more of a talking point in the UK partly to do with an evolving multi-cultural society; legal and cultural controversies over the wearing of religious objects; and how faith communities can support members of their own faith and reach out to promote a more coherent, value-driven society, but also sometimes retreat into 'tribalism'.

The word 'religion' derives from the Latin meaning 'binding obligation', and this demonstrates how much it is to do with a sense of community, altruism and social cohesion.

Religion encompasses most, if not all, of the aspects described in definitions of 'spirituality', usually in the context of belief in, and possibly a personal relationship with, a transcendent being or beings; and it provides a meta-narrative (story) which seeks to explain the origins of the world and those living in it and the questions which face human beings around life, suffering, death, and a reawakening in this world or another.

Religion can provide a 'world view' which is acted out in narratives, doctrine, symbols, rites, rituals, sacraments and gatherings; and the promotion of ties of mutual obligation. It creates a framework within which people seek to understand and interpret or make sense of themselves, their lives and daily experiences. Biologist and psychologist Robert A. Hinde provides a helpful overview of the personal and social benefits of religion even from an agnostic standpoint (Hinde, 2010), and agnostic philosopher, Alain de Botton in his fascinating *Religion for Atheists* (2012), states that religions:

'Serve two central needs which continue to this day and which secular society has not been able to solve with any particular skill: first, the need to live together in communities in harmony, despite our deeply rooted selfish and violent impulses. And second, the need to cope with terrifying degrees of pain which arise from our vulnerability to professional failure, to troubled relationships, to the death of loved ones and to our decay and demise.' (p.12)

The advantages of belonging to an organised religion include the following points.

■ Feeling that a benevolent and more powerful entity is looking after one.

■ Having a sense of 'divine empathy'.

■ The provision of specific coping resources, not least through the signs, symbols, rituals and narratives which faith communities provide to give a framework for life (see Koenig *et al*, 2012).

■ The generation of positive emotions eg. love, forgiveness, which fit strongly with the Foresight research into mental well-being, which shows that altruism or giving is a major element in a person's mental well-being (Foresight, 2008).

■ Having a sense of belonging.

■ Trust in God and in the faith community.

■ A commitment to the well-being of others, and concern for goals which are not merely materialistic (Bishops' Conference, 2010).

The downside of religion again stems from its original meaning. Organised religion can be:

■ over-controlling, and a 'straightjacket' rather than a 'framework'

■ overly paternalistic, repressive and homophobic

■ overly concerned with the needs of the organisation and not of the individual or group.

■ some of the earliest religions seem to have been female-led but the priesthoods which we know today tend to be more male-dominated

■ theistic religions can tie people into 'tribal' identities.

It is important to recall that most founders of religious traditions were actually challenging the prevailing religious and secular institutions of their day, and bringing people into a more humane and inter-connected way of looking at themselves, other people and the world in general (see Armstrong, 1999).

Swinton talks about different concepts of religion eg.:

- intrinsic, where *psyche* and *pneuma* are working positively and connected

- extrinsic religion which is around social convention and a 'self-serving, instrumental approach shaped to suit oneself'.

(Swinton, 2001, p.31)

Sometimes the term 'implicit religion' is used to denote the wide range of issues and activities with a spiritual dimension.

As we see in **Figure 1.1: Ways of mediating the spiritual dimension**, extrinsic religion can distance itself from a spiritual approach and is purely a matter of form and formulas. People with an extrinsic religious approach may be at particular risk when facing death because they lack connectedness and a deep sense of meaning.

Figure 1.3: Concepts of God/the Divine

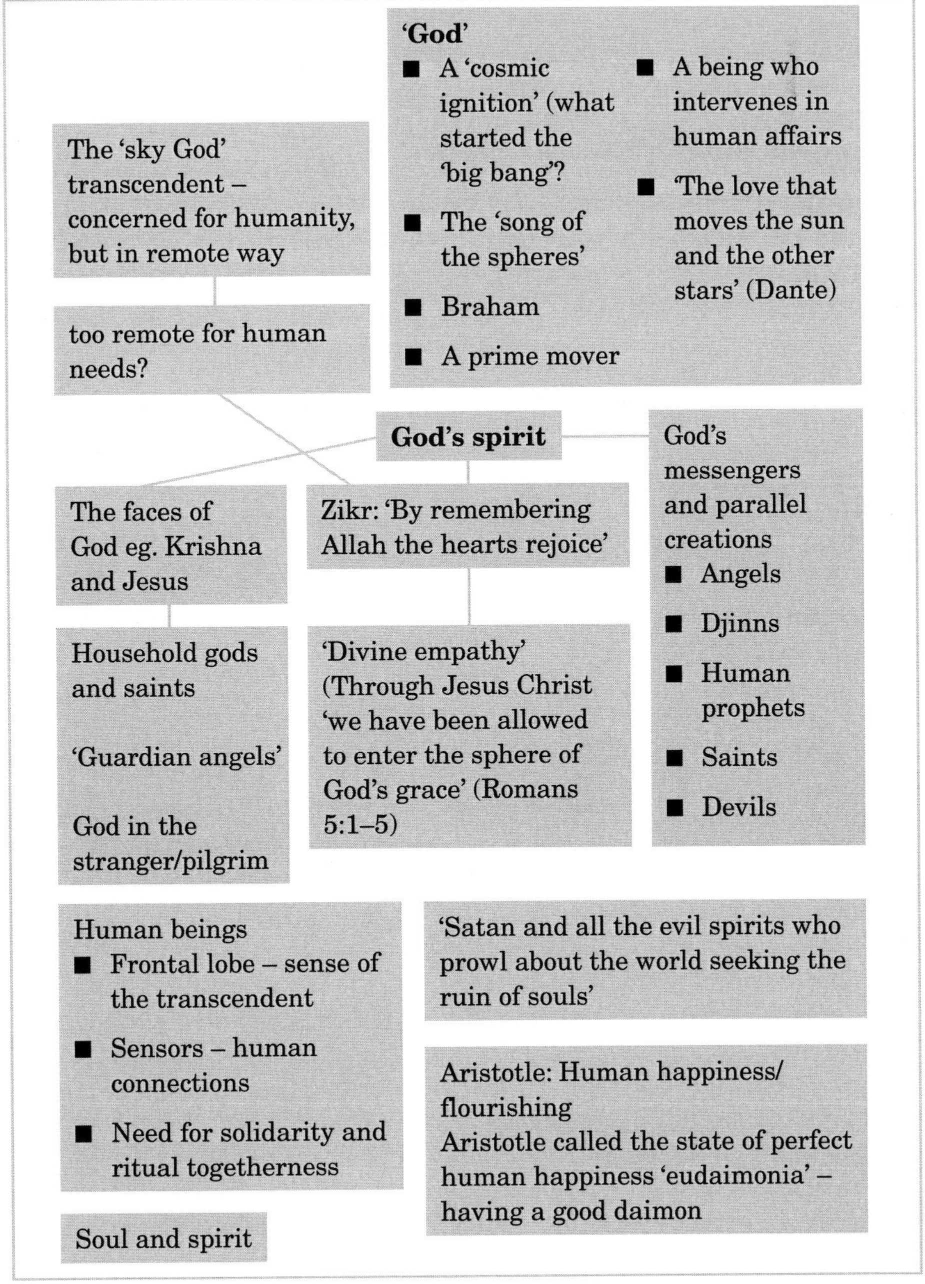

'God'
- A 'cosmic ignition' (what started the 'big bang'?
- The 'song of the spheres'
- Braham
- A prime mover

- A being who intervenes in human affairs
- 'The love that moves the sun and the other stars' (Dante)

The 'sky God' transcendent – concerned for humanity, but in remote way

too remote for human needs?

God's spirit

God's messengers and parallel creations
- Angels
- Djinns
- Human prophets
- Saints
- Devils

The faces of God eg. Krishna and Jesus

Zikr: 'By remembering Allah the hearts rejoice'

Household gods and saints

'Guardian angels'

God in the stranger/pilgrim

'Divine empathy' (Through Jesus Christ 'we have been allowed to enter the sphere of God's grace' (Romans 5:1–5)

Human beings
- Frontal lobe – sense of the transcendent
- Sensors – human connections
- Need for solidarity and ritual togetherness

Soul and spirit

'Satan and all the evil spirits who prowl about the world seeking the ruin of souls'

Aristotle: Human happiness/ flourishing
Aristotle called the state of perfect human happiness 'eudaimonia' – having a good daimon

As we can see from **Figure 1.3: Concepts of God/the Divine**, human beings have always sought some sense of connectedness with the Other, however defined (O'Grady, 2012), and there are tensions even within religious beliefs between a desire for a transcendent presence, and some form of immanence in terms of divine beings who walk the earth with human beings (Armstrong, 1999). Elizabeth MacKinlay writes that: *'As humans, we each have a unique life story, and we are part of the stories of our family'*. For people from a religious tradition we are also part of that narrative from our faith communities, *'The larger story that goes back to the beginning of time and links us with God'* (MacKinlay, 2012, p.37, see also Geffen, 2000). Woodhead and Catto's (2012) major overview of belief in the UK today demonstrates a range of belief systems and the importance of these in a crisis of health.

The ability of health and social care workers to empathise with an individual's belief system, whatever that is, is of immense comfort to the individual and their carers, and also is an opportunity for growth and development for the worker themselves. It is vital for care workers to listen to an individual's spiritual issues (Parkes & Gilbert, 2011). Specialist advice can come from the chaplaincy service (see Chapter 6; Gilbert, 2011a, Chapter 3).

What is this age?

'With cancer, she'd have something that she could fight … there was a chance that she could win. Her family … would rally behind her battle and consider it noble. And even if defeated in the end, she'd be able to look them knowingly in the eye and say goodbye before she left' (Genova (2009) *Still Alice*, p.117)

'To stand stripped of everything the world values and to see each other as we really are is a very precious and humbling experience, and which I would never have encountered were it not for the ravages of dementia. Paradoxically, Malcolm's 'losses' have turned into "gains"' (Barbara Pointon, quoted in Gilbert, 2011b, p.148)

The population in all developed countries, and many developing ones, is ageing. A recent report from the United Nations (2012) states that the global population will age so rapidly in the next 30 years that there will be more pensioners than children by 2050, when there will be two billion people aged 60 or over. This process, partly due to human beings' progress in technological medicine and other life-sciences (though in China, for example, the one-child policy has had a dramatic effect) is taking place against a cultural backdrop which defines the age we live in. With liberal capitalism being the dominant ethos, there is a danger that rather than society being something we build together for the common good, it is somewhere in which the individual sinks or swims in a 'winner takes all' paradigm.

The UK (and there are now profound differences between England, Scotland and Wales in approach to care) is situated somewhere between an individualistic USA and a more communitarian Europe. During the 2012 US presidential election, the objectivist philosophy of Ayn Rand (1964) has come into play where Rand argued that: *'money is the barometer of society's virtue'*, and that altruism undermines moral values! From a very different perspective, Robert Frank (Frank, 2007; 2008) writes about the increasing pressures on the middle class in America, especially on those with inadequate health insurance 'falling down' a gap in society; and the increasing separation into elite ghettos of the very rich, in what he calls 'Richistan'. Research demonstrates that more equal societies experience better mental health (Wilkinson & Pickett, 2009).

In the UK we tend to look back to the social cohesion brought about through the challenges of the Second World War, and the NHS, National Assistance and children's legislation which followed in the late 1940s, and set the scene for a community approach to health and welfare.

Box 1.2: Policy drivers

- Department of Health (2000) *No Secrets: Guidance of developing and implementing multi-agency policies and procedures to protect vulnerable adults from abuse.* London: DH.

- Department of Health (2001) *National Service Framework for Older People.* London: DH.

- NICE (2004) *Guidelines on Palliative Care.* London: NICE.

- Department of Health (2006) *A New Ambition for Old Age: Next steps in implementing the National Service Framework for Older People.* London: DH.

- Department of Health (2008) *End of Life Care Strategy.* London: DH.

- Department of Health (2009) *Living Well with Dementia: A national dementia strategy.* London: DH.

- Department of Health (2009) *Religion or Belief.* London: DH.

- The Patients Association (2009) *Patients Not Numbers, People … Not Statistics.* PA: London.

- NHS Education for Scotland (2009) *Spiritual Care Matters: An introductory resource for all NHS Scotland staff.* Edinburgh: NHS Scotland.

- Department of Health (2010) *Equity and Excellence: Liberating the NHS.* London: DH.

- Department of Health (2010) *Spiritual Care at the End of Life: A systematic review of the literature.* London: DH.

- Department of Health (2010) *Improving the Lives of People With Long-term Conditions.* London: DH.

- Care Quality Commission (CQC) (2011) *Dignity and Nutrition Inspection Programme: National overview.* London: CQC.

- Department of Health (2012) *Caring for Our Future: Reforming care and support.* London: DH.

- Joint Commissioning Panel for Mental Health (2012) *Guidance for Commissioners on Dementia Services.* London: RCPsych.

- Social Care Institute for Excellence (SCIE) (2012) *End of Life Care for People Living in Care Homes.* London: SCIE.

- The College of Social Work/NHS National End of Life Care Programme (2012) *The Route to Success in End of Life Care: Achieving quality for social work.* London: NELCP.

Liz Lloyd (2012) gives an excellent overview of patterns in health and ageing. And this is a complex picture as some forms of cancer are likely to reduce due to changes in health strategies and technical advances; at the same time increasing levels of ageing will have an inevitable effect on mind and body. The onset of disability, disease and dementia can result in other symptoms such as depression.

Those involved in policy and practice at a national and a local level, from the Department of Health to the local hospice or care/nursing home, need also to look at demographic changes. Research by Leeds University (Rees *et al*, 2010) indicates that ethnic minorities will make up one-fifth of the population by 2051, compared to eight per cent in 2001, with the mixed ethnic population expected to treble in size. The research team also indicated that the UK will become less segregated as ethnic groups disperse throughout the country. A city ward such as Sparkbrook in Birmingham already has over 60% of its population stating that they are Muslim. Any service designed to meet the needs of people in Sparkbrook needs to take this into account. But other towns and cities are also seeing a marked increase in diversity, and issues of faith and also culture will need to be taken into account. In September 2012 Sikh Health put on a national conference addressing the issue of stigma and mental health. Recent research demonstrates that while membership of a faith community may be very supportive to an individual and family, cultural issues may raise issues of shame and stigma and cause a barrier to seeking help from services (see Regan *et al*, 2013, forthcoming).

An ageing population may cause tensions between a working and a retired population, though many 'older' people are actually engaging in work and other pursuits well beyond the time that has been considered usual for such activity. A good example of this is Fauja Singh, the 100-year-old Sikh runner, who in October 2011 became the world's oldest person to complete a full length marathon. Singh resisted his daughter's suggestion some years ago of attending a day centre, and went back to running which he'd done as a young man. He said running has given him purpose and a sense of peace: *'Why worry about small things? I don't stress. You never hear of anyone dying of happiness'*. He goes on to say: *'It's because of the running that all these people keep showing me so much love. Look how blessed I am'*.

The invention of life's meaning

'Shorn of the rituals of old, death maroons us in grief.' (Jenni Russell *The Guardian*, 2nd January, 2009)

Newspaper columnist Jenni Russell writes movingly of how, when her father died in his 80th year, having been ill for some time, rationally she shouldn't have been startled by his death, but in fact found herself completely stunned and at a loss. As she puts it: *'I did understand that people die. I didn't understand how the loss would feel'*. She then moves on to speak cogently about the fact that in many parts of our postmodern society, we now lack the rituals to assist us with this most challenging part of life's journey. As she describes it, in the UK: *'Death has been so removed from our daily experience that it has become almost embarrassingly private'* (Guardian, 2009). Perhaps the Victorian era's approach to funerals was overly rigid, but now, as Russell puts it, we have *'No mechanisms to signal our sadness at all'* (Guardian, 2009).

Ritual can be both positive and negative. A friend of mine went to two funerals recently. The first was a church service, where the ritual was helpful, but there was very little acknowledgment of the unique personality of the deceased. On the other hand, a few weeks later she went to another funeral which was very personal, and satisfying in that way, but, as she put it: *'it was so loose in structure, nobody knew what to do!'*.

As some of the most persuasive of writers on the phenomenon of human nature put it, ritual is an essential part of human existence. For instance, geneticist Robert Winston speaks of the 'material' element to our beliefs, and how we need to approach these beliefs, whether god-centred or not, with meaningful rituals (Winston, 2006, p.156). Karen Armstrong writes of the story and structure of faiths that *'express the wonder and mystery that seems always to have been an essential component of the human experience of this beautiful yet terrifying world. Like art, religion has been an attempt to find meaning and value in life, despite the suffering that flesh is heir to'* (Armstrong, 1999, p.3).

Although in Britain some aspects of religious affiliation have declined (though others have substantially increased), Linda Woodhead and Rebecca Catto's seminal survey of *Religion and Change in Modern Britain* (2012) demonstrates that a large percentage of people still attend church for major events such as weddings and funerals. It is also interesting that at times of crisis, such as the occurrence of a heart attack to footballer Fabrice Muamba, many people without a religious faith still prayed fervently for his recovery. Pilgrimages in all parts of the world are also very popular with more than 270,000 people annually completing the Way to Santiago de Compostela in northern Spain (see also the film *The Way,* Estevez, 2011), and Hindu pilgrimages in India on the rise.

Religious faiths will have helpful guides to funerals, eg. the *Muslim Funeral Guide* by the Karimia Institute (al-Azhari, 2010), and there are helpful humanist rituals as well. Margaret Holloway and colleagues' most enlightening research into contemporary funerals (Holloway *et al,* 2010) found that with funeral services there was a need to engage in personal meaning-making; spirituality in its broadest sense was of vital importance, people without any formal religious faith might still draw on religious tradition to imbue the funeral with meaning and as a vehicle for their own spiritual experience; ritual was important in imbuing death with meaning for the individual, the family and the wider community; and funeral directors were pivotal facilitators. Research shows that where the village church closes, the whole community, religious or not, experiences a sense of loss of community focus.

As Russell (2009) concludes: *'The terrible fact of death is the loss of history, love, connection and meaning. The only consolation it offers is that the sympathy we are given, and the sorrow we share can bring us closer to the living.'*

A religious belief may assist us to hold on to history and create a connection between the living and the dead, as the *Muslim Funeral Guide* puts it: *'Death is the bridge that unites the lover with his/her beloved'* (al-Azhari, (2010) p.5).

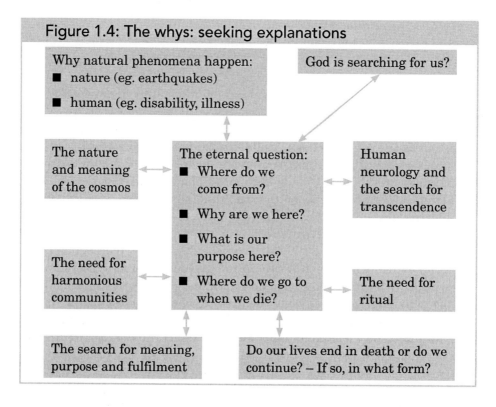

Figure 1.4: The whys: seeking explanations

Why natural phenomena happen:
- nature (eg. earthquakes)
- human (eg. disability, illness)

God is searching for us?

The nature and meaning of the cosmos

The eternal question:
- Where do we come from?
- Why are we here?
- What is our purpose here?
- Where do we go to when we die?

Human neurology and the search for transcendence

The need for harmonious communities

The need for ritual

The search for meaning, purpose and fulfilment

Do our lives end in death or do we continue? – If so, in what form?

Whose life is it anyway?

'O death where is your victory? O death, where is your sting?' (St. Paul, I Corinthians, 15:55)

'Right to die campaigner finds a victory in death?' (*The Times*, headline on the death of Tony Nicklinson, 23rd August 2012)

'Every soul shall taste death ... when their appointed times comes, not for one moment shall they hold it back, nor can they go before it.' (The Qu'ran)

Many people in Britain were moved by the story of Tony Nicklinson, a man who had been a civil engineer; a family man with a love of sports, including rugby and parachuting. In 2005, on a business trip to Athens, he suffered a severe stroke which led to him experiencing 'locked-in' syndrome. He had to be fed and moved by carers and described his life as: *'Dull, miserable, demeaning, undignified and intolerable ... I am fed up with my life and don't want to spend the next 20 years or so like this'* (Guardian, 2012).

Tony Nicklinson applied to the Courts to request that a doctor be able to assist him in dying. The Courts turned down his request and subsequently Nicklinson refused food and water, contracted pneumonia and died.

Many people, including those who believe that only God should choose the time of a person's passing, would sympathise with somebody who found that their dignity as a human being had been impaired by their disability. But there is also a major concern about a radical change in the law. The Royal College of Physicians, commenting on the Court judgment, stated that it did not back a change in the law. The Chair of the Ethics Committee said that: *'A change in the law would also have severe implications for the way society views disabled people'.*

Chapter 2: A good death deals with this vital issue in more detail, but, as medical technology preserves life for longer, this kind of issue is going to become more predominant. In a recent publication, Emily Jackson and John Keown (2012) undertake a detailed debate on the subject of euthanasia, including a consideration of jurisdictions such as in Oregon, in the United States, where physician-assisted suicide is permitted in certain circumstances.

'Euthanasia' derives from Greek for an easy or happy death (eu – 'good', plus *thanatos* – 'death'). One of the major issues to face society, which could be addressed without any changes in the law, is assisting people to die where they wish to. Currently, well over 50% of people die in acute hospitals, which are increasingly designed just to cope with acute illnesses, and where a number of scandals have broken out in recent years around the inadequacy of care for older patients, who sometimes have gone without food or water (DH, 2008). Most people wish to die in their own homes (18% of deaths occur at home) or in a hospice (4%) (see Ellershaw & Wilkinson, 2011), and Government could work towards enabling this to happen increasingly, and this would have the cost benefit of enabling acute hospitals to concentrate on areas of work they are now designed to undertake.

Sometimes, being honest with ourselves, we may have conflicting emotions and views on these vital subjects. Personally, I have to be honest and say that I would find it very difficult indeed to cope with 'locked-in' syndrome. Patience is not one of my few virtues, and as somebody who has been a runner for many years, being physically helpless would be anathema to me. On the other hand, as an historian, the current debate draws me back to the strong eugenics thrust in the 1930s, which reached its peak in Nazi Germany. Most people are familiar with the Nazi regime's attempt to exterminate the Jewish population in the Final Solution. What is perhaps less well known is that the eugenics and subsequently euthanasia programme set in place by the Nazis desensitised the German population, and was the first step on the route to the Holocaust (see Burleigh, 2000, Chapter 5). In the 1930s the regime began to identify people with physical and mental disabilities and illnesses, and gradually produced a programme of what Burleigh calls 'medicalised mass murder'. What is particularly concerning is that Germany was one of the most educationally and technologically advanced nations in the world; many medical professionals seem to have been proponents of this policy, as were lawyers; and the regime very cleverly used popular culture to promote their policy. As advances in medical technology paradoxically may see increasing numbers of people entrapped in circumstances that they themselves may view as 'undignified', societies will have to consider moral and legal frameworks which assist choice and control for individuals without undermining the essential dignity of the human person, whatever their condition.

Conclusion

'How people die remains in the memory of those who live on.' (Dame Cicely Saunders, quoted in the Department of Health, *End of Life Care Strategy*, 2008).

Though I still feel sadness at my mother's departing, and her last moments live on in my memory, I am consoled by the fact that she led a good life, and believed she would experience a life in the hereafter. I am also reassured by the care that she received at The Royal Marsden, where human and technological medicine were paired together in a way which sought a cure, if possible, while also paying attention to pain relief and attending to the holistic needs of the patient. Family and friends were welcomed in a way which enabled them to look after their loved ones, and to have attention to their own needs as carers.

As John Ellershaw and Susie Wilkinson put it, in their recent book on pathways to assist those who are dying: *'Dying patients are an integral part of the population. Their death must not be considered a failure; the only failure is that the person's death was not as restful and dignified as possible'* (Ellershaw & Wilkinson, 2011, p.30).

There are controversies around models of care, but the promotion of life needs to take into account the need for human dignity, and in both palliative care and dementia care (see Hughes *et al*, 2006).

Spiritual care, and where appropriate a religious and/or spiritual framework, will be vital especially at this time of challenge. This is not only for the person facing death, but for family carers, friends and for the staff who care. Increasingly work is being undertaken to assist staff in working with people with dementia and/or terminal illnesses, as in the imaginative *DVD: It's Still ME, Lord...* (Bano/CSAN, 2009). As the Dalai Lama points out, if someone does not belong to a set religion, more fundamental than this *'is our basic human spirituality. We have an underlying human disposition towards love, kindness, and affection, irrespective of whether we have a religious framework of not'* (Dalai Lama, 2011, p.17).

A hospice chaplain tells the story of moving through a ward and speaking with some relatives at the end of the bed of a frail older woman. The relatives say how nice it is to see the chaplain, but not to bother to talk to their mother as she has never had a religious faith; but the woman in the bed is simultaneously gesticulating urgently to him to indicate that she wants to speak to him!

Whether we believe that we have a soul, and that that soul moves on after our death, we need, in our last times, attention to our body and mind, heart and spirit. At the end some parts of our whole may feel more real than others. As EM Forster wrote in *Howard's End* (1991): *'Only connect! Only connect the prose and the passion, and both will be exalted, and human love will be seen at its height. Live in fragments no longer'.*

References

al-Azhari H (2010) *The Muslim Funeral Guide*. Nottingham: Karinia Institute.

Appleyard B (2007) *How to Live Forever or Die Trying: On the new immortality*. London: Simon and Schuster.

Armstrong K (1999) *A History of God*. London: Vintage.

Bakhshi SS (2008) *A Modern Guide to the Practice of Sikh Faith*. Birmingham: Sikh Publishing House.

Bano/CSAN (2011) *It's Still ME, Lord*. London: CSAN.

Bauman Z (2005) *Liquid Life*. Cambridge: Polity Press.

Bishops' Conference of England and Wales (2010) *Choosing the Common Good*. Stoke-on-Trent: Alive Publishing.

Burleigh M (2000) *The Third Reich: A New History.* London: MacMillan.

Dalai Lama (2011) *Beyond Religion: Ethics for a whole world.* London: Rider.

de Botton A (2012) *Religion for Atheists: A non-believers guide to the uses of religion.* London: Hamish Hamilton.

Department of Health (2008) *End of Life Care Strategy: Promoting high quality care for adults at the end of their life.* London: DH.

Ellershaw J & Wilkinson S (2011) *Care of the Dying: A Pathway to excellence* (2nd edition). Oxford: Oxford University Press.

Estevez E (2010) *The Way.* US: Filmax/Elixir Films.

Foresight (2008) *Mental Capital and Well-being.* London: Foresight.

Forster EM (1991) *Howards End.* New York: Random House.

Frank RH (2007) *Falling Behind: How rising inequality harms the middle class.* Los Angeles: University of California Press.

Frank RH (2008) *Richistan: A journey through the American wealth boom and the lives of the new rich.* London: Piatkus Books.

Geffen J (2000) *A Journey Through Cancer.* New York: Three Rivers Press.

Genova L (2009) *Still Alice.* London: Pocket Books.

Gilbert P (2011a) *Spirituality and Mental Health.* Brighton: Pavilion Publishing.

Gilbert P (2011b) 'From the cradle – to beyond the grave?'. *Quality in Ageing and Older Adults* **12** (3).

Gleeson C, Jones D, Mason P & Hanvey J (2010) *A Practical Guide to the Spiritual Care of the Dying Person.* London: Catholic Truth Society.

Guardian (2009) Shorn of the rituals of old, death maroons us in grief by Jenni Russell. *The Guardian* **2 January 2009**.

Guardian (2012) *Tony Nicklinson: fight to die with dignity 'will not be forgotten'* [online]. Available at: http://www.guardian.co.uk/uk/2012/aug/22/tony-nicklinson-die-not-forgotten (accessed April 2013).

Hinde RA (2010) *Why Gods Persist: A scientific approach to religion* (2nd edition). London: Routledge.

Holloway M (2007) *Negotiating Death in Contemporary Health and Social Care.* Bristol: Policy Press.

Holloway M, Adamson F, Argyrou B, Draper B & Mariau D (2010) *Spirituality in Contemporary Funerals.* Hull: University of Hull.

Hughes JC, Louw SJ & Sapat SR (2006) *Dementia: Mind, meaning and the person.* Oxford: Oxford University Press.

Jackson E & Keown J (2012) *Debating Euthanasia.* Oxford: Hart Publishing.

King U (2009) *The Search for Spirituality: Our global quest for meaning and fulfilment.* London: Canterbury Press.

Koenig HG, King DE & Carson VB (2012) *Handbook of Religion and Health* (2nd edition). Oxford: Oxford University Press.

Lloyd L (2012) *Health and Care in Ageing Societies: A new international approach.* Bristol: Policy Press.

MacKinlay P (2001) *The Spiritual Dimension of Ageing.* London: Jessica Kingsley.

MacKinlay P (2012) *Palliative Care, Ageing and Spirituality.* London: Jessica Kingsley.

Mental Health Foundation/Griffen J (2010) *The Lonely Society.* London: MHF.

Miles R (2010) *Ancient Worlds: The search for the origins of western civilization.* London: Allen Lane.

O'Grady S (2012) *And Man Created God.* London: Atlantic Books.

Parkes M with Gilbert P (2011) *Report on the Place of Spirituality in Mental Health.* London: National Spirituality and Mental Health Forum.

Parkes M & Gilbert P (2011) Professionals calling: mental healthcare staff attitudes to spiritual care. *Implicit Religion* **14** (1).

Rand A (1964) *The Virtue of Selfishness.* New York: Signet.

Rees P, Norman P, Wohland P & Boden P (2010) Ethnic population projections for the UK, 2001–2051. *Journal of Population Research* **29**.

Regan JL, Bhattacharyya S, Kevern P & Rana T (2013) A systematic review of religion and pathways to dementia care in black and minority ethnic populations. *Journal of Mental Health, Religion and Culture* **16** (1) 1–15.

Ross L (1997) *Nurses' Perceptions of Spiritual Care.* Aldershot: Avebury.

Rowe D (2009) *What Should I Believe?* New York: Routledge.

Russell J (2009) Shorn of the rituals of old, death maroons us in grief. *The Guardian* **2 January 2009**.

Sacks J (2011) *The Great Partnership: God, science and the search for meaning.* London: Hodder & Stoughton.

Sandel M (2012) *What Money Can't Buy.* London: Allen Lane.

Sennett R (2002) *The Fall of Public Man.* London: Penguin.

Sheldrake R (2012) *The Science Delusion: Freeing the spirit of enquiry.* London: Coronet.

St. Helen's Window (2011) Living with cancer. **15** (2).

Swinton J (2001) *Spirituality and Mental Health Care: Rediscovering a 'forgotten' dimension.* London: Jessica Kingsley.

Taylor C (2007) *A Secular Age.* Harvard: Harvard University Press.

Thomas K (2009) *The Ends of Life: Roads to fulfilment in early modern England.* Oxford: Oxford University Press.

United Nations Population Fund and HelpAge International (2012) *Ageing in the Twenty-First Century: A celebration and a challenge.* New York and London: The United Nations Population Fund and HelpAge International.

Williams M (2010) *Prehistoric Belief: Shamans, trance and the afterlife.* Stroud: The History Press.

Wilkinson R & Pickett K (2009) *The Spirit Level: Why more equal societies almost always do better.* London: Allen Lane.

Winston R (2006) *The Story of God.* London: Bantam Books.

Woodhead L & Catto R (2012) *Religion and Change in Modern Britain.* London: Routledge.

Young W, Wooley R, Hood C, Gandesha A & Souza R (Eds) (2011) *Report of the National Audit of Dementia Care in General Hospitals, 2011.* London: Royal College of Psychiatrists Centre for Quality Improvement.

Chapter 2:

A good death

David Albert Jones

The essential relationship between spirituality and ethics

To discuss what makes a death a 'good death' is to be engaged in ethics – in this case, bioethics or healthcare ethics. This raises the question of why a book on spirituality and end of life care should include a chapter on ethics at all. What is the implied relationship between spirituality and ethics? The understanding of this relationship has become more problematic in a modern context as the connotations of these terms have shifted. 'Spirituality' is now typically interpreted as something intensely private or subjective, connected to the realm of feeling and the meaning of events as experienced. In contrast, 'ethics' is thought to be concerned specifically with external relations, with duties, rights, and rules of conduct.

As soon as this supposed dichotomy is made explicit it is clear that it must be inadequate. If spirituality concerns questions of meaning then it cannot be purely private. Taken at its most general, meaning is the place of a part in relation of a larger whole, a whole that includes public events, actions, and objects. This is why, as the philosopher Wittgenstein observed, there cannot be a purely private language. Language, including the language of spirituality, is about public meanings that can be communicated.

Similarly, ethics is impoverished and misunderstood if actions are isolated from the inner life, from the wellsprings of action in our attraction to the good and the inclinations of our heart or spirit. Aristotle, whose work on ethics remains influential to this day, was clear that understanding ethics requires an account of the dispositions expressed in action, and an account of human flourishing. Ethics is not reducible to a set of rules.

This inherent relation between spirituality and ethics is perhaps seen nowhere so clearly as in the context of dying and care of the dying. The question of how to make a good death, of how to respect the good of life in the last phase of life, is one that must be both ethical and spiritual. An adequate ethical response to these issues will embody a certain spirituality and an adequate spirituality will have ethical implications.

Making a good death

There are, of course, a great variety of experiences of death: deaths at a young or at an old age, deaths by disease or by accident, deaths by violence or suicide, deaths surrounded by loved ones, deaths alone or in exile. So also, everyone must die just his or her own death, and generally with only a limited control of the circumstances of that death. Yet for all this variety, it is also true that the very fact of death is something that is common. *'There is for all mankind one entrance into life, and a common departure'* (Wisdom 7.6). On Ash Wednesday Christians traditionally queue to receive a smudge of ash on the forehead, accompanied by the words *'Remember thou art dust and to dust thou shalt return'* (Genesis 3:19). This is a Christian expression of a theme that is common to many philosophies and religious traditions: that the life of wisdom requires that we know ourselves, and that to know oneself is to know that we will die.

Death is universal. However, a good death is not universal. A good death is, rather, a challenge or a task. It is a challenge for the person dying and a challenge for those who journey with the dying, including healthcare professionals. Death is something that happens to us, but living is something we do, and the challenge is to live well in the last phase of life, aware that life is approaching its end.

Respecting life and accepting death

In relation to the ethics of dying well, and caring well for the dying, it is necessary to keep two things in mind: both to cherish the precious gift of life and to accept the inevitability of death.

Every human life is irreplaceable. This is a fundamental bedrock principle of ethics. From this it follows that every human life, including one's own, is to be cherished. The life of someone who is sick or dying is no less to be cherished than the life of someone who is healthy. Every human life possesses an inherent dignity, as is acknowledged in the preambles to many ethical codes and declarations. For example, the declaration on bioethics agreed at the United Nations in 2005 had as its stated aim, *'to promote respect for human dignity and protect human rights, by ensuring respect for the life of human beings'* (UNESCO, 2005).

At the same time as cherishing life it is important to acknowledge that life will come to an end and to prepare for this as well as we can. Elisabeth Kübler-Ross in her work *On Death and Dying* (1969) identified five stages in the process of coming to terms with death: denial, anger, bargaining, depression, and acceptance. While elements of this account have been criticised for being too formal or idealised, and while Kübler-Ross claimed that her aim was descriptive rather than normative, there is very widespread agreement that accepting death is something fundamentally healthy. This is the truth of that injunction common to many traditions of wisdom: *memento mori!*

From a naturalistic perspective, therefore, there are two elements that need to be kept in tension: cherishing life and accepting death. It might seem that Christian ethics or Christian spirituality alters this balance by making one or other of these elements stronger. However, the effect of Christian doctrine is not to alter the balance so much as to make *both* elements stronger: Christian faith gives more reason to cherish life, especially the lives of those who are marginalised or overlooked by society, while at the same time it also gives more reason to accept death, when it comes, with hope in God (Jones, 2007). It thus firmly resists the temptation to choose one or other of these elements, but keeps both in tension. As GK Chesterton (1909) remarked, *'Christianity got over the difficulty of combining furious opposites, by keeping them both, and keeping them both furious'*.

Withholding or withdrawing life-prolonging treatments

What, then, is it to make a good death? What kind of challenge is this, what kind of activity does it imply?

If we take as our starting point the need both to cherish life and to accept death, then it should be clear that a person will not always have a duty to maximise his or her length of days. Indeed, as death becomes inevitable the attempt to *'rage, rage against the dying of the light'* (Thomas, 1951/2002) would seem to be a kind of denial of reality, and thus a moral failure. Now failures of courage in the face of death are very understandable and this may represent the furthest a person has reached in his or her journey. Nevertheless, if the ultimate aim is to hold together the cherishing of life and the acceptance of death then this implies we need to qualify or constrain our constant striving to extend life.

It is reasonable then to refuse life-prolonging treatment if, for example, the treatment would be excessively burdensome in relation to its expected benefits. This is widely acknowledged:

'Discontinuing medical procedures that are burdensome, dangerous, extraordinary, or disproportionate to their expected outcome can be legitimate: it is the refusal of "over-zealous" treatment. Here one does not will to cause death; one's inability to impede it is merely accepted. The decisions should be made by the patient if he is competent or, if not, by those legally entitled to act for the patient, whose reasonable will and legitimate interests must always be respected.' (Catechism of the Catholic Church, paragraph 2278).

If life need not always be extended, might it be legitimate in some cases deliberately to hasten death? Could there be a justifiable act of suicide by omission? If the aim of making a good death is to continue to affirm the value of human life, even to the end, then to deliberately bring about death will not be a good death in this sense. It will be a failure to respect humanity *'in your own person'* (as the philosopher Immanuel Kant once put it). Contemporary discussion tends to regard suicide as an expression of autonomy; that is, as an affirmation of the self. However, in reality suicide seems more generally to be an overcoming of the self by despair – a desperate flight from the world. Thus from a religious perspective it is considered to be wrong to refuse treatments *in order* to hasten death, though there may well be good reasons to refuse treatment, especially as death approaches and the prospective benefits of treatment become more limited.

Healthcare professionals need to consider which treatments will prolong life or address symptoms without causing undue burden. They too should never withdraw treatment *with the aim of* hastening death. If a person's death is imminent then it will generally be futile to attempt to prolong life. If a person's death is not imminent then the prolongation of life will be a reason to offer at least some interventions, but with a realism about the burdens or risks and the limitedness of the benefits. In cases where burdens and benefits are finely balanced the wish of the patient will usually be the deciding factor. It is the patient who desires the benefit and endures the burden.

From an ethical perspective, is there a difference between deciding not to offer a treatment and stopping a treatment which has been started? There is at least a psychological difference between withholding and withdrawing treatment. It may feel more difficult emotionally to stop something than deciding not to start it in the first place. However, we cannot always know whether a treatment will work until we have tried it. We should not discourage people from starting treatment simply to avoid anxiety about discontinuing it. Instead, it may be more helpful, and is good clinical practice, to discuss beforehand in what circumstances a treatment or intervention would be stopped.

What should a doctor do in circumstances where a patient refuses treatment that the doctor thinks would be beneficial? In such circumstances if the person is well-informed and competent to make the decision then the refusal has, and ought to have, the final word, at least if there is no question of suicidal motivation. The importance of taking responsibility for decisions affecting oneself, which is a feature of the whole of life, is still more significant in the last phase of life. On the other hand, the doctor has a duty to explain to the patient the benefits of treatment and must seek to encourage him or her to act well. A failure to challenge bad decisions can be a kind of abandonment: neglect disguised as respect.

There are particular problems with decisions that have been made in advance, especially where these are formalised and prevent the doctor, by law, from giving certain treatments. In such a case, where the doctor has no opportunity to dissuade the patient, the law ought to allow the doctor to act in the best interests of the patient. However, if the doctor does not have the support of law, then he has reason to respect the refusal, not only to protect himself from what may be serious legal repercussions, but also because acting in the face of a refusal is analogous to coercion or constraint and this seems to require communal sanction, at least of a tacit kind.

In England and Wales the current legal framework for these issues is given by the Mental Capacity Act (2005). This legislation and associated Code of Practice have much to commend them in relation to helping people to make decisions where they are able, and in relation to what to consider when assessing best interests. They also give safeguards and requirements for any advance refusal of life-sustaining treatment. However, in relation to advance refusals that are not only unwise but are explicitly suicidal, the legislation is flawed and creates a problem for the conscientious doctor. It does not always give a doctor the legal power he or she would need to override such a refusal.

Clinically assisted nutrition and hydration

Even though the need for nutrition and hydration will decline in the last few days of life, the human meaning of eating and drinking needs to be borne in mind. Offering or sharing food and drink can be a sign of care and affection: it is an archetypal expression of solidarity or hospitality.

All patients should therefore be offered food and drink of adequate quantity and quality and, where necessary, the help they need in order to eat and drink (GMC, 2010). If there are risks because the patient has difficulty swallowing, these should be explained. The decision about whether to switch from oral to clinically assisted nutrition and hydration (CANH) ie. tube feeding should be made by realistically weighing up the risks and benefits. This judgment will be influenced by the patient's stage of illness and how close they are to death. CANH will not be effective for all patients (RCP, 2010).

When considering the meaning of CANH some people focus on the clinical aspect and regard it as a medical treatment, which just happens to be related to nutrition and hydration. Other people understand CANH primarily as the provision of nutrition and hydration and thus as basic care, which just happens to be delivered clinically. Those who hold that CANH is medical treatment are generally concerned that patients should be permitted to refuse CANH, and/or that CANH can be withdrawn when it is no longer effective. Those who insist that CANH is part of basic care are generally concerned that patients might be unjustly deprived of food and fluids in cases where it would have been effective.

Pope John Paul II was a prominent defender of the opinion that CANH is part of the basic care due to the sick.

'I should like particularly, to underline how the administration of water and food, even when provided by artificial means, always represents a natural means of preserving life, not a medical act. Its use, furthermore, should be considered, in principle, ordinary and proportionate, and as such morally obligatory, insofar as and until it is seen to have attained its proper finality, which in the present case consists in providing nourishment to the patient and alleviation of his suffering. The obligation to provide 'the normal care due to the sick' in such cases includes, in fact, the use of nutrition and hydration.' (Bishops' Conference, 2010: 2.8)

It is important to note that the Pope did not say that CANH could *never* be refused or withdrawn. Nutrition and hydration, including CANH, is regarded as normal care due to the sick and thus as *'in principle … morally obligatory'* (Bishops' Conference, 2010: 2.8). However, this obligation would cease if the means used were not effective in *'providing nourishment to the patient and alleviation of his suffering'* (Bishops' Conference, 2010: 2.8). If in the last hours or days of life CANH has little or no effect in prolonging life, and if symptoms can be addressed equally well by other forms of care (including mouth care), then it could perhaps be withdrawn. Similarly, even if CANH is classified as a medical intervention, this does not mean there is no obligation to provide it. Doctors have a duty to assess the needs of the patient for nutrition and hydration, and find a way to address these needs. CANH may well be obligatory where clinically indicated.

Thus while the classification of CANH either as a medical intervention or as basic care is important to people, and affects decision-making in this area, whichever way it is understood, there should not be a blanket rule in favour of or against CANH. Instead, each case should be *judged on the basis of the needs of the particular patient*, with nutrition and hydration assessed separately (GMC, 2010; RCP, 2010).

A dispute may also occur when a patient or a relative wishes the healthcare team to provide CANH but the team do not think that it would effective. It is important to recognise the human and spiritual meaning of food and fluids to the patient and/or the relatives as they often represent life, comfort, hope and the avoidance of suffering. In these circumstances it is unhelpful to frame the dispute in terms of the 'legal right' of doctors to withhold medical treatment that they do not think is indicated, and the legal classification of CANH as 'medical treatment'. This approach does little to alleviate concern and may well inflame a situation.

What is needed instead is an honest assessment of benefits and burdens of different kinds of CANH and the clear communication of these options. The patient or relative may overestimate the benefits of CANH for prolongation of life or for symptom relief. It is also possible that the healthcare team may underestimate the benefits or overestimate the burdens of hydration or have other, even discriminatory, reasons for withholding it. In cases where burdens and benefits are finely balanced the wishes of the patient will usually be the deciding factor.

A dispute might also arise if the patient or relative is unwilling to believe he or she is dying, and fears that withdrawing CANH would make the prognosis a self-fulfilling prophecy. This may be a reflection of unwillingness to face reality, but it may also be a genuine concern about misdiagnosis. The team should assure themselves of the diagnosis and reassess the situation. The patient or relative may also wish to pursue a second opinion and the team should be open to this, as misdiagnosis does sometimes happen. In this situation, clinically assisted hydration should generally be given while re-assessment takes place.

Palliative sedation and analgesia towards the end of life

Analgesia towards the end of life has often been cited as an example of 'double effect'. It was widely believed that the use of opiates might hasten death but nevertheless be justified if the aim or intention was to relieve pain. However, we now know that this example is misleading. The evidence is that the use of analgesia towards the end of life does not generally shorten life if it is prescribed and used according to current best practice. In reality, therefore, the anxiety that analgesia may hasten death leads to a false dilemma. Where this anxiety is present, healthcare workers should be clear that their interventions are unlikely to hasten death.

Under-treatment of pain or distress can cause considerable physical, emotional and spiritual suffering. However, overtreatment or inappropriate treatment can also cause problems, rendering people unconscious or semi-conscious when this is not necessary for effective symptom relief. This could deprive people of the opportunity to make a good death: setting things right as much as they can, making peace and saying their goodbyes.

Supporting someone to make a good death

The first ethical duty of those who accompany the dying, more than symptom control or withdrawal of futile interventions, is to help the person find meaning in this last phase of life, to support his or her spiritual needs (in the broad sense of that word). The task of those who accompany the person facing death is to help them to live well – not to take over. Someone else can manage decisions about care for me, but if I am to make a good death then this must be my action. It is simply not possible for someone else to die my death for me.

For the dying person, the avoidance of futile treatments is not only a matter of comfort: it is a matter of honesty to self and justice to others. Similarly, the provision of sufficient but not excessive medication to alleviate symptoms of pain or distress, in addition to being legitimate care for oneself, can also be a means to find lucidity and consider the care of others. Discussion of death in modern philosophy is often flawed because it is concerned only with the individual who is dying, whereas in death, people are, and ought to be, concerned with those they leave behind. People are rightly concerned with how the manner of their death may affect others. The word martyr means 'witness' and sometimes in the face of death people are given an opportunity to witness to what they most care about in life. This is a general truth not necessarily related to overt religious belief.

If, as many religious traditions proclaim, death is not the end but is a moment of judgment and the transition to the life of the world to come, then this constitutes a further reason why the approach of death is an ethical and spiritual challenge. This is why Christians have traditionally prayed for protection against sudden and unforeseen death and for the grace of a happy death, to be able to say, with Jesus, *'Father, into thy hands I commit my spirit!'* (Luke 23.46).

References

Bishops' Conference of England and Wales (2010) *A Practical Guide to the Spiritual Care of the Dying Person.* London: Catholic Truth Society.

Catechism of the Catholic Church (1993) *Catechism of the Catholic Church* [online]. Available at: www.vatican.va/archive/ENG0015/–INDEX.HTM

Chesterton GK (1909) *Orthodoxy.* New York: John Lane Company.

General Medical Council (2010) *Treatment and Care Towards the End of Life: Good practice in decision making.* London: GMC.

Jones DA (2007) *Approaching the End: A theological exploration of death and dying.* Oxford: Oxford University Press.

Kübler-Ross E (1969) *On Death and Dying.* London: Macmillan.

Royal College of Physicians and the British Society of Gastroenterologists (2010) *Oral Feeding Difficulties and Dilemmas: A guide to practical care, particularly towards the end of life.* London: RCP.

Thomas D (1951/2003) *Dylan Thomas: Collected poems 1934–1953.* London: Phoenix.

UNESCO (2005) *Universal Declaration on Bioethics and Human Rights* [online]. Available at: http://www.unesco.org/new/en/social-and-human-sciences/themes/bioethics/bioethics-and-human-rights/ (accessed April 2013).

Chapter 3:

'Why me?' and 'Whose good death?': Anger and values-based practice in end of life care

Bill (KWM) Fulford and Jan Cooper

'Do not go gentle into that good night,
Old age should burn and rave at close of day;
Rage, rage against the dying of the light.'
Dylan Thomas (1951, 2003)

This chapter is about anger. That may seem a surprising focus for a chapter on values in a book on spirituality and end of life care. True, anger is often one of the many emotions expressed in that all-too-familiar question for those facing death: 'Why me?' But aren't the values of end of life care about 'managing' emotions like anger – 'dealing with', 'working through' and the like?

Well, we hope anger does come as a surprise. For values-based practice is all about surprise. It is about being and continuing to be surprised by the truly remarkable extent to which people's values – their beliefs, hopes, fears, needs and strengths – may differ radically from what we might expect them to be. Faced with questions like 'Why me?' values-based practice does not provide ready-made answers. Instead, as the story of (our imaginary) 'Jim Smith' below will illustrate, values-based practice helps us to come to a deeper understanding of the often surprising diversity of values lying behind such questions, and, hence, to a more person-centred approach in end of life care. No 'good death' then, we will conclude, without asking 'whose good death?' But just what is values-based practice?

What is values-based practice?

Values-based practice is a new skills-based approach to working with complex and conflicting values in healthcare. Set within a person-centred and multidisciplinary model of healthcare, values-based practice supports balanced decision making within frameworks of shared values.

Values-based practice is thus more about 'how to do it' rather than 'what to do'. This is why it does not give us ready-made answers. The beliefs and values of ethical, religious and other 'creeds' can certainly help us to find answers in difficult situations. Values-based practice starts instead from the fact that in many situations the beliefs and values of those involved may be very different with resulting potential for misunderstandings and conflict. So, values-based practice says, rather than trying to adjudicate, let's use our clinical skills to better effect in building mutual understanding as a basis for genuine team work and partnership in delivering person-centred care.

The first practical training manual for values-based practice was published by Kim Woodbridge and Bill Fulford in 2006 for use in mental health. Its title, *Whose Values?* (2004), reflected the particularly diverse values of stakeholders – people who use services, carers and service providers – in this area of practice. But values-based practice is now being extended to the many other areas of healthcare where complex and conflicting values come into play (see http://www2.warwick.ac.uk/fac/med/study/research/vbp). The story of Jim Smith that follows shows some of the ways in which values-based practice supports stakeholders in end of life care.

Your values too!

You may find it helpful in reading Jim Smith's story to think about it from your own point of view. To this end we have included some questions to think about rather than just giving our own reactions to the issues raised.

'Making it personal' is important because values-based practice is about mutual understanding – and mutual understanding depends on understanding our own values as well as those of others. So whether you are reading this as a professional, or as someone facing death, or as someone caring for a friend or relative in that situation, your values matter too!

Anger and 'Why me?'

Jim Smith is a 50-year-old man who lives with his wife and three children aged 20, 18 and 15. He initially saw his GP three months ago with vague symptoms of abdominal discomfort and had a follow-up appointment a month later when there had been no improvement. At this point he was referred for further investigations, which confirmed a diagnosis of inoperable carcinoma of the stomach with liver metastases. He is currently undergoing palliative chemotherapy. When he meets the palliative care nurse, he is extremely rude and angry and becomes distressed, asking her 'Why me?'

Reflection points

- If you were Jim's nurse, how do you think you would deal with his anger towards you?
- How might you respond when he asks 'Why me?'?

Three different responses

Given Jim Smith's story it may seem obvious why he is angry. But there are different ways in which we might respond to this. Here are three responses from three different people. Again, as you read through these ask yourself to which response you relate most strongly. Which response from your point of view most closely reflects the values of end of life care?

We will first set out the three responses and then look briefly at our own answers to the above two questions and at what the responses tell us about values-based practice.

Response 1 – setting boundaries

Sue Boundaries says: 'I would explain that I understand how he (Jim) is feeling but there is no need for him to be angry with me because it is not my fault and that everything is being done to help him. If he continued to be angry and rude I would leave and say that I would return when he had the chance to calm down. If he calmed down I would explain that I don't know why it has happened to him – that it is just bad luck but I will do everything I can to support him.'

Response 2 – sticking to the facts

Sue Facts says: 'I would explain that what has happened to him is unfortunate but there was nothing else that could be done and that the GP's response was reasonable given the vagueness of his original symptoms – all too often GPs are accused of causing unnecessary anxiety by rushing in when it turns out there was nothing wrong! If he realises the rationale behind the GP's decision it should help him to not be so angry. In terms of responding to why this has happened to him, I would explain the various causes of stomach cancer to see if we can identify possible causative factors. I think it is the healthcare professional's responsibility to always explain things to clients.'

Response 3 – sitting with Jim Smith

Sue Sitting-with says: 'I would sit with Jim and ask him if he is able to explain what he feels angry about. I think I might also say that I am sorry that this has happened to him as this is clearly very distressing. I am not sure that I could answer his question 'Why me?', but I might ask him if there is something that he thinks may have caused his illness and discuss this with him.'

Sue Sitting-with

Some experienced practitioners working in end of life care will relate most readily to the third response. Sue Sitting-with after all exemplifies empathic engagement that will allow her to see beyond Jim Smith's anger and its 'apparent cause' in his GP's failure to refer him on first presentation, to possible underlying issues; and the importance of allowing these issues to surface not through direct questions but by sitting with him and encouraging him to talk about what he is feeling.

In all this, too, Sue Sitting-with exemplifies excellent values-based communication skills. Among other elements (see below), values-based practice depends critically on and in turn helps to strengthen communication in two main areas: eliciting values, and conflict resolution. Sue Sitting-with shows both of these in good measure. By sitting with Jim Smith she shows that she can accept and cope with whatever it is that is driving his distress – this makes it easier for him to 'open up' because he will feel reassured that if he does, he will not be misunderstood, censured or, worse still, patronised. And by sitting with Jim Smith, Sue Sitting-with shows that she is willing not only to understand but also to accept his anger, acceptance being often a key first step towards conflict resolution.

But ...

And, yes, there is a values-based 'but', more than one 'but' in fact. The first 'but' is that the responses of Sue Facts and Sue Boundaries no less than that of Sue Sitting-with, illustrate important aspects of values-based practice:

■ **Sue Facts** illustrates one of three key principles of values-based practice underlining the close links between it and evidence-based practice.

The principle in question (it's called the 'squeaky wheel principle', see **Figure 3.1: Summary of values-based practice**) reminds us that however value-laden a situation may be, we should go back always to the relevant facts: thus, faced with Jim Smith's understandable anger at an apparently missed diagnosis, Sue Facts tries to bring him back to the clinical facts (that his GP had to balance precipitous and potentially harmful intervention against the small possibility of something serious) and present realities.

■ **Sue Boundaries** illustrates that mutual respect in values-based practice does not mean 'anything goes'.

The key point here is that mutual respect is just that, ie. *mutual* respect. This means that some rather extreme forms of disrespect for the values of others – the values of racism for example – can never be values-based practice-able. But it is also why values-based practice works within frameworks of shared values; and an important shared value at least in our society is that we do not subject each other to violence, physical or, as in this case, verbal.

In any real life situation it is of course likely that there will be other complex and, in part, conflicting values in play influencing how each Sue responds to Jim: this is why awareness of our own values is important for mutual understanding. Thus, Sue Sitting-with's ambivalence about 'saying sorry' may well reflect possible conflicting values. Sue Boundaries, on the other hand, may be reacting defensively because she feels that as health care professionals we let clients down when 'there is nothing we can do' or that everything was done to try and treat Jim appropriately; or she may just not feel comfortable with anger as an emotion. Sue Facts, similarly, may believe that healthcare professionals are 'professional' just to the extent they can provide relevant information.

In each of these three responses then it is likely that complex and conflicting values are in play. Our first values-based 'but', nonetheless, is that natural as it is to identify initially with Sue Sitting-with's response, further reflection shows that Sue Boundaries' and Sue Facts' responses could be important as well.

Three different Jim Smiths

But, you may be thinking, coming now to our second values-based 'but', if all three Sues are 'right', where do we go from here? After all, in the 'real world' of clinical work we have to decide what to do. There is little scope in practice for sitting on the values fence.

This second values-based 'but' is where Jim Smith comes in – or rather three Jim Smiths. For which Sue is 'right' depends on the values of the Jim Smith in question and how these play out in the anger and distress of his 'why me?'

One Jim Smith, believing in his heart of hearts that, say, a double-cross he had played on a business partner many years ago had finally caught up with him, needs a Sue Sitting-with to break through his distress. But a different Jim Smith who prides himself on being a 'rationalist' and is angry that he is being kept at arm's length by his GP (fearful perhaps of a complaint to the GMC) is looking for the straight-talking offered by Sue Facts. Yet a third Jim Smith is, well, used to getting his own way and needs Sue Boundaries' firm handling to bring him up against the reality that this time no amount of shouting will get him what he wants.

But ... how do we pull it all together?

Different values, different approaches, then. There is no one-size-fits-all with values. Nor should there be, for values are at the very heart of our uniqueness as individual human beings. But this still leaves open the question of how to make sense of all this in practice. How can we pull all this diversity of values together in a given situation into a coherent and effective care plan?

Figure 3.1: Summary of values-based practice

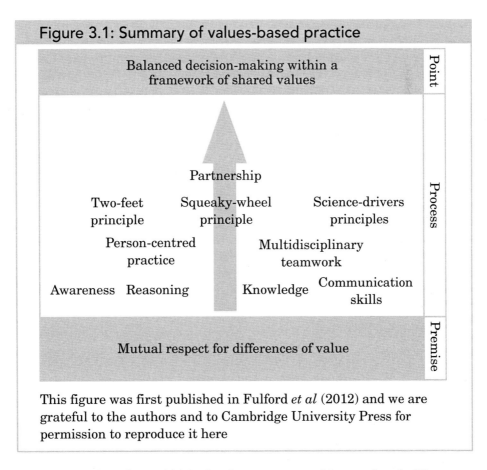

This figure was first published in Fulford *et al* (2012) and we are grateful to the authors and to Cambridge University Press for permission to reproduce it here

'Enter values-based practice', is the short answer to this question. As **Figure 3.1: Summary of values-based practice** shows, the process of values-based practice includes a number of distinct elements. We do not have space here to go into each of these in detail. In brief, as **Figure 3.1** indicates, the elements of values-based practice come together through a particular model of partnership in decision making, called 'dissensus', that allows individual decisions to be taken in a balanced way reflecting the particular values of those concerned.

As with other skills-based approaches, values-based practice works best when its elements are used together in a well joined up way. Any of its elements however may be helpful used independently. We touched above on the importance of values-based communication skills (shown by Sue Sitting-with), of Sue Facts' return to the evidence, and of Sue Boundaries' embodiment of the values-based premise of mutual respect.

Collectively, our three Sues show the importance of a further element – multidisciplinary teamwork. As team members working in a values-based way, we bring to the clinical encounter a range not only of different skills and knowledge, but also of different values. The values in question may be professional or, as with our three Sues above, personal. Either way, it is the different values offered by team members, as well as their different areas of knowledge and skills, that are the basis for an approach to care planning that in meeting the distinct needs of each unique individual is genuinely person-centred.

Surprised by anger

We hope that our focus in this chapter on anger as a perhaps surprising topic in a book on spirituality has brought out the 'itch' behind values-based practice: the often surprising diversity of individual human values; and our pressing need as healthcare professionals to find ways of understanding and working more effectively with that diversity as the basis of care that is genuinely person-centred.

We hope too that our various Sue and Jim stories of anger and 'Why me?' will have shown the importance in all this diversity of our own values. Nothing in values-based practice requires subordination of self to other. This is not a 'my customer right or wrong' approach. To the contrary, 'Your values too!' means as we have seen that in values-based practice, the diversity of our values as individual healthcare practitioners is a key resource for team work and partnership in providing person-centred care.

'Your values too!' is nowhere more important than with spirituality in end of life care. Spirituality after all is about finding meaning and meaning is nothing if not uniquely personal and, hence, often surprising. As a nowadays-not-quite-respectable emotion, anger is just one sometimes surprising portal to meaning. The 20th century Christian apologist (and Oxbridge professor), CS Lewis, described his own spiritual awakening as being surprised by another nowadays-not-quite-respectable emotion, joy. Writing in a similar vein from a secular perspective, the French poet and pioneering aviator Antoine de Saint Exupery (1995), said that: *'It is only with one's heart that one can see clearly. What is essential is invisible to the eye.'* Such spontaneity, such breaking through of the unique individual, may sit uneasily with those for whom religious (or other) convictions mean as it were 'my values right or wrong'. Yet as the now suffragan bishop of

Stockport and former Benedictine, Robert Atwell, has pointed out, each of the great religious faiths includes healing traditions in which deeply held personal values and beliefs are the very foundations for an open and respectful acceptance of the values and beliefs of others.

So, be surprised. Be surprised by how very different other people's values may be from what you might expect. Be surprised by your own values. Be surprised by how building on your own values you can extend your skills of understanding and engagement. But don't be surprised that thus extended you find there really is no 'good death' without first asking 'whose good death?'

Where can I learn more?

Clinical stories illustrating the way values-based practice supports person-centred decision making in a wide range of clinical contexts are given in Fulford *et al* (2012): Chapter 13: A good (enough) death: dissensus in end of life care, illustrates in more detail the role of values-based practice in palliative care.

Warwick Medical School's website has useful information on Values-based Practice (http://www2.warwick.ac.uk/fac/med/study/research/vbp) and provides resources including a PDF of *Whose Values?* (2004): http://www2.warwick.ac.uk/fac/med/study/research/vbp/resources/library/whose_values_complete_workbook.pdf

For further reading on anger as an expression of spirituality, see:

Connor KM, Davidson JRT & Lee L-C (2003) Spirituality, resilience, and anger in survivors of violent trauma: a community survey. *Journal of Traumatic Stress* **16** (5) 487–494. Available at: http://onlinelibrary.wiley.com/doi/10.1023/A:1025762512279/abstract (accessed March 2013).

María Márquez-González, López J, Romero-Moreno R & Losada A (2012) Anger, spiritual meaning and support from the religious community in dementia caregiving. *Journal of Religion and Health* **51** (1) 179–186.

References

de Saint Exupery A (1995) *The Little Prince.* Hertfordshire: Wordsworth Editions Limited.

Atwell R & Fulford KWM (2006) The Christian tradition of spiritual direction as a sketch for a strong theology of diversity. In: J Cox, AV Campbell and KWM Fulford (Eds) *Medicine of the Person: Faith, science and values in health care provision.* London: Jessica Kingsley Publishers.

Fulford KWM, Peile EP & Carroll H (2012) *Essential Values-based Practice: Clinical stories linking science with people.* Cambridge: Cambridge University Press.

Lewis CS (1966) *Surprised by Joy: The shape of my early life.* New York: Houghton Mifflin Harcourt.

Thomas D (1951/2003) *Dylan Thomas: Collected poems 1934–1953.* London: Phoenix.

Woodbridge K & Fulford KWM (2004) *Whose Values? A workbook for values-based practice in mental health care.* London: The Sainsbury Centre for Mental Health.

Chapter 4:

Dignity in end of life care

Wilf McSherry

'Very many of us have now witnessed the real peace of a dignified death from a personal or a professional perspective – long may this continue.' (Hornett, 2012, p.1295)

The above quotation highlights that significant developments and improvements over several decades have ensured that those caring for the dying and their families create environments and outcomes that have a positive and lasting impression in the memories of those who live on. Yet, and probably more importantly, the quotation highlights that these developments have enhanced the last days and hours of those who are dying.

However, despite all the attention accredited to death, dying and end of life care, both within society and more specifically within health care, it still remains an extremely sensitive and emotionally charged area. It is an area that touches, pervades and provokes primeval fears and feelings. Many of these feelings are aroused if individuals sense that they or their loved ones have not been treated in a dignified, comfortable and humane way during their last days of life. Part of this fear may originate because dignity and end of life care necessitate an engagement with taboo areas such as suffering, pain and loss. As Porock (2011, p.132) asserts, suffering is not well understood from the dying person's perspective and yet suffering and dignity are integrated concepts.

Therefore, this chapter provides a brief overview of the meaning of dignity and its role, place and relationship within end of life care. Dignity is a term used repeatedly within policy and guidance documents (DH, 2008; 2012) and indeed by many contemporary health and social care professionals (as reflected in the edited book *Dignity in Healthcare* by Matiti & Baillie, 2011). But, like many words used liberally in healthcare, consideration must be given to both understanding and 'actioning' dignity in end of life care otherwise it will remain rhetorical, with limited impact and outcome. This is captured so beautifully in the following quotation by Magee *et al* (2008, p.9): *'It is easier to make pronouncements about dignity than to ensure dignified care happens.'*

Defining dignity

This section explores some of the meanings of dignity by highlighting their implications for end of life care. Fenton and Mitchell (2002, p.21) provide a conceptual definition, describing the main attributes of dignity: *'Dignity is a state of physical, emotional and spiritual comfort, with each individual valued for his or her uniqueness and his or her individuality celebrated. Dignity is promoted when individuals are enabled to do the best within their capabilities, exercise control, make choices and feel involved in the decision-making that underpins their care.'*

This definition has a direct relevance to end of life care as it presents a total/holistic approach to care delivery highlighting the interdependence and integrated nature of our humanity. End of life care involves an engagement with all dimensions of a person; physical, psychological, social and spiritual (consideration must also be given to the impact of culture and environment). Failure to address each of these dimensions in a meaningful and therapeutic way can have disastrous consequences on the perceived quality and outcome of care and the dignity of the person. This is certainly evident in the national media. For example, the article written by Max Pemperton (2013), *The Liverpool Care Pathway to Dignified Death,* highlights the fears and misgivings and inconsistencies of implementing the Liverpool Care Pathway for the Dying Patient (LCP) and the important role that all health care professionals play in preserving people's dignity.

However, it must be emphasised that despite recent controversies surrounding the LCP, if implemented and used appropriately it can have a positive impact for the dying person. This is reflected by several authors:

Hornett (2012, p.1295) writes: *'It enables the kind of care health professionals want to give and allows people to die as peaceful a death as possible.'*

While The Right Reverend Thomas A Williams (2013, p.18), talking about health care professionals' experiences of using the LCP, states: *'In my experience the LCP can be applied successfully, but only if it is used well by skilled and caring professionals. There is reason to be cautious but also reason to affirm the good example given by many Catholics working in palliative care and applying the LCP well.'*

Four notions of dignity

Nordenfelt and Edgar (2005) offer a useful model of dignity that may assist those caring for dying people to provide dignified care. They suggest that dignity may be explained by the following terms.

Menschenwürde: The translation from German means 'humanness'. This refers to the dignity inherent in every person, highlighting it is something universal, affirming why it is enshrined within the Human Rights Act (1998) and legislation.

Dignity as merit may be formal or informal implying that dignity is something conferred by others perhaps as a result of merit or rank. This aspect of the model has come under some scrutiny within health care as it implies that some people are more deserving of dignity than others (Baillie, 2009). In end of life care there can be no discrimination because there are no shades or degrees of dignity; all dying people should be afforded the same level of dignity and respect irrespective of rank or merit. Rank and merit must not be totally discounted as these may influence the identity of the dying person.

The dignity of moral stature is about people's own moral stature and integrity. This can be lost if a person fails to act in accordance with one's principles and values. This has relevance to those providing end of life care since professional conduct and behaviour communicate trust, compassion and caring. Attention must be given to how moral stature and integrity can be safeguarded, protected to uphold and always act in the best interests of the dying person, their family and friends.

The dignity of personal identity: This addresses the identity of the person. This aspect of dignity may be violated by physical assault and humiliation. Central to this are the values of integrity, autonomy and inclusion that shape and preserve the person's identity. This type of dignity is of fundamental importance within the context of end of life care. Closer inspection of this form of dignity reveals how any health care professional's actions, attitudes and behaviours can either preserve the dying person's identity or even compromise it.

Nordenfelt and Edgar's (2005) four notions of dignity suggest dignity involves and permeates every aspect of life: physical, psychological, social, spiritual and environmental. Reinforcing dignity is multifaceted or layered, it is something that is innate and constructed through the interaction of all these dimensions, which shape identity. They also imply that preserving dignity is relational, meaning how people relate with each other is fundamental to preserving a sense of self and esteem. Disease and illness can strip away the dying person's dignity leaving them vulnerable and exposed. It is the role of those caring for the dying person and their families to safeguard and preserve dignity.

Therefore, careful consideration must be given to interventions and interactions when caring for the dying person since professionals and carers must be mindful that actions, behaviours and attitudes can preserve an individual's sense of dignity and self-esteem.

Primary dignity domains

When one looks at recent controversies surrounding the inappropriate use of the LCP (Ellershaw & Murphy, 2003; Ellershaw & Ward, 2003), it can be said that several of the primary domains associated with dignity-preserving care have not been adhered to or implemented in an open, honest and transparent manner.

McSherry and Coleman (2011) adapt the work of Magee *et al* (2008) to suggest that there are nine primary dignity domains.

1. **Autonomy:** Involving the dying person and their family in decisions at every stage of the end of life care pathway. Provision must be made to discuss personal wishes and preferences associated with end of life care, for example treatment choices and place of death. Attention must be given to advance directives and 'living wills' and arrangements for lasting power of attorney.

2. **Communication:** Using interpersonal and communication skills to promote an open and positive dialogue with the dying person and their next of kin. Developing attitudes and behaviours that are not patronising, but are courteous and respectful. Communication is the foundation for the delivery of dignified end of life care and promoting positive and therapeutic relationships.

3. **Eating and drinking:** Ensuring that the dying person is not nutritionally compromised. It is important that individuals are involved in decisions about supportive interventions. Independence and choice about selection of food and drink is very important. Appropriate and sensitive assistance with eating and drinking should be given as required.

4. **Privacy:** Individuals should be afforded maximum privacy but not isolated and segregated and devoid of interaction. This will necessitate giving priority to the individual's preference regarding place of death. Health care professionals should plan visits and intrusions by medical and allied staff should be kept to only what is absolutely necessary. Individuals should be supported as necessary when using wash or toilet facilities and independence should be maintained. Consent should be obtained before any care or treatment is given.

5. **Personal hygiene:** The dying person should be offered timely assistance as required. Individuals should be given choice regarding bathing and independence should be maintained.

6. **Pain:** There should be timely and appropriate intervention and management of symptoms, pain or discomfort. Allowing the dying person to be involved and where possible responsible for the management of their own pain is desirable. They should be included in all aspects of their care and fully informed.

7. **Social inclusion:** It is vital that personal, religious and spiritual beliefs are considered towards the end of life. These areas may be a valuable source of strength, hope and comfort to the individual and their family. Contact and access should be maintained with family, friends and community, and any religious or spiritual needs involved if requested.

8. **Safety:** Good end of life care must include a thorough individualised assessment of each person, identifying any potential environmental or personal risks.

9. **End of life care:** There needs to be recognition that death and dying are inevitable aspects of life. There needs to be openness and willingness to discuss and support individuals with decisions made with regard their own death. Attention must be given to advance directives and 'living wills' when these exist. End of life care must be culturally sensitive to people's religious and spiritual needs. Therefore, it is imperative that all those providing end of life care have an awareness of how such issues may impact upon attitudes to death and care of the person following death. Throughout the end of life care pathway, provision must be made to discuss personal wishes and preferences and include the dying person (where possible) and their next of kin or family in treatment choices and decisions concerning end of life care.

All nine domains are interrelated and have a fundamental impact on the quality, standards and people's levels of satisfaction with the end of life care provided. Interestingly, it could be asked: Why is end of life care a discrete domain? This may be explained by the fact that each of the primary domains take on a different meaning and significance when caring for individuals and their families as they approach the end of life. Each of the domains presents a unique set of challenges and opportunities for those caring for the dying person and supportive care offered to family and friends. For example, one of the alleged criticisms surrounding the LCP is that dying people are placed on the pathway without explicit explanation or involvement of next of kin or family; this practice contravenes all principles and practices that preserve and promote dignified care.

Wainwright (2011, p.35) argues *'that there are three classes or categories of objects, in the context of health care to which dignity is relevant'*. These classes certainly have relevance within the context of delivering end of life care.

- **The dying person** and all those associated with them demand dignity and respect because of their inherent worth as fellow human beings. End of life care should safeguard and value the unique individuality and identity of each person.

- **The individual professional** is entitled to dignity; they must behave with dignity acting in a professional manner adopting attitudes and behaviours reflecting their role and function.

- **The practice of end of life care** has a specific value and function and as such has moral worth and demands respect.

Each of these classes must be considered because each plays a fundamental role in preserving the dignity of the dying person. Failure to consider each of these classes will see a breakdown in the provision of end of life care meaning the dignity of individuals could be compromised or violated.

Dignity integral to end of life care

In England the Department of Health launched the *End of Life Care Strategy Promoting High Quality Care for All Adults at the End of Life* in 2008. A search of the document using the word 'dignity' reveals 11 usages. Reviewing the context in which the word is used affirms that dignity is seen as an integral part of developing an end of life care strategy that is respectful of the dying person and inclusive of their family/friends. This strategy strives to embed the same level and standards of end of life care across the full spectrum of sectors. Dignity is afforded priority in that it is the second objective: *'To ensure that all people are treated with dignity and respect at the end of their lives'* (DH, 2008, p.33).

Therefore, dignity in all its manifestations and composite elements is seen as fundamental to the delivery of high quality end of life care where people feel safe, valued and comforted, having choice and preference on where they want to spend their last months or days of life, and importantly being supported in the place of death that they choose.

Dignity conserving care at the end of life

One of the pioneers exploring the relationship between dignity and end of life care is Harvey Max Chochinov, a professor of psychiatry at the University of Manitoba, Canada. Chochinov has researched and written extensively on the subject of dignity and palliative care (see Chochinov, 2002; 2007; Chochinov *et al,* 2002; 2008; Sinclair & Chochinov, 2012). He provides a simple acronym termed the A, B, C, D of dignity-conserving care (Chochinov, 2007).

A. **Attitudes**. Those caring for the dying must examine their own attitudes and assumptions towards death and dying. This is crucial since what they believe will either positively or negatively influence the potential of the dying person. Chochinov (2007, p.185) captures this, stating: *'In other words, patients look at healthcare providers as they would a mirror, seeking a positive image of themselves and their continued sense of worth. In turn, healthcare providers need to be aware that their attitudes and assumptions will shape those all-important reflections.'*

B. **Behaviour** stems from attitudes and values. Behaviour should be predicated on kindness and respect. This can be reflected in the way small acts of care are performed, for example giving a glass of water, greeting the individual with a 'good morning' and smile affirming their worth and self-esteem.

C. **Compassion** is about recognising the suffering and pain in another and having the desire to alleviate and relieve this for the dying person. Compassion is more than just an intellectual awareness, it is something far deeper. Compassion moves beyond physical acts of care as it is felt and experienced emotionally and spiritually. Compassion may be intuitive and innate in some people while for others it may develop through professional practice and life experience. Compassion is communicated through verbal and non-verbal channels, for example the way we approach the dying person or use touch to convey presence offering reassurance.

D. **Dialogue** is the outcome of A, B, C working synonymously and effectively since attitudes, behaviours and compassion will lead to a deeper engagement and understanding of the needs of the individual and their family and friends. Dialogue is about elucidating the personal narrative and biography of the individual. It is about knowing who they are and glimpsing their own unique dignity and identity. Therefore, dialogue is essential if the dying person is to be understood and have their personhood affirmed. Dialogue is not a one-off activity but a continuous and cyclical process that captures and supports the dignity of the dying person as situations and needs change.

This is reflected in the following quote by Chochinov (2007, p.187): *'The practice of medicine requires the exchange of extensive information, within a partnership whose tempo is set by gathering, interpreting, and planning according to new and emerging details. As such, dialogue is a critical element of dignity-conserving care. At its most basic, such dialogue must acknowledge personhood beyond the illness itself and recognise the emotional impact that accompanies illness.'*

This simple acronym provides a useful tool/framework for promoting and preserving the dignity of the dying person. It involves the healthcare professional being reflective and introspective, being prepared to change perhaps long established attitudes and behaviours that may have a negative and detrimental impact on end of life care. The tool places the dying person and their dignity/identity at the centre of care delivery, encouraging dialogue and a compassionate approach. The A, B, C, D can foster an environment and relationships where trust, honesty and openness flourish and dignity is conserved. Brown *et al* (2011) have used this framework as a basis for their research within a community context identifying care actions that can be adopted to conserve dignity in end of life care.

Conclusion

This chapter has demonstrated that dignity is a word that is frequently used within health and social care. Dignity is universal to all people transcending all societies, pervading every aspect of human existence and life. It is not constrained by age, gender, religious belief, ethnicity or any other factor since there are no shades of dignity, since all people are deserving of dignity.

The chapter has described how dignity has an array of meanings and interpretation, and consideration must be given to these within the context of end of life care. The key dignity domains described must be addressed if the dignity of the dying person and their family and friends is to be conserved within the delivery of end of life care.

Dignity is not an optional extra but is a fundamental element of end of life care, which if absent will leave the dying person and their family and friends feeling isolated and disconnected from the partnership of care. Focusing on dignity places the dying person at the centre of any care pathways. This encourages all those involved to see the person and to develop a plan of care that upholds their personal identity, reviewing all the factors that have influenced and shaped this throughout their life.

References

Baillie L (2009) Patient dignity in an acute hospital setting: a case study. *International Journal of Nursing Studies* **46** 22–36.

Brown H, Johnston B & Östlund U (2011) Identifying care actions to conserve dignity in end-of-life care *British Journal of Community Nursing* **16** (5) 238–245.

Chochinov HM (2002) Dignity-conserving care – a new model for palliative care: helping the patient feel valued. *Journal of the American Medical Directors Association* **287** (17) 2253–2260.

Chochinov HM (2007) Dignity and the essence of medicine: the A, B, C, and D of dignity conserving care. *British Medical Journal* **335** 184–187.

Chochinov HM, Hack T, McClement S, Kristjanson L & Harlos M (2002) Dignity in the terminally ill: a developing empirical model. *Social Science Medicine* **54** (3) 433–443.

Chochinov HM, Hassard T, McClement S, Hack T, Kristjanson LJ, Harlos M, Sinclair S & Murray A (2008) The patient dignity inventory: a novel way of measuring dignity-related distress in palliative care. *Journal of Pain and Symptom Management* **36** (6) 559–571.

Department of Health (2008) *End of Life Care Strategy: Promoting high quality care for all adults at the end of life.* Available at: http://www.dh.gov.uk/prod_consum_dh/groups/dh_digitalassets/@dh/@en/documents/digitalasset/dh_086345.pdf (accessed March 2013).

Ellershaw JE & Murphy D (2003) The national pathway network of palliative care pathways. *Journal of Integrated Care Pathways* **7** (1) 11–13.

Ellershaw JE & Ward C (2003) Care of the dying patient: the last hours or days of life. *British Medical Journal* **326** 30–34.

Fenton E & Mitchell T (2002) Growing old with dignity: a concept analysis. *Nursing Practice* **14** (4) 19–21.

Hornett M (2012) Dying to care: dignity at end of life. *British Journal of Nursing* **21** (21) 1295.

Magee H, Parsons S & Askham J (2008) *Measuring Dignity in Care for Older People.* London: Picker Institute Europe for Help the Aged.

Matiti MR & Baillie L (Eds) (2011) *Dignity in Healthcare: A practical approach for nurses and midwives:* London: Radcliffe Publishing Ltd.

McSherry W & Coleman H (2011) Dignity and older people: In: MR Matiti and L Baillie (Ed) (2011) *Dignity in Healthcare: A practical approach for nurses and midwives:* London: Radcliffe Publishing Ltd.

Nordenfelt L & Edgar A (2005) The four notions of dignity. *Quality in Ageing* **6** (1) 17–21.

Pemberton M (2013) *The Liverpool Care Pathway to Dignity in Death*. Available at: www.telegraph.co.uk/health/elderhealth/9796968/The-Liverpool-Care-Pathway-to-dignity-in-death.html (accessed April 2013).

Porock D (2011) Dignity and the end of life. In MR Matiti and L Baille (Eds) *Dignity in Healthcare: A practical approach for nurses and midwives*. London: Radcliffe Publishing Ltd.

Sinclair S & Chochinov HM (2012) Dignity: A novel path into the spiritual landscape of the human heart. In: M Cobb, CM Puchalski and B Rumbold (Eds) (2012) *Oxford Textbook of Spirituality in Healthcare*. Oxford: Oxford University Press.

Wainwright P (2011) Professional and ethical expectations for dignity in care. In: MR Matiti and L Baillie (Ed) (2011) *Dignity in Healthcare: A practical approach for nurses and midwives*. London: Radcliffe Publishing Ltd.

Williams TA (2013) Palliative care – light of experience. *The Tablet* **26 January 2013**.

Chapter 5:

Belief and palliative care

Andrew Goodhead

In the minds of many, hospice care and belief go hand in hand. This has undoubtedly arisen because Cicely Saunders, the founder of the modern hospice movement, which gave rise to the specialism of palliative care, had an active Christian faith. The name of the hospice she opened in 1967, St Christopher's, is resonant of the idea of a journeying, in which Christ is a central character. In this case the journeying is towards death and Christ might be seen as the accompanier of the one who is dying. In the Muslim tradition, making the Hajj (pilgrimage) to Mecca is one of the five pillars of Islam, and the Hindu tradition of pilgrimage is seen most recently (2013) in the Kumbha Mela in Uttar-Pradesh Puja. These pilgrimages are not inner religious journeys suggested by the story of St Christopher, but lively, faith-developing gatherings. Today, St Christopher's Hospice actively engages with the cultural and religious context in which it is geographically placed, with an emphasis towards a broad recognition of faiths. This enables the hospice to reach a diverse, multicultural and complex community effectively.

As palliative care has developed, into care in people's homes, specialised units in hospitals and more recently in care homes, care for patients with life-limiting illness has retained much of its earliest ethos. As a chaplain, I would argue this is good. Not just because a patient in their home can ask to see a faith leader, but because the wider concept of spiritual care, inherent in the creation of St Christopher's Hospice, has continued as an element of palliative care. I focus on spirituality and spiritual care in **Chapter 15: The caring professions**. Here I aim to unpack more of belief in the context of palliative care.

Religious belief and spirituality (see **Chapter 1: Rage against the dying of the light, or a new light shining?**) are often conflated so that the two are fused into one; or separated out, so belief loses any sense of vitality which spirituality brings to it and spirituality itself is left undefined and often ignored. A belief system provides '*a framework for understanding the human* *experience of death and dying for patients, family members and healthcare professionals'* (Daaleman & VandeCreek, 2000, p.2514). It is within that framework that the difficult questions of dying and death are framed; 'Why is God allowing this?', 'Has God given me this disease to test my faith?' Questions of ultimate value, meaning and purpose in the milieu of belief are usually framed within a relationship to a transcendent being or beings.

Men and women with a religious belief will bring to the clinical setting the ethics which their belief has instilled within them, and patient care must reflect those personal and/or community ethics. The care of the patient depends on the belief system followed by an individual and their family. A Muslim female would expect personal care from a female nurse or doctor, respecting the Muslim ethic of modesty. A Roman Catholic patient would expect the ministry of his or her priest to focus on the sacraments: reconciliation, Holy Communion, anointing and the Sacrament of the Sick. The Buddhist patient may expect to be fully aware of the process of dying and therefore, for the attending doctors, the reduction of medications which cause sedation could be requested. For patients from the Hindu tradition, rituals around the end of life include reading and chanting in preparation for death (Dom, 1999). In these contexts, the ethic of the patient is an expectation that their care will be dignified and their belief and its practice will be respected.

There is research available which shows that a belief ethic influences decisions for end of life care. In studies around physician-assisted suicide, the responses of older adults suggest that a strong religious belief is a marker for disagreement with the concept of euthanasia. Religious teachings which discuss the value of life impact on the person who, although reaching the end of life, does not see physician-assisted suicide as a means of controlling the time or place of dying (Daaleman & VandeCreek, 2000). An opposite view was taken by Philip Wetherell, an Anglican priest who was diagnosed with motor neurone disease in 2007. For Wetherell, his ethic changed because of his experience of life-limiting illness. In his book *When You are Dying* (2011), Wetherell argued that, with the right safeguards and checks, assisted suicide would not be imposed on those who are facing death. He believed that when his quality of life, an important argument for those who disagree with assisted suicide as a reason not to allow this, was no longer as he would want it to be, dying at a time of his choosing was preferable to living longer (Wetherell, 2011).

In recent years in the UK, the NHS has produced guidelines through the End of Life Care Strategy (EOLC) implementing pathways for discussion of end of life wishes. Advance care planning (ACP) specifically encourages healthcare professionals to discuss a patient's faith and belief systems and the resulting plans reflect the wishes of the patient for treatment or its withdrawal (including cardiopulmonary resuscitation), personal concerns and place of care and death. Those who have a belief will respond to the ACP through a prism of ethics and morals drawn from that belief. Responses will reflect this. At the time of dying, the Liverpool Care Pathway (LCP) specifically requires healthcare staff to address a patient's religious beliefs and call a chaplain or faith leader from the community to support the patient and their family.

A challenge to the healthcare professional is to be sufficiently skilled to initiate a difficult conversation about the end of life, and be able to explain treatments and their withdrawal sensitively, respecting a patient's right to make what the professional might consider a 'wrong' choice (cardiopulmonary resuscitation, for example).

For those who are reaching the end of life, particular wishes may become paramount. Monroe (2011) described a female patient experiencing respiratory failure who requested immersion baptism. Physicians considered this dangerous as the likelihood of survival once extubated was poor. Other members of the multi-professional team, including the chaplain, worked to ensure the patient's wish was fulfilled. The patient's Christian belief and last wishes were respected by her medical team and a form of advance care planning took place; a wish was expressed, those who were able to fulfil this did so.

Quality of life will feature in segment on chaplaincy in **Chapter 15: The caring professions**, but I mention it here, as belief is a marker for an individual's quality of life at the time of illness or dying. What gives quality to a person's life is intensely subjective. The social aspect of believing by attending worship or prayers; an intrinsic activity, spills into the extrinsic life by the creation of social networks beyond the place of worship, with those who form part of the same religious community. At times of illness or dying, those social networks can become a helpful support, both practically and emotionally. Disease need not be faced alone, but with others who share the patient's belief and can support the patient and carer(s) at times when hope seems lost.

Finally, within the individual's belief there is the personal dialogue between that individual and their God. Within that dialogue there will be questions of meaning about disease or dying (Daaleman & VandeCreek, 2000). There will also be, for some, the handing over of control to God which can enable happiness to be found in suffering (Koffman *et al*, 2012).

Within the world of palliative care, belief is brought by the individual to the services being offered. The individual's belief cannot and should not shape the service. However, that belief which forms an integral part of the patient's understanding of themselves, their ethics and wishes, must be respected by the healthcare provider to ensure that each patient is cared for holistically and with dignity.

References

Daaleman TP & VandeCreek L (2000) Placing religion and spirituality in end of life care. *The Journal of the American Medical Association* **284** (19).

Dom H (1999) Aisnava Hindu and ayurvedic approaches to caring for the dying: an interview with Henry Dom by AL Romer and KS Heller. *Innovations in End-of-Life Care 1* (**6**). Available at: www.edc.org/lastacts

Koffman J, Morgan M, Edmonds P, Speck P, Siegert R & Higginson JI (2012) The meaning of happiness among two ethnic groups living with advanced cancer in South London: a qualitative study. *Psycho-Oncology* doi: 10.1002/pon.3108.

Monroe C (2011) Spirituality shines through in a magnet moment. *Critical Care Nurse* **31** (4) 98–99.

Wetherell P (2011) *When You are Dying: A personal exploration of life, suffering and belief.* Malton: Gilead Books.

Further reading

Humphrys J with Jarvis S (2009) Chapter 14: Who decides? In: J Humphrys and S Jarvis *The Welcome Visitor.* London: Hodder & Stoughton.

NHS (2013) *Improving end of life care* [online]. At: http://www.endoflifecareforadults.nhs.uk/ (accessed March 2013).

University of Liverpool (2010) *What is the Liverpool Care Pathway for the Dying Patient* (LCP)? [online] Available at: http://www.liv.ac.uk/media/livacuk/mcpcil/migrated-files/liverpool-care-pathway/updatedlcppdfs/What_is_the_LCP_-_Healthcare_Professionals_-_April_2010.pdf (accessed March 2013).

Part 2:

End of life care
in practice

Chapter 6:

Birmingham Children's Hospital: Paediatric end of life care and the bereavement care pathway

Paul Nash

'Do not worry about saying the wrong thing. Nothing can be worse than what has already happened to us.' (Bereaved parent)

The untimely death of a child is one of the most tragic events encountered in life, bringing with it an exaggerated sense of injustice, loss of role and identity, and possibly feelings of blame, guilt and shame. When I became senior chaplain at Birmingham Children's Hospital (BCH) we offered end of life support and sent out invitations to have an inscription included in the remembrance book. Our provision has grown significantly since then and we now offer in the region of 1,000 episodes of care a year. Our vision is to offer the very best practice in multi-faith and spiritual end of life and bereavement care. Our objectives are:

■ to ensure differences between adults and children and young people are known and acted upon

■ to communicate that the child will never be forgotten by the hospital

■ to continue to name the child and give permission for the family to continue to mention the name without judgment

■ to give age and belief-appropriate resources to families.

BCH bereavement care pathway (BCP)

A care pathway is a medical term used to describe the protocol or processes for staff to follow in a particular context. This pathway has been developed by observing similar organisations, listening to other professionals and perhaps most importantly, listening to bereaved parents. There are both proactive and reactive elements in the design and BCH has developed unique contributions such as faith-specific gift booklets and virtual training rooms. The pathway is a work in progress and we expect it to evolve in response to new understandings of best practice and feedback from families.

Figure 6.1: BCH Chaplaincy: End of life and bereavement care pathway

The imagery that we find useful in chaplaincy is that of accompanying and sharing the bereavement journey with families. We don't seek to offer easy answers or platitudes to their grief or questions, but to travel with them, supporting them from alongside. We seek to work with other staff in drawing out from families how they appreciate others supporting them.

Before and at the time of death	A. End of life care including on call, prayers, blessing and offer of literature and resources	
	B. Notification of death form arrives	
	C. Visits to the bereavement suite	
After death	Support offered through:	
	Events	Literature and resources
Within a week after death	E. Funerals	D & F. Booklets and condolence cards
Within a year after death	I. Christian memorial service	G. Memorial book inscriptions and subsequent visits
A year after death	J. Memorial walk and picnic	H. Anniversary cards

Guidance

NICE (2011) and Department of Health (2009) end of life quality standards and the *Together for Short Lives Charter* (2012) and *Integrated Palliative Care Pathways Standards* (Together for Short Lives, 2011) suggest that holistic spiritual and religious support is offered to patients, their families and carers. NHS guidance suggests that the quality of the bereavement service is enhanced if different forms of spiritual care are offered and these may be equally important as other forms of support. It is proposed that such spiritual care may be best offered through chaplaincy working closely with others involved in bereavement care.

Research

Our BCP is evidence-based, drawing on research and conversations with families. We ran a Listening into Action event where bereaved families advised us and we also drew on feedback from events. There is a range of literature which informs bereavement care on topics as varied as parental grief (Kriecbergs *et al*, 2007), supporting children and young people (Pearson, 2010), particular religious needs (Heydayat, 2006), offering contact cards (Clarke & Pearson, 2010), hospice support services (Wilkinson *et al*, 2007) as well as literature reviews (Harvey *et al*, 2008; Kendall & Guo, 2008) and studies of spiritual care at the end of life (DH, 2010a) and bereavement care services (DH, 2010b; Chaplin, 2009). Bereavement care is best started before the child dies as part of an end of life care plan (Kriecbergs *et al*, 2007). A particularly significant finding for our pathway is that parents wanted a flexible, ongoing bereavement service from the hospital where their child was treated (D'Agostino *et al*, 2008) and that bereaved parents value follow-up so as not to feel forgotten (Collins-Tracey *et al*, 2009).

Underpinning principles

There is a wide range of principles which underpin our BCP, such as seeing the child who has died as continuing to be 'our patient'; ensuring we know and differentiate between care for adults and children, particularly from a faith perspective; multidisciplinary team work; and self-care for staff. We are also committed to the extended family, particularly acknowledging the double grief of grandparents. However, what is acutely important for us at BCH is differentiating between different types of care and to offer multi-faith not interfaith care.

Each time I approach a patient or their family I make an assessment as to what sort of care is needed. Others offer medical care, as a chaplain I tend to offer pastoral, spiritual or religious care, although they may overlap at times. The different types of care may be defined thus:

- pastoral care refers to care given to address the cares, concerns, problems, needs and issues of an individual or family

- spiritual care concerns itself with the big questions of life involving who someone is, their purpose, their destiny, their identity and their relationship with the transcendent

- religious care relates specifically to the tenets, practices, rituals and conventions of a particular religious faith (Nash, 2011).

While there are some religious professionals who offer interfaith care, my experience as a chaplain in a large multicultural city is that people want faith-appropriate care.

A significant aspect of end of life hospice chaplaincy care involves being an attentive presence to others in the present moment. This is a deceptively simple way in which adults can connect with children, which the playwright Dennis Potter illuminated. For, if children have the capacity to *'live almost entirely in the present tense,'* he suggested that, as adults, we too can experience this through playing or acting, singing or dancing, and in these ways find ourselves *'outside "normal" time … in the cauldron of the actual minute'* (1987, p.50). Attentiveness, then, can draw us into the child's world and enable us to engage with them in the moment.

Bereavement care pathway overview

The quality of the relationship between the chaplain, the patient and their family can impact on how many or which elements of the pathway can be delivered.

As Ben became less well, his cat made hospice visits from home and Ben was able to stroke the cat as he snuggled on his lap. His room was set up with his own photographs and belongings. Because of Ben's complex family background, staff supported his wishes with regards to visitors. He allowed his mother and sibling to visit once and enjoyed visits from friends and teachers. An organised trip home enabled Ben to say 'goodbye' to all that was familiar to him there for one final time. After his death, he was moved to a special bedroom set up with his photographs and music. The family were given a photo-book of his time at the hospice and they were able to stay at the hospice until the funeral. His dad wanted Ben dressed in his new football kit, a favourite cap and with a photograph of his cat; Ben's music was played at the funeral. Staff attended Ben's funeral, which his dad organised with the community children's nurse, who gave Ben's eulogy. On-going support was offered, but not taken up by the family. Ben had a 'good death' and his wishes were fulfilled throughout. It was a good example of person-centred holistic care, integrating spiritual, emotional and physical support.

A. End of life care

Our end of life and bereavement care pathways overlap. At end of life we have multi-faith 24:7 availability to support families when their child is about to die. Most of our deaths at BCH are through withdrawal of treatment, so plans can be made for prayers, blessings, baptisms etc. The Paediatric Chaplaincy Network (PCN) have written Christian books for children with life-limiting illness and bereaved siblings and we offer these to patients, families, siblings and friends. These are also available online (www.paediatric-chaplaincy-network.org) narrated by Bear Grylls. Such resources give confidence to families in engaging with the issues. Islamic and spiritual books are also available.

Danny was a 10-year-old slowly dying from a life-limiting cardiac condition. When asked what he wanted to do, he would say go and play football with Grandad. The problem was that Grandad had died the year before! Danny used this image of playing football with Grandad to communicate that he had had enough of his illness. He was ready now and wanted to do what he used to do with Grandad, when both of them were well. Clearly his image of death was one where he would be well, free and happy.

B. Notification of death form

Chaplaincy receives this form usually within a day of death. It provides the date of death, religious affiliation, parents' address(es) and details of siblings. We add the family to our database and start the bereavement care pathway.

C. Visits to the bereavement suite

We accompany families to the bereavement suite and this can be done by appointment until the body has been collected. Faith resources are available and staff are trained in their use.

D. Condolence cards

These are given out around the time of death or when family visit the bereavement suite. We have two personalised cards, including one for Muslim families, which is designed to be given in the first three days of bereavement, during the significant time of mourning.

E. Funerals

We do about 10 funerals a year. Our policy is not to offer but, when asked, we normally try to stay within the Midlands. We try to include local clergy if possible to facilitate local spiritual support for families. We also do burials of ashes.

F. Gift booklets

'If I had been given this book when I lost my babies, I think it would have saved me years of suffering. I would have carried it with me all the time', said a bereaved Muslim mother about our booklet.

We send a booklet to parents within two weeks of a death. We have BCH faith-specific booklets for Muslims and Sikhs and have a further five in draft form. We use booklets from other publishers for Christians and those with no reported faith. In the accompanying letter, we explain when we will be in touch and give the option to opt out of further contact (which happens very rarely). We also stock booklets for different age siblings and make these available to staff in the hospital or community to give out. There are many ways to support families shortly after the death of a child; other hospitals send flowers, an information booklet, an invitation to a support group etc.

G. Remembrance book

We have a remembrance book in the chapel with short inscriptions and the book is always open at today's date. The invitation to have a child's name inscribed is sent out at around three months after the death.

H. Anniversary cards

We send cards to Christian and Muslim families. The Muslim card uses the same design as our gift booklet and condolence cards and the Christian card is overprinted with our details. Originally we only sent them out for the first anniversary, but families told us that everyone remembers for a year, but they feel forgotten after that, so we are sending cards for another year now. We take advice from different faith chaplains as to the appropriateness of anniversary cards.

I. Memorial service

These are held annually in the Cathedral. Bereaved families are invited from the previous year up until three months before the service on the advice of psychologists. Next year's date is on the order of service so families can return if they wish. Some have returned for four years. Families can participate by sending a poem for a booklet, lighting a personalised candle during the service, and bringing up a leaf for the prayer tree. They readily engage with these activities. We also have a children's worker doing activities with children.

A family member commented: 'I would just like to thank you on behalf of my family for inviting us to the memorial service yesterday. We found it beautiful; the service was lovely, with words that touched our hearts. I was touched by how many parents and families did turn up and it was not just us who have had such a tragedy. We hope to come as a family next year.'

J. Memorial walk and picnic

'Just a BIG THANK YOU for the lovely afternoon on Saturday. We found the end of the day very moving when we gathered around the tree. The National Memorial Arboretum (NMA) is certainly a very beautiful setting!'

We developed a relationship with the NMA, which is about 15 miles from BCH. We have the riverside walk as our memorial with a signpost at one end, a bench and memorial tree at the other, and some seed-shaped sculptures en route. There is also an area where families can buy a tree and plaque to remember their child.

We wanted a place with a peaceful environment where families could come without appointment, not on the hospital site. Annually we have a walk and a picnic and all our bereaved families are invited. Up to 200 family members attend, many coming back each year. It is not a religious event and dog collars are not worn. It is an opportunity for pastoral and spiritual care, which is offered according to the needs of families. After the walk we have a picnic (provided by the hospital) and a short ceremony at our memorial tree. Children blow bubbles as families lay sunflowers. In a similar way, a bereavement organisation offers a memorial walk and annual carol concert in a park near their offices.

A chaplain colleague uses terms such as 'the creative energy of life' and 'the benevolence of life', despite what is happening. She may say 'there is a love that holds all of life, even in the midst of the pain and suffering'. Her experience is that people are not upset by or do not challenge such language. In talking in this way she seeks to give people a sense of hope in something bigger than themselves, a hope that sustains her too.

Enhancing the environment

The wider bereavement team, of which we are a part, has gained funding for artwork for our counselling room, the Rainbow suite and NMA. We extensively consulted bereaved families and schoolchildren to produce beautiful glass works for our rooms and seed-shaped iron memorials, signifying among many things, the beginning and end of life, at the NMA.

Deaths in the community

For deaths in the community, we send the booklet and remembrance inscription invitation out about two to three months after a death. We are also developing a resource to help churches support bereaved families in their community.

Partnerships

Much of our pathway is a good illustration of how we have needed and benefited from external partnerships and we always seek to work in partnership when we can. We now work with the local palliative care team, for example. They have our books and cards and give them to families they work with. They let us know who has had what so we do not duplicate. This, again, ensures the most appropriate resources get to as many families as possible. We have also worked with the Kings Fund (environment), MidTech (Muslim booklet) and Staffordshire University (virtual rooms) in developing our provision.

Other dimensions of bereavement care pathways

Staff training and support

Wider paediatric staff feedback suggested that staff were sometimes so debilitated by the fear of offending families who had a faith they were unfamiliar with, that care was not offered. Initially we were reactive in providing training but have now begun to produce blended learning resources to equip staff to use our BCP and offer appropriate religious and spiritual care. We use faith-specific virtual rooms covering skills, attitudes, knowledge and ethics. Thus the Islamic end of life care room has a compass, prayer mat, holy water, prayer beads, the Qur'an, and information booklet with care pathways, plans, FAQs, etc. There are videos in many of the artefacts on organ donation, daily prayer, end of life recital, etc. We also do lunchtime choir, meditations and day retreats to give staff involved in the BCP the opportunity to reflect, be reinvigorated and to model self-care.

Faith care pathways

We have now written the day-to-day, palliative, end of life and bereavement care pathways for Buddhist, Christian, Hindu, Jewish, Muslim, Sikh and generic spiritual care. We piloted the Muslim pathways in our hospital by way of testing if and how well they worked. They have received very good feedback: 'This gives me the confidence of asking the right questions'. Families told us 'it was nice to be asked about what we wanted'. Our plan is to produce a hard copy and electronic resource pack for each ward for staff to be able to easily refer to.

Christian resources for funerals and memorials

The PCN has written 12 new songs for funeral and memorial services. They have been written to well-known tunes, so at least they might be known a little. Our aim is to have these on our website and produce a CD. Research suggested that it was only Christians who wanted such a resource.

Integration into the wider hospital bereavement service

Along with the chaplaincy, BCP we are also involved in bereavement more widely in the hospital. This includes a monthly meeting of all staff involved in bereavement, attending the group which reviews all deaths, a bereavement interest group which looks at service development and a bereavement-specific training group.

Costs

A BCP such as ours is not cost neutral. We estimate the costs to be around £4k a year plus staff time. We have had to negotiate with different parts of the hospital in funding the different elements.

Future development

We hope to provide web-based bereavement support where our families can get information when they want it, be kept up-to-date with resources and events, and which would include a peer bereavement support blog. We also hope to do more work with siblings including appropriate resources for others to use. Some chaplaincies are part of a rapid response or emergency referral scheme for all child deaths and this is something we would like to explore. We would also like to do a longitudinal study into our BCP to explore benefits and potential gaps.

Conclusion

The comprehensive BCP we now have and the positive feedback we have received about it from families has raised the credibility of chaplaincy within the hospital. A good quality BCP can help to provide personalised and comprehensive care for the family. It may contribute to people being able to grieve well and mitigate against the grief becoming pathological, with the potential additional costs to the NHS of this.

The lessons we have learnt from our BCP are that we need to ask, not assume we know what families need. We have got a long way on goodwill, and in part this has enabled us to access further funding. It is really helpful to have a personal worldview or a theology of the death of a child which enables you to be effective in self and staff care and which enables you to stay in the job for the long haul.

We hope this pathway is transferable into other settings where bereavement care is offered and that it can be appropriately contextualised to meet the short and long-term religious and spiritual needs of bereaved families, communities and caring staff.

Acknowledgements

Thank you to colleagues Mark Clayton, Dorothy Moore Brooks and Penny Sherringham for sharing stories for this chapter.

References

Chaplin D (2009) Developing an end-of-life care pathway to improve nurses' bereavement care. *Nursing Times* **105** (1) 20–21.

Clarke K & Pearson N (2010) Providing contact cards for relatives following bereavement. *Nursing Standard* **24** (44) 35–37.

Collins-Tracey S, Clayton JM, Kirsten L, Butow PN, Tattershall MHN & Chye R (2009) Contacting bereaved relatives: the views and practice of palliative care and oncology health care professionals. *Journal of Pain and Symptom Management* **37** (5) 807–822.

D'Agostino NM, Berlin-Romalis D, Jovcevska V & Barrera M (2008) Bereaved parents perspectives on their needs. *Palliative and Supportive Care* **6** (1) 33–41.

Department of Health (2009) *End of Life Care Strategy*. London: Department of Health.

Department of Health (2010a) *Bereavement Care Services: A synthesis of the literature*. London: Department of Health.

Department of Health (2010b) *Spiritual Care at the End of Life: A systematic review of the literature*. London: Department of Health.

Harvey S, Snowdon C & Elbourne D (2008) Effectiveness of bereavement interventions in neonatal intensive care: a review of the evidence. *Seminars in Fetal and NeoNatal Medicine* **13** 341–354.

Heydayat K (2006) When the spirit leaves: childhood death, grieving and bereavement in Islam. *Journal of Palliative Medicine* **9** (6) 1282–1291.

Kendall A & Guo W (2008) Evidence-based neonatal bereavement care. *Newborn and Infant Nursing Reviews* **8** (3) 131–135.

Kreicbergs UC, Lannen P, Onelov E & Wolfe J (2007) Parental grief after losing a child to cancer: impact of professional and social support on long-term outcomes. *Journal of Clinical Oncology* **25** (22) 3307–3312.

Nash P (2011) *Supporting Dying Children and Their Families*. London: SPCK.

National End of Life Care Programme (undated) *Draft Spiritual Support and Bereavement Care Quality Markers and Measures for End of Life Care*. London: NHS.

National Nurse Consultant Group Palliative Care (2011) *Guidance for Staff Responsible for Care after Death*. London: NHS End of Life Care Programme.

NICE (2011) *Quality Standards for End of Life Care for Adults* [online]. Available at: http://publications.nice.org.uk/quality-standard-for-end-of-life-care-for-adults-qs13/ (accessed April 2013). See particularly statements 6 and 7. There is a statement within the document which says they are applicable for paediatrics also.

Pearson H (2010) Managing the emotional aspects of end of care life for children and young people. *Paediatric Nursing* **22** (7) 32–35.

Potter D (1987) The other side of the dark. In: M Mayne *A Year Lost and Found*. London: DLT.

Together for Short Lives (2011) *Integrated Palliative Care Pathways Standards: Service self-assessment tool* [online]. Available at: http://www.togetherforshortlives.org.uk/professionals/resources/2443_standards_framework_for_childrens_palliative_care (accessed April 2013).

Together for Short Lives (2012) *Charter* [online]. Available at: http://www.togetherforshortlives.org.uk/professionals/resources/2446_together_for_short_lives_charter_2012 (accessed April 2013).

Wilkinson S, Croy P, King M & Barnes J (2007) Are we getting it right? Parents' perceptions of hospice child bereavement support services. *Palliative Medicine* **21** 401–407.

Chapter 7:

The power of presence – spiritual accompaniment in dementia end of life care

Ben Bano

The end of life in dementia

Dementia is the third most likely cause of death in older age. And yet death from the effects of dementia is not often a 'noble' death where the dying person has both the capacity and the insight to reflect and make their peace both with themselves and their loved ones. Those close to someone who is dying from the effects of dementia see the body almost literally wasting away. Even with our best efforts in palliative care, the end of life from the effects of dementia is often a distressing experience for those close to the dying person. It is in this context we need to consider the spiritual accompaniment of someone who is dying from the effects of dementia. The way in which we accompany someone with dementia as their life ebbs away is crucial in upholding their dignity and worth as a person.

A focus on personhood

When we are unable to speak and our mental and bodily functions seem to be failing, it is more important than ever that our personhood is understood and promoted by those around us. The phrase 'See ME rather than my dementia' is particularly relevant at this time. As Zizioulas (1991) points out, our personhood is what makes us unique. Kitwood (1997) suggested that our personhood is 'sacred and unique' to each of us and forms the basis of the need for each of us to be treated with respect. Personhood can also be said to be 'transcendental' – in some religions and belief systems people are said to have an 'inner self' that transcends and continues beyond death.

When Kitwood defined personhood (1997) he was heavily influenced by Martin Buber and his concept of the 'I-Thou' relationship: *'In dementia … identity remains intact, because others hold it in place, thoughts may have disappeared, but there are still interpersonal processes, feelings are expressed and meet a validating response, and if there is a spirituality, it will be likely to be of the sort which Buber describes, where the divine is encountered in the depth of I-thou relating'* (Kitwood, 1997).

A focus on personhood does not always mean that it is always respected and understood. As dementia advances, and particularly towards the end of life, it is all too easy to assume that the real 'person' is no longer present. A sense of bereavement in loved ones and family may already have taken place as an assumption grows that 'there is nobody still there'. Members of families may feel – but hesitate to articulate – that it would be better if their relative with dementia is released from their suffering as quickly as possible.

We often see people with advancing dementia in care homes cared for physically in the best way possible, but care of the 'inner self' is more of a challenge as dementia advances. As the 'self' seems to be ebbing away from our eyes we need to understand and reaffirm the personhood in and behind this fragile body. The challenge which is presented to us is the question 'Can life flourish in the presence of this living death?' I am convinced from my own experience in spiritual accompaniment that even as life ebbs away we can still recognise familiar prayers and hymns from our childhood and that we can still recognise the power of experiences such as handling flowers and other natural experiences.

Being the 'other' in spiritual accompaniment

Kitwood pointed out the unique role of the 'other' in understanding and promoting the personhood of the person with advancing dementia. He reminded us that the 'other' is needed to offset degeneration and fragmentation. Kitwood and Bredin (1992) remind us that *'The further the dementia advances, the greater is the need for that "person work" – we are needed to hold the fragments together'*. Radden and Fordyce (2006) point out that *'Others must remember, reinforce, and reinscribe the identity of the person with dementia … we must preserve the person's identity as the person's own grasp on it weakens…'*

This chapter will explore how we may be that 'other' in the task of spiritual accompaniment of the person dying from the effects of dementia. Spiritual accompaniment is not just for the minister or priest – it is a task for all of us whether we are a relative, carer or volunteer. It is for the kitchen assistant bringing a cup of tea as much as for the night care worker comforting someone who is dying in the early hours. We might have a caring role in a hospital ward or residential home – our task is be the 'other' so as to show our respect for and draw out the personhood of the dying person at this final stage of their life journey.

We look at how we might understand both the personhood and the 'inner self' of the dying person and how we can use this understanding to ensure that the spiritual needs of the dying person are met and that the final stages of life are endowed with a sense of meaning for all who are involved, in particular those who are close to the dying person.

In the work of spiritual accompaniment with a person who is dying we need to start from the perspective that our spiritual being is still there even as our body fails. Jewell (2009) suggests that we undertake a *journey into the divine*, with all its adventures and uncertainties. Even when the dying person does not have a religious belief, the spiritual self still needs to be recognised and affirmed. Zizoualis reminds us that at this stage we should not see capacity as compared to incapacity – instead we should see 'capacity in incapacity'. Psalm 139 reminds us that God remembers us whether we are waking or sleeping.

Understanding the spiritual story

At a time when there is a focus on advanced care planning in dementia care, it is not always easy to help someone to reflect on how they wish to be treated at the end of their life. But wherever possible we should develop a profile of someone's spiritual life story well in advance of their terminal phase, so that we can be aware of their preferences at this important time. As Gilbert explains in **Chapter 1: Rage against the dying of the light, or a new light shining?**, spirituality is a much broader concept than religious belief. Using life story techniques, a 'spiritual' life story will focus on what provides purpose and meaning to someone's life. In a spiritual memory box or story book we might find reminders of key events in someone's life, such as wedding pictures or the picture of a favourite pet.

What interests have they had? What has been important for the person? A spiritual life story may tell us about someone's favourite hymns or prayers, which can be a comfort as dementia advances. For instance, if there is an opportunity it could be helpful to discuss funeral arrangements in advance. A funeral can be a much more genuine memorial of someone's life, as well as being of comfort to their loved ones, if we know their preferences for prayers and hymns.

The power of presence

As those involved in spiritual accompaniment of someone dying from the effects of dementia, our question may be: 'What do we actually do?' Perhaps the first aspect of spiritual accompaniment of which we are aware is that we will be working in silence, with someone who has most likely lost the power of speech. In spending time with the dying person we need to be the 'other' in a way that helps us to put to one side our daily concerns. This is not the time or place for phone calls or text messaging!

We may be involved in a physical care task such as feeding or helping to make the dying person comfortable. In this situation, can we free ourselves, even for a few minutes, from the daily demands of the care setting? Daniel O'Leary (2012) writes about some of the qualities we need at this time. He refers to the power of presence. Even if we cannot spend more than a short period at a time with the dying person, our presence can heal and will often be of great comfort to the dying person as well as to loved ones. As Christine Bryden (2002) reminds us, *'I need you to minister to me, to be my memory for me'.*

Presence requires a conscious desire to put ourselves in the right frame of mind: O'Leary (2012) reminds us again:

'The role of the body in revealing Presence … is central; the graciousness of your eyes – windows out and windows in; the touch of your hands – extensions of your heart; your body – the dignity of composure; your body betrays the inner state of your soul; the dignity of your voice, a radiance from your physical presence, a reverence for the Presence of the other. Then you release a healing Presence in the other. That is the key.'

As the dying person will usually have lost the power of speech, much of our time may be spent in silence. This is something which we may well find challenging in our busy lives! But we may well come to welcome these precious moments not just for the person who is dying but for ourselves as well. These are the times when we might want to think about, as Gilbert reminds us in **Chapter 1: Rage against the dying of the light, or a new light shining?**, what brings meaning and purpose to our own lives. Some of us may have parents or grandparents who have been or are going through a similar experience. How would we want them to be treated? How would we want to be treated ourselves in these circumstances?

Presence gives a new and more complete dimension to the caring process. Sheila Cassidy (1988) talks about the *'prophetic nature of caring for those who are, in economic terms, useless. Caring is a lavishing of precious resources, our precious ointment ... on the rejected and the dying...'*

Reflection point

Our presence will always make a difference – our compassion and concern will show through.

As the last days and hours approach

Presence, and helping family members to keep a vigil at this stage are all important. This does not necessarily mean that we have to sit in the room or ward without anything to do. We might want to engage in some gentle and soothing touch, even if we are not aware of an immediate response. It is very possible that our touch will alleviate some of the physical and emotional distress of the dying person. Touch forms part of religious rituals – for example the last rites of some Christians involve touch through anointing. A person dying from the effects of dementia can be comatose or agitated, or resting quietly when they take their last breath. Agitation may well be due to discomfort or pain that cannot be expressed in any other way – and we need to be alert to signs and symptoms which point the way as to how distress might be alleviated.

Different parts of the body will feel hot or cold. For example, a person may feel hot to the touch on their forehead, but be cold on their hands and feet. Alongside medications, touch or a gentle hand massage can be of value. We need to be sensitive to the response – we will soon know if it feels right to continue.

Over recent years we have become much more aware of the power of someone with advancing dementia to respond to a particular stimulus, for example familiar prayers and hymns from their childhood. We need to be alert to signs of a response, even if it is the flickering of an eyelid.

A beautiful and powerful example of this is the YouTube film clip of Naomi Feil, the founder of validation therapy, communicating with Gladys Wilson, an older woman with advancing dementia, who has lost the power of speech. Through a combination of gentle touch and a few words, Naomi helps Gladys to remember a familiar hymn from her childhood. You can view the clip at: http://www.youtube.com/watch?v=CrZXz10FcVM. Pastoral visitors often notice that even when the power of speech is no longer present, symbols such as a crucifix are recognised and cherished.

Reflection point

Glenys, an 85-year-old woman, was dying in her room in a residential home. Even though she was unable to speak, her family ensured that there were fresh flowers in her room which she could smell.

Can you think of any other ways in which we can provide stimulation for the dying person?

We can also help to create an environment in which familiar memories can be re-awakened. Some time ago I was with a woman with dementia who was dying. There seemed to be no communication but Songs of Praise was being shown on TV. Her eyes flickered as she remembered a familiar hymn. Afterwards I prayed some familiar prayers with her and I noticed that she became quite calm as the prayers progressed.

Reflection point

Margaret, a 90-year-old woman with Alzheimer's disease, is dying in her room and Tracy, who is a care worker, has been asked by her shift leader to be with her, comfort her and help her to be comfortable. Margaret has lost the power of speech but her eyelids are flickering and Tracy is wondering how she might communicate with her. She finds a version of Abide with Me on her iPad and connects it to the TV in the room. As the music of the choir fills the room, Tracy notices that Margaret's eyelids are moving. A communication has been made.

Have you had any similar experiences?

The physical surroundings in which end of life care takes place are also an important issue to consider. We need to strike a balance between privacy and isolation and ensure that while privacy is respected, the dying person is not left isolated. A sensitive discussion may be needed with colleagues and relatives on how best this can be achieved.

> ### Reflection point
>
> An older woman with dementia was dying from pneumonia in a corner of the acute medical ward. The staff drew the curtains round the bed to ensure privacy for the family at this difficult time and to avoid distress for other patients and visitors. I was visiting another patient in the bed opposite. As the evening progressed her daughter asked me if she could open the curtains as she was finding her time with her mother somewhat claustrophobic. The others present on the ward, who were still awake, were happy to agree and her daughter thanked us for helping to ensure that her mother did not die alone.

The significance of rituals

A person dying from the effects of dementia has a need like anyone else to connect with rituals. Rituals are the way in which we connect with meaning in a more ordered way. These may be part of religious traditions, each of which has their own rituals. For example, for many Christians last rites and anointing as well as reconciliation and Holy Communion are important. Prayer and religious music can be important aspects of ritual, even in the advanced stages of dementia, and in the Orthodox tradition prayer is an important part of the grieving process.

There are important cultural issues to consider at the end of life. We need to know how someone would like to be addressed. Modesty issues are also important – for example a Muslim woman may not wish to be cared for by a male carer. At the end of life there are requirements in different religions involving washing and dressing the body, as well as the ways in which funeral rites are to take place. Rituals need not necessarily be religious. They can equally be part of a process in which we value those things which are most dear to the dying person.

Saying our farewells

Spiritual care does not end with the death of the person with dementia. As well as performing religious rituals, where appropriate, we need to think about how the person who has died can be remembered as a unique and precious person. Other residents or patients may want an opportunity to remember the person who has died through a quiet time of reflection or prayer. Some residents – as well as staff – may want to attend the funeral or at least say their farewells if there is an opportunity.

Reflection point

In a care home run by a Christian social care agency, staff put out a book of remembrance for both staff and residents to write down their memories of a resident who had died if they so wished.

Can you think of ways in which your care setting can remember someone who has died?

Being present to loved ones

The end of life from the effects of dementia is a distressing time for loved ones and families. The physical appearance of someone when the body appears to be wasting away can be very distressing. This is a time when the sensitive input of a chaplain or pastoral worker can be very beneficial, even for those without a religious faith. There may be feelings of guilt regarding the failure to love and acknowledge their family member who is dying, particularly if this is taking place in an institution rather than at home.

There may be questions as to how a person who has lost contact with all reality can be accepted and loved by God. Is there such a thing as the 'good news' in the presence of a 'living death' when the person concerned can no longer articulate their feelings? As Keck (1996) reminds us, loved ones need reassurance that their relative who seems to be withering away is still loved and cherished by God.

Even without the input of a chaplain or pastoral worker there is still much that can be achieved in spending time with loved ones at the terminal stages of dementia as well as after death. Relatives may need to be encouraged to share some of their complex and sometimes conflicting emotions. They may find comfort in being encouraged to remember and share memories of happy and fulfilled times as well as difficult times in the past. They may need support in thinking through how funeral arrangements can best reflect the parent or spouse they have lost.

As Cassidy (1988) points out, there is no blueprint for loved ones in being with their dying relative, particularly someone dying from the effects of dementia. Some might want to keep a constant vigil, while others may be very distressed and need encouragement to leave their relative, going home if needed. A sensitive approach is also needed where families have become divided or estranged.

Conclusion

End of life care in dementia is a particular challenge. We need to understand and acknowledge the personhood and uniqueness of the person who is dying. In this way we can provide prompts, such as familiar prayers and hymns, as well as symbols which the dying person may recognise even if they have lost the power of speech. We need also to understand the spiritual and religious needs of the dying person in order to ensure that these needs are met as carefully and respectfully as possible. We need, in being with the dying person, to be aware of the gift and privilege of the power of our presence as we accompany the individual in their last days and hours. Finally, we need to be aware of the often complex needs of loved ones as we accompany them as well as the person who is dying. In these ways we may help in promoting as good a death as possible for a person with dementia.

References

Bryden C & Mackinlay E (2002) Dementia – a spiritual journey towards the divine: a personal view of dementia. In: E Mackinlay (Ed) *Mental Health and Spirituality in Later Life*. New York: Haworth Press.

Cassidy S (1988) *Sharing the Darkness – the Spirituality of Caring*. London: Darton, Longman and Todd.

Jewell A (2009) *Spirituality and Personhood in Dementia*. London: Jessica Kingsley Publishers.

Keck D (1996) *Forgetting Whose We Are: Alzheimer's disease and the love of God*. Nashville: Abingdon Press.

Kitwood T (1997) *Dementia Reconsidered: The person comes first*. London: Open University Press.

Kitwood T & Bredin K (1992) Towards a theory of dementia care: personhood and well-being. *Ageing and Society* **12** (3) 269–287.

O'Leary D (2012) From a talk given at the Conference: 'The Journey of Hope – Catholic Chaplaincy in Mental Health Services' - Liverpool, March 2012. Available at: http://www. welcomemeasiam.org.uk/the-journey-of-hope-conference-03-2012.html (accessed March 2013).

Radden J & Fordyce J (2006) Into the darkness: losing identity with dementia. In: J Hughes, S Louw, S Sabat *Dementia: Mind, meaning and the person.* Oxford: Oxford University Press.

Zizioulas J (1991) On being a person: towards an ontology of personhood. In: C Schwöbel and C Gunton (Eds) *Persons, Divine and Human: King's College essays in theological anthropology.* Edinburgh: T&T Clark.

Chapter 8:

Don't forget me!: Questions of death, bereavement and accompaniment for people with an intellectual disability

Cristina Gangemi

My day in the office had just begun when the phone rang. On the line was a parish priest in the diocese for whom I worked as a disability adviser.

They told me: 'Cristina, I have a family in my parish that needs a little help. The mother is dying from cancer and has a daughter with a learning disability. They have tried to find support and advice, but can find no one that can help. The mother is becoming desperate and I really don't know how to be of service'.

In this chapter I hope to take the reader on a journey that will draw out insights that are both *'faithful and transformative'* (Swinton & Mowatt, 2006). I will seek to explore with the reader why dilemmas, such as the one I have narrated above, might occur and how attention to the spiritual can transform dilemma into hope. I do not aim to locate the chapter within any particular religious tradition, but I do recognise that the insights from my own experience of the Christian faith may colour the road as we travel.

My aim is to explore the human story and spirituality of a person with an intellectual disability and examine why the issue of death and bereavement may seem such a difficult area for people to discuss and work through. My hope is that at the end of our journey the reader will have encountered the call of the person who is disabled and in so doing turn back into their own lives, cultures and traditions, asking themselves vital and *enabling* questions. I hope this chapter will help us all reflect and act in a way that will make it possible for a person with an intellectual disability to die well, knowing that their life has had meaning, or as they grieve, be accompanied in a way that respects who they are and who they are born to be.

The journey begins: Questions, questions, questions...

As I sit to write, I do so accompanying my father who has cancer and who is presently undergoing radiotherapy treatment at a cancer hospital. The weeks following his diagnosis were filled with agonising appointments and an array of doctors, letters, information leaflets and unending visits to various hospital departments. It was a time filled with fear and questions. Could he be cured? Would he die? How would he and we cope with treatment? Was it for the best and, indeed, is cancer hereditary? Not only did I face my father's death but somehow it unveiled my own finite mortality. In the forward to this book, my colleague, Professor John Swinton, asks the question 'Why are we so nervous of death and all of those things in life which seem to remind us of it? In the hospital I noticed copious amounts of information aimed at helping people face their fear of dying, but something was missing.

My experience with disabled people leads me to ask: 'How would a person with an intellectual disability cope with all of this written information?' Looking around, everything was designed for people who could read and write within a certain level of intellectual ability. It was as if people who 'think in pictures' (Isanon, 2001) and who make sense of their illness using 'books with no words' (Hollins, 1998) simply didn't exist and if they did exist, they certainly didn't get ill or need support! (See Mencap, 2012).

The assumption seemed to be that we exist in a world filled with people who are basically all the same. This seems rather odd as all of us know that human beings are diverse and often quite different in their experiences, desires, hopes and expectations. The lack of readily available and accessible material, missing from the information-loaded shelves and tables, begs the question 'How do we accompany a person with an intellectual disability through death and bereavement, and why do accessible resources seem so invisible?'

Loss and disability: When is a person a person?

It is fair to say that the lives of people with disabilities have been and continue to be touched by the *experience of multiple losses* (L'Arche UK, 2012), the greatest of which I fear is the denial of their full personhood;

body, mind and spirit. In her provocative and inspiring book *Loss and Learning Disability* (2003) Noelle Blackman writes of the way that '*through the centuries there have been many words used to name people with learning disabilities*'. Labels assigned to the human person. This was also an observation made by Nancy Eiesland in her book *The Disabled God* (1994). Eiesland, a Christian sociologist writing about finding God '*not in spite (of) impairments but through them*' (Eiesland, 1994), notices that historically, disabled people have been '*named by medical and scientific professionals or by people who deny their full personhood*' (Eiesland, 1994) and that the use of euphemisms camouflages disability so as '*to make it acceptable for public discourse*' (Eiesland, 1994).

Let us explore now why does disability have to be made 'acceptable'?

In her book, Nicolle Blackman dedicates a whole chapter to the idea that society places a '*high value on beauty, intelligence, independence, youth and wealth ... in its "drive towards perfection,*' (Blackman, 2003), which sets up a hierarchical image of perfection into which (owing to our different) not all people may fit. The person who is '*visibly different through the manifestation of disability*' (Blackman, 2003) may therefore carry a mistaken image of 'imperfection'. An example of this was powerfully revealed to me by my friend, John McCorkell, who shared that at his birth the sight of his disability saw all expectations removed from him, so what was there to strive for?

But where did this 'hierarchy of ability' begin?

For hundreds of years philosophers and theologians have pondered upon 'what defines the human being'. This has been interestingly chartered in works such as *The Soul of the Embryo* (Jones, 2004) and in *Disability in the Christian Tradition* (Brock & Swinton, 2012), in which, starting with conception, the status of the human person is traced. Each records the approach of classical Greek and Roman philosophers for whom a person's value was largely defined in social terms (Brock & Swinton, 2012). For them, to be able (or indeed presumably unable) to contribute to society required the human to look, reason and act in a certain way if they were to be of any worth. Thus the disabled body was held within the realm of loss, with habitual infanticide practised upon disabled newborns (see Jones, 2004).

From this we can surmise that, from influential ancient philosophies, a *measurable* way of perceiving personhood has emerged and has caused 'loss and disablement' to certain human beings. Indeed the Eugenics movement, which has had *'long term effects ... on the lives of people with disabilities'* (Waldron, 2012; Blackman, 2003; Diane & Moore, 2010), demonstrates how the striving to achieve a perceived *perfection* had catastrophic and fatal outcomes. It is fair to say that this image of human existence continues to influence the 'loss' of personhood for people society chooses to disable because of their bodies, communication styles and ways of being.

John Wyatt, a professor in ethics and perinatology, has recently published a fascinating book that explores contemporary, human and spiritual dilemmas facing the person in matters of life and death. He suggests that we have begun to see the world from within a mode of 'scientific reductionism' which leads to a 'mechanistic view' (Waldron, 2012) of humanity and the human body (see Wyatt, 2009). Wyatt argues that there is an unwritten implication (in modern day medical practice) whereby if an *'abnormality is detected, it is morally responsible to carry out an abortion'* (Wyatt, 2009). While I make no moral judgment upon this, I seek to use this issue in agreement with Blackman and Wyatt, to unveil the fact that there seems to be a certain way of being human, implicit within the legislation and medical screening, which indicates what is or is not 'normal' and sets up a *'hierarchy of ability'* (Gangemi, 2006) within human existence. Hence, the person whom *'we choose to label'* (Swinton, 2006) as having an intellectual disability, experiences even further loss of status, expectations, loss of services, of available and accessible resources but most importantly, loss of a sense of belonging. The paradox within this loss, however, is that, once born, the person with a disability is totally protected by disability legislation, assigning them with full human status, dignity and the right to access all that the world offers.

My argument is that the 'gift of the presence' (based upon Reinders, 2008; Tuffrey-Wijne, 2009) of disabled people within our human story must intend that there is one human story to which we all belong. If their history and treatment has been recorded throughout time, it must be that they have always been present; they belong! (Gangemi, 2012; Swinton, 2012)

However, as we have explored, from the moment of their very beginning *'the giveness of'* (see Wyatt, 2009; Tuffrey-Wijne, 2009) the human person can be disabled by attitudes, medical opinions, financial implications (Wyatt, 2009) and an experience of loss which is to accompany them throughout life.

The influence of this *'approach to relationships between the body and society'* (Waldron, 2012) is at the very foundation of the dilemma named at the start of this chapter. In society's effort (that is each one of us) to make provision for the people that fit into the perceived model of perfection, we have somehow forgotten that ours is a world, coloured by the fact that *'difference does not diminish; it enlarges the sphere of human possibilities'* (Sacks, 2002). For sure, if disability was an issue in times of antiquity and recorded from the beginning of time, it is a way of being human that is part of our story. As people with differing bodies and ways of being have always existed, is it not fair to say that it is a very usual way of being human?

A society where access, provision and acceptance is reliant upon social inclusion, rather than a knowledge of *belonging*, speaks of *who we are* and shapes how we welcome and say farewell to those with whom we share this world. This is powerfully echoed in the speech that lay the foundations for disability legislation:

> *'Mr Speaker, if we could bequeath one precious gift to posterity, I would choose a society in which there is genuine compassion for long-term sick and disabled people; where understanding is unostentatious and sincere; where needs come before means; where if years cannot be added to their lives, at least life can be added to their years; where the mobility of disabled people is restricted only by the bounds of technical progress and discovery; where they have the fundamental right to participate in industry and society according to ability; where socially preventable distress is unknown; and where no one has cause to be ill at ease because of her or his disability.'* (Morris, 1969).

At the end of the journey

Having journeyed through personhood and intellectual disability, we will now turn to the issue of death and bereavement, but first a story.

I met a young man with Down's syndrome waiting, daily, outside the cemetery. He shared with me that he had been told that his mum had gone away, and thus for years he waited there for her to return. No one had told him she was dead.

In this book's foreword, Swinton suggests that we *'don't just die; we are taught how to die ... by family, friends, the media and culture'*. An important thesis, by Liam Waldron, exploring issues of friendship and loneliness among people with intellectual disabilities, discovered that, while people with intellectual disabilities may now be legally 'included' more, they continue to remain alone (see Waldron, 2012). Their lives can be *socially isolated with few friends and little practical support*' (Hollins, 1995; Gangemi *et al*, 2012). If this is so, then the accompaniment that is available, as they approach death or grieve, may also be touched by this disabling loneliness, as will the chance to be 'taught' and accompanied.

Will anyone care when I die?

This question, which burrows into the very consciousness of Blackman's book on loss and learning disability, suggests that the *'significance a person gives to dying is based upon the personal philosophy he or she acquired during life'* (Raji, 2000). Knowing, therefore, that your life has value and quality is vital if a person is to die well. This means that our programmes of palliative and bereavement care can no longer occur within a hierarchy of personhood, but must be available for all in ways that are meaningful. In an article about palliative care and intellectual disability, Swinton writes that the *'spiritual and palliative needs of people with learning disabilities are the same as anyone else's'* (Swinton, 2006). The article is a thoughtful, unfolding of the way in which an attention to the spirit and body, of the person with intellectual disability, requires journeying with them and that *'journeying demands that we enter into meaningful, empathic, relationships that enable us to understand'* (Swinton, 2006)

As a result of disabled people insisting that they are not forgotten, recent history has seen an emergence of literature, resources and guidelines concerning issues of health and palliative care. A foundational voice in this, Maureen Oswin identified pressing needs in 1970. In her book *Am I Allowed to Cry?* (1991), Oswin highlights the issue of people in institutions and their imminent social inclusion. The book unveils insights and guidelines aimed at helping service providers of the day. Years later, the findings in *A life Like No Other: A national audit of specialist inpatient healthcare services for people with learing difficulties in England* (Health Care Commission, 2007) make for sombre reading with the words 'poor' and 'lack of service' dominating throughout. Clearly not enough has changed. In most of the legislative documents read, concerning health and palliative care, the issue of spirituality is almost as invisible as the people I did not see in the hospital.

Accompaniment: Attending to the spirit

It is clear, however, from many sources of research that people with *'learning disabilities in general want spirituality incorporated into the care and support they receive'* (Swinton & Powrie, 2004). The privileged experience of sharing my life with people who have intellectually disabilities is that they have an intuitive sense of their inner being (Gangemi *et al*, 2012). There are indeed many models of spirituality and how *'it is understood and defined has a variety of meanings ascribed to it'* (Swinton, 2006).

My own research – undertaken in partnership with people with intellectual disabilities (Gangemi *et al*, 2012) – has uncovered some important insights. The research aims to enable communities to meet people with intellectual disabilities and respond to their spiritual and religious needs. Our insights suggest that the 'encounter' with a disabled person, as with any other human person, is indeed a meeting of 'being'. As a result of the narration and exchange of stories, recorded over a period of time, we had shared in their 'sense of life'. In this we had noted a quality of life that valued every day and every experience, including death. We were all given, irrespective of presumed structures of ability, an opportunity to enter into unique and creative relationships with each other, *'discovering innovative and agreeable ways of expressing the spiritual experiences, which we shared as equal human beings'* (Gangemi *et al*, 2012). The spirituality that emerged from this *'sense of life was present before any intellectual effort to discover or uncover meanings'* (Gangemi *et al*, 2012). We noted that in many definitions of spirituality there was a requirement for a certain use of cognition and processing information, which could disable a person if how they are does not meet those requirements. This could account, I feel, for the way in which people find it difficult to express 'spiritual empathy' (Swinton, 2006) within in palliative care.

Our research partners – people with intellectual disabilities – revealed a spirituality 'of being' rather than 'of mind', 'of presence' rather than 'of ability', encouraging us to view spirituality as **being present and attentive to the other, reciprocal exchange and real, authentic encounter.** *'Spirituality, in its original and more basic reality, is presence. It is a dialogue, being in relationship with meaningful dimensions without any word being spoken, before any rationalisation, of what is being experienced by the person, takes place'* (based upon Gangemi *et al*, 2012) We found, therefore, that throughout life there seems to be a cyclical movement where by the reaching towards the transcendent is something that never ends and that redirects each person back into their own self, only to rediscover significance within and reach out to share that with others. In the receiving, welcoming and holding of each other's story the sense of life becomes real and vibrant and in that, no one can be forgotten. However, within any sense of life lies the reality that, while we live we also die.

Death is a difficult concept for all of us and *'grief is a universal feature of human existence'* (Foundation for People with Learning Disabilities, 2005) and yet, within this, our research uncovered yet another worrying paradox. While being able and seemingly relieved to share freely about death, our research partners did not seem to have the space or the correct resources and methods to express their experiences. Professionals such as Sheila Hollins, Oyepeju Raji, Sue Read and Stuart Todd agree that people with intellectual disabilities *'will come to a dying phase in their lives, yet care professionals may be uncertain how to talk (and support) people at such sensitive times'* (Read & Todd, 2010; Hollins, 1995; Raji *et al*, 2003). As a person approaches death or bereavement, creative resources and guidelines have become available, though, worryingly, the absence of friends, who may receive their story, has not.

Communities such as L'Arche, St. Joseph's pastoral centre and many others, who share life with people of all abilities and faiths, witness to the wisdom of attending to the spirituality within palliative care, sharing becomes a two-way exchange (Tuffrey-Wijne, 2009).

'Some people, despite suffering a variety of losses, are also able to grow in wisdom and self-acceptance. Perhaps the main precondition for this maturity is not being left alone. Being alongside people with learning disabilities, especially as they face their own death, often reveals the essential quality of relationships and show us what matters most in our lives.' (L'Arche UK, 2012).

Each person born will die and in that we are all equal. People who have intellectually disabilities, through the lack of accompaniment and accessible ways of expressing their grief, will remain bewildered and indeed continue to ask *'will anyone care when I die'* (Blackman, 2003). Where a society forgets some of its members, it loses out on the profound witness and unique, spiritual insights that each person offers and as such is *'poorer for it'* (Hollins, 2012)

John Paul II came to the end of his life as a disabled man. As a witness to his own spiritual writings on the body, he claims it not as machine but *'created to transfer into the visible reality of the world, the mystery hidden since time in memorial'* as such it is a sign which *'speaks of the ineffable, whispering to us of something of the deepest secret hidden in God from all eternity'* (John Paul II, 1980).

Is it not so, therefore that as we remain present to one another, accompanying each other towards death and in moments of grief, there we meet God, no matter what our ability.

The end of our journey

My aim in this chapter was to journey with you, the reader, into issues surrounding personhood, spirituality and disability. In so doing I invited you to look back into your own life, culture and faith tradition, not forgetting people with intellectual disabilities but indeed enabling them to be present. As you read through the wisdom of this book, which *'opens a window into the meanings of death and the practices of dying'* (Foreword), remember those who are disabled so that ours will be a faithful journey, which will 'reclaim a positive meaning' for the lives and deaths of people who are intellectually disabled.

References

Blackman N (2003) *Loss and Learning Disability*. London: Worth Publishing Ltd.

Brock B & Swinton J (2012) *Disability in the Christian Tradition*. Michigan/Cambridge: Wm. B. Eerdmans Publishing Company.

Diane BP & Moore J (2010) The Darwin context: evolution and inheritance. In: A Bushford and P Levine (Eds) *The Oxford Handbook of the History of Eugenics*. Oxford: Oxford University Press.

Eiesland N (1994) *The Disabled God*. Nashville USA: Abingdon Press.

Foundation for People with a Learning Disability (2005) *Dying Matters: A workbook on caring for people with learning disabilities who are terminally ill*. London: FPWLD.

Gangemi C (2006) *The Body-Human or machine?* Masters essay, St Mary's University London.

Gangemi C (2012) 'Everybody Has A Story'. Lecture to the summer Bethesda institute in Chicago. Available at: http://bethesdainstitute.org/Theology2012Presentations (accessed April 2013).

Gangemi C, Swinton J, Vincenzi G, Tobanelli M (2012) *Enabling Communities to Meet People with Intellectual Disabilities and Respond to Their Needs and Hopes*. University of Aberdeen. Available from c.gangemi@abdn.ac.uk (in press).

Health Care Commission (2007) *A Life Like No Other: A national audit of specialist inpatient healthcare services for people with learning difficulties in England*. London: Commission for Healthcare Audit and Inspection. Available at: http://archive.cqc.org.uk/_db/_documents/LD_audit_report1.pdf (accessed March 2013).

Hollins S (1995) *Managing Grief Better: People with intellectual disabilities* [online]. Available at: http://www.intellectualdisability.info/mental-health/managing-grief-better-people-with-intellectual-disabilities (accessed March 2013).

Hollins S (1998) *Why Pictures?* [online] Available at: http://www.booksbeyondwords.co.uk/background (accessed March 2013).

Hollins S (2012) The disabled are becoming invisible to Britons. *The Universe* **28** September.

Isanon A (2001) *Spirituality and the Autism Spectrum: Of falling sparrows.* London: Jessica Kinsgley Publishers.

John Paul II (1980) Theology of the body. In: C West *Theology of the Body Explained: A commentary on John Paul II's 'Gospel of the Body'.* Boston, MA: Pauline Books and Media Ltd.

Jones D (2004) *The Soul of the Embryo.* London and New York: Continuum.

L'Arche UK (2012) *Celebrating Life in the Face of Death* [online]. Available at: http://www.larche.org.uk/pdf/Celebratinglifeinthefaceofdeath.pdf (accessed April 2013).

Mencap (2012) *Death by Indifference: 74 deaths and counting. A progress report five years on* [online]. Available at: http://www.mencap.org.uk/campaigns/take-action/death-indifference (accessed March 2013).

Morris Lord (1969) The Right Honourable Lord Morris of Manchester from the Chronically Sick and Disabled Persons Bill to the House of Commons on 5 December, 1969.

Oswin M (1991) *Am I Allowed to Cry: A study of bereavement amongst people who have a learning difficulties.* London: Souvenir Press.

Raji O (2000) *Losing the Self and Finding the Soul.* Available from SIPSIG/RCPSych.

Raji O, Hollins S & Drinnan A (2003) How far are people with learning disabilities involved in funeral rites? *British Journal of Learning Disabilities* **31** (1) 42–45.

Read S & Todd S presentation (2010) *Thinking about Death and What it Means: Conversations with People with intellectual disabilities* [online]. University of Glamorgan. Available at http://hesas.glam.ac.uk/media/files/documents/2010-07-28/Sue_Read.ppt

Reinders H (2008) *Receiving the Gift of Friendship: Profound disability, theological anthropology and ethics.* Grand Rapids: Wm. B. Eerdmans publishing company.

Sacks J (2002) *The Dignity of Difference: How to avoid the clash of civilizations.* London: Continuum.

Swinton J (2006) *Spirituality, suffering and palliative care: a spiritual approach to palliative care with people who have learning disabilities.* In: S Reed *Palliative Care and People with Learning Disabilities.* London: Quay Books.

Swinton J (2012) 'Symposium on Qualitative Research and People with Profound Disabilities' and 'Theology and Dementia'. Lecture to the summer Bethesda Institute in Chicago. Available at: http://bethesdainstitute.org/Theology2012Presentations (accessed April 2013).

Swinton J & Mowatt H (2006) *Practical Theology and Qualitative Research.* London: SCM Press.

Swinton J & Powrie E (2004) *Why Are We Here?: The spiritual lives of people with learning disabilities.* London: Foundation for People with Learning Disabilities.

Tuffrey-Wijne T (2009) Am I a good girl?: dying people who have a learning disability. *Journal of End of Life Care* **3** (1) 35–39.

Waldron L (2012) *I Came That They May Have Life, and Have it Abundantly: Reimagining life-giving responses to the problem of loneliness among people with learning disabilities.* Aberdeen University, Doctoral thesis.

Wyatt J (2009) *Matters of Life and Death: Human dilemmas in the light of the Christian faith.* Nottingham: Inter-Varsity Press.

Chapter 9:

Making sense of grief

Neil Thompson

Experiencing a significant loss can be an extremely challenging aspect of life. We can be left feeling overwhelmed by what has happened. Our reaction will generally incorporate not only biological, psychological and sociological elements, but also a spiritual one (Thompson, 2012). This is because a major loss can produce 'identity disruption'. That is, we can temporarily lose our sense of who we are and how we fit into the wider world: we lose our spiritual bearings.

Grief can therefore be seen as a spiritual or existential challenge; it can have a profound effect on our spiritual well-being, and, while that effect is generally painful and distressing, it can at times produce a positive effect in some ways. This chapter therefore explores how grief disrupts our (spiritual) frameworks of meaning; how we can use different (theoretical) frameworks of meaning to make sense of the complex processes that characterise grief; and how grief can have a long-standing detrimental effect on our spiritual well-being (complicated grief) as well as potentially a positive impact in certain circumstances (transformational grief).

Theorising grief

Grief is a topic that has a wide literature base associated with it, incorporating both practice guidance elements and attempts to develop theoretical understandings. A comprehensive review of that theory base is beyond the scope of this chapter, and so I am going to limit myself to a summary of what I see as some key theoretical issues that can help us make sense of grief.

Beyond the stages approach: dual process theory

The idea that people grieve in stages derives from the work of Elisabeth Kübler-Ross (1969). This conception has become strongly entrenched in both academic discourses and practice settings (on training courses, for example), despite the fact that there is little or no empirical evidence to support it and much dissatisfaction with its implied 'one-size-fits-all' approach (Thompson, 2012).

There have now been many theoretical developments that have sought to replace this popular but flawed approach. One notable example of this is the dual process approach put forward by Stroebe and Schut (1999). This involves recognising the presence of two processes that occur at a time of grieving: (i) loss orientation – a process of focusing on whom or what has been lost, characterised by a wide range of potential emotions: sadness, anger, bitterness, guilt and so on; and (ii) restoration orientation – a process of looking forward and attempting to rebuild after the loss – for example, by making the adjustments that the loss has necessitated (such as having to undertake tasks previously the responsibility of the person who has died). Stroebe and Schut argue that people do not grieve in stages, but, rather, oscillate between the two orientations. That is, grief can be understood as a process of swinging backwards and forwards between loss and restoration, with more time gradually being spent in restoration orientation – but with the possibility that, even years after the loss, we can still move into loss orientation at times (at anniversaries of a death, for example).

This is an important theoretical development, as it helps to explain the dynamic, ever-changing nature of grief experiences while also allowing for significant variation across individuals and groups. The fact that someone can be in loss orientation in the morning (perhaps crying and distressed), in restoration orientation in the afternoon (making arrangements relating to financial matters previously handled by the person who has died, for example) and back in loss orientation in the evening captures well the confusion and 'disorientation' associated with grieving.

Assumptive worlds

A further important concept is that of the 'assumptive world'. This refers to how we become enmeshed within our own life experiences and create a sense of our own reality based on the assumptions we make. Our assumptions both shape and are shaped by our experiences. Attig (2011) explains this as follows: '*We weave unique daily life patterns. And we live out and embody unique life stories. Through caring engagement we "assume" places in the world; we become caught up in living in it. We establish and orient ourselves in the world in and through the needs, wants, emotions, motivations, abilities, habits, dispositions, interaction patterns, expectations, and hopes that arise within and shape our caring engagement with it.*' (pp. xli-xlii)

A major loss can be seen to turn our assumptive world upside down, leaving us feeling all at sea because aspects of what we have taken for granted for so long no longer apply – for example, if someone we have relied on for comfort and/or security is no longer with us precisely at a time when we need comfort and security most.

The notion of 'assumptive worlds' fits well with dual process theory, in so far as 'restoration orientation' can be understood as a process of rebuilding our assumptive world and establishing some degree of stability and a new sense of normality.

Meaning reconstruction theory

The work of Neimeyer and his colleagues (see Neimeyer, 2001, for an introductory overview) has taken our thinking forward on grief by emphasising that a major loss necessitates a change to our biographical narrative. The notion of meaning reconstruction chimes well with Attig's work on 'assumptive worlds', in so far as it proposes that loss disrupts our frameworks of meaning and thereby presents us with the challenge of constructing new (post-loss) meanings, enabling us to construct a new narrative in a sense.

This is also consistent with dual process theory and helps us to recognise that restoration orientation is not simply a process of making practical adjustments (although these are certainly part of it), but also incorporates a broader process of making sense of our changed circumstances. In this regard, all three conceptual frameworks (dual process theory; assumptive worlds; meaning reconstruction theory) can be understood to have spiritual dimensions and thus potentially significant consequences in terms of our spiritual well-being. It is, therefore, to the topic of grief and spirituality that we now turn.

Grief and spirituality

Key aspects of spirituality include meaning, purpose and direction, and hope. All of these can be lost, temporarily at least when we experience a major loss. The relationship between grief and spirituality is therefore one that is worth exploring if we are to develop a better understanding of grief.

The dimensions of grief

Grief is traditionally understood as primarily an emotional response to loss. However, this reflects only one part of one aspect of our responses to loss. First of all, it is important to recognise that our psychological response to loss is not just emotional. Grief can, and often does, have a significant effect on us cognitively (that is, in terms of our thought processes and memory functioning) as well as behaviourally (we can display very different patterns of behaviour when we are grieving compared with our normal behaviours). We can therefore see that there is more to our psychological response to loss than emotion. However, our psychological response is, in itself, only one part of our broader grief reaction.

We also have to consider the biological response (for example, effects on appetite and/or exacerbation of medical conditions, such as asthma) and the social response (for example, how people respond differently to someone who is grieving compared with how they normally would, plus different cultural and gender expectations in relation to grief). We can therefore recognise that the tendency to see grief as primarily, if not exclusively, a matter of emotion is far too narrow a conception of grief, as that neglects the cognitive, behavioural, biological and social aspects of grief as a response to loss. It also neglects the spiritual dimension, for, as we have seen, a major loss is likely to disrupt our frameworks of meaning, our sense of purpose and direction, and so on.

It could also be argued that there is an important link between spirituality and grief in terms of how grief experiences can have a long-term effect on our spiritual well-being, whether positively or negatively. I shall return to this point below.

Loss as an existential challenge

Life is full of challenges, but existential challenges are those that in some way relate to our very being, to what it means to be human (facing up to the fact of our own mortality, for example). Coping with loss experiences can therefore be understood as an existential challenge, an inescapable aspect of our humanity.

An important part of this is the concept of 'ontological security'. Ontology is the study of being, and so ontological security could also be called existential security. It refers not to specific forms of security (avoiding being a victim of violence or crime, for example), but rather to a deeper sense of security about our life overall – it is about feeling secure with who we are and how we fit into the wider world, and is therefore a concept that speaks to spirituality. We can therefore say that grief places us in a position where we encounter the existential challenge of maintaining ontological security – maintaining a thread of meaning through a period of significant change, disruption, pain and confusion. It is for this reason that social support can be such a key factor when it comes to coping with the demands of grief. It is also why it is quite common for people who are deep in grief to feel that they are going mad, in so far as they associate their sanity closely with ontological security.

Loss experiences can also throw our frameworks of meaning into sharp relief. For example, it is not unusual for people who have a near-death experience to show a deeper understanding of their lives and therefore to feel more appreciative of what they have got and what their life means. Similarly, when we experience a bereavement, the result can be immense pain, but it can nonetheless highlight aspects of our lives that would otherwise remain out of focus. Tomer and Eliason (2008) capture this idea well when they write of the poignancy of death contributing to meaning.

An example of this phenomenon would be a man I once met who had been considering leaving his wife because he felt the relationship had gone stale and he wanted more excitement. However, when a close friend of his died, he changed his mind and decided that it would be much wiser to work on his existing relationship and try to rekindle it, rather than face the losses that would be involved in ending it.

Spiritual impoverishment: complicated grief

I made the point earlier that grief experiences can be positive or negative when it comes to our spiritual well-being. Complicated grief is something that can be very detrimental in so far as it relates to situations where people are somehow stuck in their grieving, where the process of healing associated with grief (Thompson, 2012) is inhibited in some way. This can manifest itself as delayed grieving, as if the person concerned is somehow 'holding off' grief, or as prolonged grieving where there seems to be little or no progress in coming to terms with the loss (the concept of complicated grief is itself quite complicated and open to considerable oversimplification and misunderstanding – see Neimeyer *et al*, 2011, for a useful overview).

Complicated grief is generally (but not exclusively) associated with:

- **Cumulative losses:** This refers to situations where people encounter loss after loss after loss in fairly rapid succession and therefore become overwhelmed by the experience.

- **Multiple losses:** This refers to situations where a number of losses are experienced at the same time – for example, where someone may lose several members of their family in a house fire. The result can be the same as cumulative losses: a sense of being overwhelmed that can get in the way of healing.

- **Traumatic losses:** These are losses that inflict a psychosocial or existential wound (Thompson & Walsh, 2010). This includes losses that involve violation of the person, being victim of a crime, losing one's home and/or witnessing a death.

Schneider (2012) points out that while grief is a very painful process, it is also a positive one in the sense that it is a process of healing, preparing us for coping with life without the person or thing we have lost. However, the kinds of losses I have outlined here can so easily prevent that grieving from taking place, producing a wide range of psychological, interpersonal, familial and workplace problems – and, of course, problems in terms of the diminution of spiritual well-being.

Spiritual enrichment: transformational grief

Despite the potentially destructive impact of grief on spiritual well-being we need to recognise that there is also potential for spiritual enrichment. Schneider (2012) discusses the importance of transformational grief. This refers to grief responses which, although they may be extremely painful, exhausting and disorientating, may also offer scope for improving ourselves and our lives in some way. Schneider puts it this way: *'When transformations happen, we relinquish reliance on certainty, authority and empty ritual. Our lives regain a spiritual openness. We connect – to previous lifetimes, to future ones, to people we've never met, to loved ones long gone, to a purpose for living that goes beyond individual existences.'* (p.304)

Transformational grief gives us a new vista on life by forcing us to reframe our current understandings – to write a new narrative. Consider the following examples.

Mark had had a troubled life during his teenage years and was well on the way to a life of crime when he was involved in a serious car accident in which his best friend was killed. He struggled to cope with his grief and needed professional help for a while for the sake of his mental health. However, he also benefited from the experience, in so far as he lost the 'devil may care' attitude that had got him into so much trouble before. He became much more cautious in his life and therefore much less likely to take the risks involved in criminal behaviour. This then gave him a much firmer foundation on which to make something of his life.

Amanda had set her sights on following in her father's footsteps by becoming a doctor, but the medical training she was undergoing was proving very stressful for her and she was beginning to doubt whether she was cut out for such a career. However, when her mother died just before Amanda was due to sit her end-of-year exams, she went to pieces and failed every single one. She was given the opportunity to re-sit them, but she decided not to, as her grieving had made her realise that her heart was not really in a medical career and she had just been trying to please her father. The loss of her mother had led her to review her relationship with her parents. She decided that, from now on, she would be in charge of her own life and go where she wanted to go, not where other people wanted her to.

Shahid was something of a workaholic who paid minimal attention to his roles as husband and father to his three children, until his youngest child was killed in a freak accident. This significant loss led to Shahid reviewing his life and realising how mistaken he had been to take his family life for granted while losing himself in his work.

One of the practical implications of the idea that loss can transform us positively in some way is that professionals involved in helping people who are grieving need to be tuned into the opportunities presented and not play a part in stifling them by encouraging grieving individuals to get back to normal as soon as possible.

This concept can also be linked to wider theoretical issues as well as practice concerns. For example, Dobson and Wong (2008) argue that coping with grief can involve learning from suffering and finding a degree of spiritual benefit from adversity. This reflects Nietzsche's philosophy of 'self-overcoming' by engaging with adversity – that is, seeing suffering as a potential source of growth, rather than just of pain (Wicks, 2002).

Transformational grief does not take away the immense pain, anguish, confusion and suffering of loss, but it does enable us to recognise that positives can emerge from negatives.

Conclusion

We can see that, when it comes to making sense of grief, there are two sets of challenges. One relates to the existential challenge of maintaining or rebuilding a coherent thread of meaning that enables us to have a sense of biographical continuity and thereby sustain or re-establish a sense of spiritual rootedness and ontological security. The other is the challenge of developing a theoretical understanding of the complexities of grief that goes beyond the oversimplifications associated with the stages approach, so that we are able to ensure that practice efforts geared towards supporting grieving people do justice to the subtleties involved and do not try to shoehorn people into an artificial set of stages.

References

Attig T (2011) *Relearning the World: How we grieve* (2nd edition). Oxford: Oxford University Press.

Dobson WL & Wong PTP (2008) Women living with HIV: the role of meaning and spirituality. In: A Tomer and GT Eliason (Eds) *Existential and Spiritual Issues in Death Attitudes*. New York: Lawrence Erlbaum Associates.

Kübler-Ross E (1969) *On Death and Dying*. New York: Macmillan.

Neimeyer RA (2001) Introduction. In: RA Neimeyer (Ed) *Meaning Reconstruction and the Experience of Loss*. Washington DC: American Psychological Association.

Neimeyer RA, Harris DL, Winokuer HR & Thornton GF (Eds) (2011) *Grief and Bereavement in Contemporary Society: Bridging research and practice*. London: Routledge.

Schneider J (2012) *Finding My Way: From Trauma to Transformation: The journey through loss and grief*. Traverse City, Michigan: Seasons Press.

Stroebe M & Schut H (1999) The dual process of coping with bereavement: rationale and description. *Death Studies* **23** (3).

Thompson N (2012) *Grief and its Challenges*. Basingstoke: Palgrave Macmillan.

Thompson N & Walsh M (2010) The existential basis of trauma. *Journal of Social Work Practice* **24** (4).

Tomer A & Eliason GT (2008) Existentialism and death attitudes. In: A Tomer & GT Eliason (Eds) *Existential and Spiritual Issues in Death Attitudes*. New York: Lawrence Erlbaum Associates.

Wicks R (2002) *Nietzsche*. Oxford: One World.

Part 3:

User, carer and professional perspectives

Chapter 10:

The patient's story: ends and change

Christopher Jones and Arthur Hawes

The late Christopher Jones was policy adviser for Home Affairs for the Archbishop's Council for the Church of England, and co-vice chair of the National Spirituality and Mental Health Forum. He was previously chaplain and fellow of St Peter's College, Oxford.

Before he died on 9th May 2012 Christopher engaged in a conversation with Arthur Hawes, in which they reflected on the diagnosis of cancer which Christopher received in 2009. In 2010 the diagnosis changed to terminal cancer. The two were close friends who valued each other and celebrated what each brought to the Christian church and the world it is called to serve. They invite you to share their conversation and enjoy sharing in their friendship.

The conversation

Arthur began by saying how much he valued having Archbishop Anthony Bloom as his spiritual director for a year when he was studying in London. The archbishop had been a surgeon in Paris during the Second World War before becoming a Russian Orthodox monk, priest and bishop. He said that never, when you are visiting someone in hospital, should you say that you know what their suffering is like.

AH: So, Christopher, let me begin by asking how have you approached the cancer which has been diagnosed?

CJ: I decided to take a high profile line and share openly all that I know without hiding anything either from myself or from other people, but to endeavour to be transparent. This makes it easier for other people and for me because we are all aware of what we are confronting.

Knowing what is entailed in any illness helps the coping process enormously and some have said it goes more than half way to dealing with the situation.

When I was a child, people would speak of cancer in hushed tones, avoiding dealing with an open and honest appraisal of what was happening to the patient with the cancer. In answer to your question, my first direct experience was when I was 23. My 85-year-old grandmother died of bowel cancer and this raised a number of issues for me.

It was my first bereavement of a person who was very close to me. She was a forceful character who played an important part in my life and I was very close to her. Furthermore, she died within a week of being given the diagnosis. Until this point she had concealed the illness and its symptoms, as people of her generation did. This did not help the family because they stumbled across the news of her illness and (for them) sudden death was totally unexpected.

I also realised that it is a shock to be reminded of mortality and, even when you know someone is dying and may have been for a long time, death still comes as a shock. As often happens, my grandmother's bowel cancer only became real at the point of diagnosis.

Between the ages of 20–37, I thought a certain amount about dying and this was for two reasons. First, as a priest, death is something you cannot avoid. While serving my title at St Margaret's, Putney, I quickly came into contact with premature death and this included babies and young children. The parish, which was a mixture of middle and working class people, was a good training ground for the pastoral ministry.

Secondly, while on the staff at Cranmer Hall in Durham, I taught the module on death and dying and fully participated in it. I also taught the second module on sexuality. I am always indebted for this part of my teaching programme because both are areas of human living which people find difficult to speak about and with which the church has had to grapple.

Belief in resurrection is about belief in God and God completing everything in His own economy. There is paradoxically the element of knowing and not knowing. Christians know in faith that Jesus is risen, but we do not know the full extent of the resurrection life and often struggle to describe it. The nature of the resurrection life described in the New Testament includes belief in the resurrection of the body. For me this is important because resurrection of the body is a means of expression and communication, and so it is social in nature.

AH: Christopher, I have always relied on this particular understanding of resurrection because it enables us to identify people. Very recently this was brought home to me forcibly, when I visited a friend who was dying of cancer and has since died. He had lost so much weight that, had I not known whom I was visiting, I would not have recognised him.

CJ: I agree and this links to the continuity and discontinuity we find in the New Testament, especially in the gospels. One moment Jesus is there and the next he is gone. Perhaps the best moment is the post-resurrection appearance of Jesus on the road to Emmaus. He interprets the conversation of the two travellers for them and then, when he breaks the bread at the supper table, they realise who he is and then he is gone. Without a body, they would never have recognised Jesus. I do so love Rembrandt's painting of the scene.

AH: How do you react to the link some people make between sin and sickness?

CJ: It is a red herring and often worse.

AH: You can say *that* Christopher. I remember one older lady telling me that she had mentioned to her vicar, who was a returned missionary and very much 'born again', that her knees hurt a great deal. He told her that it was because she was a sinner and should spend more time on her knees! Sometimes I do despair of those charged with preaching the gospel.

CJ: It might help if I spent a moment talking about my background, which explains why I describe myself as a liberal evangelical Anglican.

I was brought up in the Shropshire village of Coalbrookdale, which was home to the ironworks. I attended the Tractarian church of the Holy Trinity which was built in 1854. It was, ironically, moderate in churchmanship without vestments and the central act of worship was the Parish Communion. This is important and explains why I remain a sacramental Christian.

When I was 17, a friend who attended a revivalist church in the evangelical tradition persuaded me to make a personal commitment to Christ. I have to say that it was a real experience and I shifted from being a passenger in the church to a pilgrim – so my journey had begun. On the journey I have been greatly helped by Archbishop Michael Ramsey. His book *The Gospel and the Catholic Church* (2008) is very Anglican. Ramsey was rediscovering catholic, liberal and evangelical theology because he was a synthetist combining the three strands of scripture, tradition and reason. I was so fortunate to study with him. He gave me a real sense of Anglicanism.

AH: I too have memories of Michael Ramsay and particularly his phenomenal memory. He would remember years later names of a person's family and this, of course, made them feel very special. It is a wonderful gift. At the same time he was ethereal. See him at worship and he was in a different place – halfway to heaven.

CJ: I have already written my funeral service and one reading is from Bonhoeffer. It is not about becoming a saint but about having a faith. My faith includes a very strong commitment to the secular world, which is why I try to hold together creation, incarnation and redemption. In terms of spirituality, I turn to Irenaeus. Perhaps it is because I was ordained priest on his feast day – 28 June.

AH: Yes, Christopher, the great Irenaeus who said that God became man so that we could become divine. I am fascinated by your threefold package of creation, incarnation and redemption.

CJ: I soon became more inclined towards contemplative prayer rather than a prayer life that is an anxious badgering of God. I remember Ramsey again saying that it may take you half an hour to prepare to approach God and one minute to pray. So it is really about listening and less about talking and remembering that, only when we give, do we receive. My spirituality changed quite a bit and was developed extensively in my second curacy where my work involved the chaplaincy at the nearby remand centre. I learnt that you find Christ there. You do not bring Him into a situation because He is already there. It is about being more reciprocal than unilateral and is well described in St Matthew, Chapter 25.

AH: So then Christopher, mission is ministry in action and you learn about Christ and how to share the gospel by ministering. As you know we were involved in a road traffic accident 10 days ago and were so fortunate to escape with just bruises, aches and pains from a car that was written off. For six hours we had to put ourselves in the hands of others – police, paramedics, hospital staff, and taxi drivers. All of them cared for us and we were totally dependent on them. It seems to me, Christopher, that as we experience new dependencies, our view of the world changes and there are times when we shall experience darkness and uncertainty.

CJ: I think this is why I have a particular affection for, and appreciation of, St Teresa and St John of the Cross. Like them, I am in the darkness and can only trust in God. The feeling is one of being stripped of all that you know and all that you are certain of. It really is a huge change and *(mutatis mutandis)* this stripping of certainty and knowledge was certainly true of the remand centre and, indeed, the world of mental health.

AH: Christopher, as you know, there are innumerable definitions of spirituality. My own is 'the awakening in each person of the other side of themselves'.

CJ: I like that because it encapsulates both the other side of what you are and of what you are not. You see, evangelical spirituality is self-centred, and my experience was one of being de-centred in order to become God-centred – open to God means, of course, being open to others.

I want to spend a little time talking about my own experience of illness, especially during these last three years. For 27 years I have enjoyed excellent health and, in that time, have never had a day off. I saw myself as indestructible and indispensable. In 2007 I suffered from gout and then a range of physical problems. I should have reflected more upon these physical ailments in order to decipher the message that lay behind them. Then in the autumn of 2008 I had pains in my abdomen which made daily living quite difficult. For almost a year the doctors would not agree that I was suffering from a serious condition. There was no evidence of bleeding or weight loss. I told the physicians about my grandmother and about my own 'gut' feeling that there was something serious happening inside me. I did have tests, but it was a year before I underwent a colonoscopy.

In a way, the diagnosis of cancer was a relief rather than a shock because it named the problem. I felt pleased that, at last, something might be done. At the same time, it was a huge shock which turned my world upside down; but I was helped by the fact that events moved very quickly and that I underwent surgery within three weeks. I recognised that there was a possibility that I would not survive the operation and so found myself trying to say goodbye to family and friends. The realisation of an end means finishing unfinished business and so I checked my will, wrote my funeral service and completed outstanding work. I was confident that I would recover but, before the CT scan, I did not know how far the cancer had advanced. The surgeon was confident that he would be able to remove all the cancerous tissue.

The process of becoming used to a new identity now began in earnest. From this moment onwards I was a 'cancer patient'. I found very helpful two books – *The Enduring Melody* (2006) and *The Questioning Country of Cancer* [sic]. Both were written by Michael Mayne, who was the Dean of Westminster Abbey. The picture in my mind was of carrying something inside myself which could kill me. As you know, Arthur, I have always had a penchant for detail and have always been interested in medical detail. What the scan showed was a large tumour in the splenic flexure, not a well-known organ, which is why it took so long to discover.

In November 2009 I underwent surgery and half my bowel was removed. My role simply was to put myself in their hands as God's instruments and, by having faith in them, I was also having faith in God. My understanding of the operation is that it is sacramental. As I entered the anaesthetic room I died, as it were, and then rose again in the recovery room. When I regained consciousness, I was relieved, and risen.

Sadly, this was not the end, and there were signs of more cancer from the results of the histology. The treatment recommended was chemotherapy. I have to say that I felt disappointed, having taken a fairly charitable view of doctors who are highly skilled and fallible and who have a difficult calling. I did not blame anybody, not even God. To do this is a fairly futile sort of business.

AH: This means, Christopher, that we are back to the old chestnut of sin and sickness, and we have already agreed that God does not visit his people in this way, nor does he punish them. It is all very Jenkinesque and it was, of course, Bishop David Jenkins who stated unequivocally that he did not believe in an interventionist God; otherwise, why was it that God had not intervened in the Holocaust during the Second World War.

CJ: Exactly so, and, Arthur, it reinforces my own very strong theology of the created order which God works through and through which he restricts himself. I do take the natural order very seriously. As we speak, 300 people in Turkey have died because of the volcano. I really cannot conceive of this as an expression of God's anger. Rather, we need to be much more realistic about the natural order and the world in which we live and, as a consequence, face it unflinchingly. We know from reading Romans, Chapter 8, that God is present in frailty, pain and despair, and the journey is a scary one.

AH: Christopher, I do so agree with taking the natural order and the world in which we live seriously because it is, par excellence, an expression of the Incarnation and what it means for God to dwell among us and engage in human affairs. We must, at all costs, avoid 'spiritualising' the Gospel, as though it exists separately from the Kingdom of God and the world he created.

As you say, Christopher, we have to take the natural order seriously, and this means taking our own bodies seriously and trying to understand them. My own view of cancer has always been of rogue malignant cells that cause chaos wherever they happen to be located in the body.

CJ: Listening to you, Arthur, I am reminded of what Archbishop John Hapgood said when he linked heresy and cancer. He said that the mark of a cancer cell is that it has lost the power to discriminate. The image in my mind is of St Paul's description of death being at work in us and the notion of carrying death in our bodies.

From January to July 2010, I received 24 treatments of chemotherapy and felt very positive about the whole thing. The main side effect was neuropathy and I still suffer from this today. Of the rest of 2010, I reflected upon the treatment I had received and how it had begun to change me as a person. I realised that I was far less inhibited, was experiencing a new-found freedom and becoming much more daring.

AH: Christopher, I am interested that you use the word 'daring' because when the wife of a colleague of mine died at a young age with cancer, I remember how much it changed his preaching. In your words, Christopher, he became much more 'daring'. I think now, Christopher, it is time to turn to your family and those close to you.

CJ: Jenny (Christopher's wife) is the most important person to me, and I have what I describe as both a sacramental and covenantal relationship with her. This means that I am bound to her, and indeed she to me.

'End and change' are going to mean something very different for her. I try very hard not to make demands upon her and also to try to retain some of my own autonomy. For example, I always take myself off to chemotherapy by myself. However, I am very conscious that my dependency upon her is growing and this, of itself, causes tension. Given my own profession and new status as a cancer patient, there is the ever-present danger of people treating me as a holy figure, talking in hushed tones and saying things like 'he is so brave'. They forget that Jenny, too, is a holy figure. The role of the carer/spouse is not an easy one, and that person is not in the limelight. Jenny has to be strong for me and I am the person over whom everyone else is fussing. Her outlet is her music, which she takes into schools, and I think that maybe she chooses different music depending upon how she is feeling. My hunch is that music might, at a later stage, become a very real source of support for her. Music has also been an increasingly important aspect of my own life and it gives me great comfort and solace.

In the marriage service we read that 'as husband and wife give themselves to each other throughout their lives…', and these words underlie the vocational aspect that we find in marriage. In a crisis, the calling to be bound to one another is taken and stretched to new levels. I am conscious that in 2003 Jenny herself had breast cancer. Neither of us wants to be defined by cancer. Consequently, each of us is committed to keeping our own lives going and, at the same time, ensuring that our identities are rich and complex. My own fear stems from the realisation that cancer has a narrowing down effect, and theologically this can mean losing sight of resurrection. It is difficult for Jenny to know what effect all this is having on her, and also for me to know. There are, and will continue to be, many unanswered questions, some of which might be understood better with hindsight, but hindsight is perhaps something that will be denied to me. Understandably, Jenny is worried about practicalities. I have always been the main breadwinner and, when I am no longer here, Jenny will need to work more in order to earn more. There is also the question of where she will live in future. I am conscious that my part in the drama will come to an end, but this is not the case for Jenny, and I really do not know how to deal with this.

Rachel is in Reading and Andrew in Upminster, and we meet regularly. Both children are quite reticent, though that is not to say that they do not take an interest in me and ask a range of questions. I suspect that they are trying to keep their feelings at bay. I think back to conversations I had with my grandmother and I am aware that children are sensitive to not saying too much, and sometimes not knowing what to say. Rachel and Andrew have shown me a great deal of affection and are pleased that the chemotherapy is keeping the cancer at bay.

At work, colleagues have been tremendous and shown a great deal of support, kindness and humour in a very straightforward way. I realise that

I may have been sublimating a great deal of my own feelings, but do, at the same time, value Malcolm, our director, who takes a great deal of pressure off me. At the same time, Philip, the chairman of the Mission and Public Affairs Council, has been very kind and thoughtful. In general, colleagues do not exaggerate the situation and show pleasure when the news is good, and weep with those who weep. It really is an expression of solidarity.

AH: Christopher, I imagine that this is because they both know and see the real Christopher?

CJ: Yes, that is a good way of putting it. It is different when I go to church, and sometimes I groan inwardly because of being afraid of being put through the third degree, but then, of course, people at church do not know me as well as colleagues at work.

In November and December 2010, just two months after receiving the all clear, following a scan, an antigen was discovered. Bad news like this provides the most negative part of the reality. Until then I had been making plans and felt a sense of reprieve. It is about being 'recalled to life' as in Charles Dickens' *A Tale of Two Cities* (1859). What followed were the results showing three active growths in the liver, which left me with the feeling of being dismissed from life. It was certainly the biggest shock I had ever had, and I began to exhibit classic symptoms of, for example, a cold feeling in my stomach, a sense of despair, and what followed were six weeks of huge difficulty which, as it happens, coincided with a spell of awful weather (how British!). There is a sense in which the weather became sacramental, by which I mean there was a coldness in the atmosphere which matched my inner coldness, and there was a barrenness in the landscape which reflected my own inner life; all of this both reduced and reinforced my sense of loss and desolation. I sat full of self-pity in front of the television.

Then, as we have already said, I realised that God does not visit his people in this way, nor is my cancer personal; rather, God gives us burdens, aches and pains in order that we may gain his blessing. One of the lessons I have chosen for my funeral is the wrestling Jacob, and this helps me face my own reality and recognise that I am not the only person with terminal cancer.

AH: Christopher, do you remember Bob Champion, the jockey, who contracted cancer and, as a result of the chemotherapy, lost all his hair? When in hospital, he found himself wandering down to the children's ward, where he discovered that so many of them were like him – they did not have any hair either. From that moment onwards, Bob Champion saw life in a very new and different way.

CJ: It is, as you say, Arthur, the young people who make you stop and think. For me, particularly, it is young people with a fiancée or a wife, or very young children. What I have found among fellow cancer sufferers, whether they are young, middle-aged, or elderly, is tremendous support, and people who are stoical, brave, realistic, persevering, and often humorous. All of this provides me with a realistic context and a framework in which I can safely ask: why should I think that I might be exempt more than anyone else?

There is a place for self-pity and self-compassion, and therefore compassion for others. For, as the poet John Donne wrote: 'no man is an island'. I had to face and work through the harsh reality of terminal cancer and I did this by finding the resources to cope and then accepting the situation, rather than resenting, denying or fighting it. The process can take a long time to reach this point (in my case two months) and often it is gradual; sometimes it bites you on the ankle and feels very much like a bereavement.

AH: As you know, Christopher, there are four stages to bereavement and I suppose my question is whether you felt you had to work through all four, viz. – shock, depression, withdrawal, and readjustment?

CJ: It is very similar, and I now think I have reached a place of acceptance and understand terminal cancer as part of the natural order. Like Saint Paul, I can say that I know how to be content.

AH: Christopher, thank you very much indeed for having this conversation with me. I hope that your description of living with terminal cancer will be a help, support and inspiration to other sufferers. So may we finish by blessing one another as we say together the words of the Grace – The grace of our Lord Jesus Christ, and the love of God, and the fellowship of the Holy Spirit, be with us now and forever. Amen.

References

Dickens C (1859) *A Tale of Two Cities*. London: Penguin Classics.

Mayne M (2006) *The Enduring Melody*. London: Longman and Todd.

Ramsey M (2008) *The Gospel and the Catholic Church*. Eugene, OR: Wipf and Stock.

Chapter 11:

Carers and end of life care

This chapter provides insight about caring for children and adults who are at the end of their lives.

Child care: A parent's experience

Contributed through Paul Nash

It was a beautiful spring morning and I held on to the precious hand of my Ibraheem as I walked him to school. It was his birthday; he was eight and he was so excited he could hardly contain himself. We talked about his birthday party after school and all the friends he had invited, and the presents he was going to open. I waved goodbye at the gate and watched as he turned, smiled and waved before he disappeared out of sight.

I began to walk back from school, occupied with the thoughts of preparation for the party. I turned the key to the front door and I heard the phone ringing, little did I know that my life was about to change forever. It was the school, 'So sorry Mrs Ahmed, but Ibraheem has collapsed and is unconscious. Mr Dean has accompanied him to the hospital in the ambulance'. I could not believe what I was hearing – he was fine a few moments ago!

I walked into hospital with my husband; it all seemed surreal. We kept vigil by the bed, hoped and prayed for a miracle but the days passed and there was no change. What sustained us through the whole experience was the kindness and competence of the staff. I knew they were doing the best they could. However, they were busy in their work. I felt lonely; there were so many questions constantly repeating in my mind. There was also confusion, pain and bewilderment.

Amidst the darkness and anguish I felt that God sent me help in the form of the Muslim chaplain. Here was someone from my own faith who understood my frame of reference, gave me time, so unhurried, even when I repeated the same thing again and again. I could see from her eyes and demeanour that she really cared. I received answers from the sources of authority which I believed were true and indisputable. She showed us the prayer room and liaised with other staff to provide help, advise us what was available, and answer our enquiries. I received practical, emotional and spiritual care as well as friendship and a confidante.

We were told that there was no hope of recovery and that it was only the machines which were keeping Ibraheem alive. The chaplain was there for us and helped us to gain an understanding on the Islamic perspective of removing life support. This made it easier on our conscience to give consent for the removal of life support. We needed a few days, so family and friends could be present.

The chaplain discussed the Muslim belief of life after death, in particular the death of a child, how the child would take the parents by the hands into paradise. She also told me about a book that she had written – *A Gift for the Bereaved Parent* (2010) – that was sent to parents three days after their child had died. She explained that it contained verses from the Holy Scripture that would help in making sense of what was happening, and provided solace and comfort after losing a child. She offered to give us a copy if we would like. I felt an eagerness to have the book, I needed something tangible, something, anything, that would help me.

The book was so beautiful that I felt God and his Prophet were speaking from the pages and holding my hand. In particular, the letter the Prophet Mohammad wrote to a companion whose son had died. I felt had been written to us; I read it again and again. The verse *'On no soul does God place a burden greater than it can bear'* (Qur'an, 2: 286) gave me courage and strength, as did so much of the rest of the pages.

Ibraheem passed away after three weeks in hospital. We had requested to be taken to the Rainbow room at Birmingham Children's Hospital. The chaplain had shown us this room before and we had thought it provided a homely and normal setting as well as privacy. I remember how I had longed for things to be normal when I had seen it.

We had to have a coroner's report. Ibraheem was kept overnight and we made an appointment to come back the next morning. I held him in my arms for hours, cherishing each second.

On the third day after the funeral, we received a condolence card and another copy of *A Gift for the Bereaved Parent* (2010). It was so touching to know that we were remembered; the card still sits on our mantelpiece alongside the anniversary card that we received a year later from the chaplaincy.

We subsequently received an invitation to have a short inscription put into the remembrance book. We accepted this as a way of keeping his memory alive. We also accepted an invitation to a memorial picnic. Attending the memorial picnic helped us realise that we are not the only ones walking with grief. Over 100 of us walked amongst the presence of nature, sharing a common bond. I tried to absorb the healing as the tears flowed and my heart ached.

We are grateful to Birmingham Children's Hospital for all the help and support we received. It was not just a case of medical treatment, but a story of human compassion. We are grateful for the follow-on contact and support, and knowing that our child was not forgotten.

References

Hussain Z (2010) *A Gift for the Bereaved Parent: A remedy for grief from the Islamic perspective using quotes from the Qur'an and Ahadith.* London: Ta-Ha Publishers.

Adult care

Contributed through Jen Close, with Mark Jackson

'Where is the sunshine
Now cancer brings the darkness
God only knows why'
Anon

The Haiku above was written by a carer from St Richard's Hospice Carers Group as part of a Carers Voice project for Carers Week in 2012. While supporting and acknowledging carers' needs, both emotionally and physically, what attention do we pay to their spiritual needs, and the often, strong faith that sustains them?

For carers, the everyday practicality of living and caring overtakes their life and emotions, but life goes on, one precious day at a time.

The overwhelming realisation that carers can do nothing to halt the process or relieve the pain can lead to despair, anger and a sense of helplessness. From somewhere they need to draw on a place of resilience and strength to help them make sense of their caring journey and to provide support and give them the ability to continue. This may come in the form of religious or spiritual belief, or from a humanistic determination not to give in.

Some carers relate that the strength and support can come from a deep and loving relationship they have developed with the cared for and their wider family. Some people relate that although they attend church, it doesn't always provide them with the strength to care; what does provide that strength is love – knowing that why and how they care is because of the love they have for their spouse and their spouse for them.

For others, illness has brought change to their loved ones and support comes in other forms. The following is the story of Janet and her husband Jack. Jack has suffered from Parkinson's disease for the past 18 years and is now deteriorating more quickly, needing 24-hour care. He exhibits mood swings and unpredictable behaviour, often subjecting Janet to vicious verbal attacks – he is no longer the man she knew. Reluctantly, Janet has employed care staff as she can no longer physically or emotionally manage Jack's personal care needs. However, she continues to care for him at home following a promise she made to him during the early days of his illness.

Janet's story

'Stand tall and it will all slide off' – my grandmother used to tell me this when I was little. It doesn't make it go away but it somehow makes it easier to bear. I had a difficult childhood in children's homes and foster care, with periods of return to an abusive family situation. I learnt to develop a core of inner strength and standing tall helped me to survive and become strong. This wasn't the only thing though. I always knew I had somebody – a presence – guiding and supporting me; something giving me strength and purpose to carry on. Although I attend church occasionally, I do have trouble believing in God; especially the vengeful God of fire and brimstone, so some of the Christian teaching I have had does not help me. However, there is something here around me that I cannot explain – I just accept the presence of my angels.

'During the years of caring for my husband they have continued to be with me, mostly nearby. On a few occasions I have felt very low and wondered why I carry on, and I can feel them become troubled and start to move away.

This is quite scary and I feel alone and frightened. Gradually they come back, filling the room with a sense of security and safety, and I can breathe again.

'I talk to them every day and I know I have heard 'someone' tell me everything will be alright. A sense of calm and peace helps me to face a difficult moment and to 'stand tall'.

'There have been at least two occasions when I am sure I have seen them, but I don't need this proof to know they are there and that I am held and cared for.

'I am a firm believer that we are all assigned a pathway in life that we have to follow. If we are aware we will know there is someone to guide us along this pathway and help us when times are difficult. I experience times when I falter, especially when I have no control over what is happening. The angels 'touch me' and remind me it's time to move on.

'When my husband dies I shall grieve and I will feel very lost. I grieve now for the man he once was. I know my angels will be there, comforting me and helping me take the next step along my pathway. They are my light in the darkness. I haven't spoken of this before but I recognise how much I need them and how much strength they give me.'

Janet's story helped me realise that one of the important things was that she was able to tell it. When deciding how to help carers it reminds us of the importance of the holistic approach to their needs. Janet didn't need me to believe in angels, her strength of belief was enough but she did need me to hear what she was saying and affirm the strength they give her.

Another carer in our group gives a different, although no less poignant, picture.

For Dorcas, her belief in God is strong and it is what has helped her through a difficult few years. She has cared for her mother, mother-in-law and very recently, her husband, George, during a painful and difficult struggle with several forms of cancer. They journeyed together on a rollercoaster of diagnosis, misdiagnosis, treatment, respite, operations, and finally his last weeks in 2012 receiving hospice palliative care. Not one to give in easily, George fought for his life, taking every opportunity offered by medical science to seek a cure. Dorcas, however, recognised the seriousness of his illness but was determined to support him in any decision he made. For her, the involvement of St Richard's Hospice and the move to palliative care to alleviate the pain improved the quality of the end of his life and gave her considerable support. She is thankful they always had an open relationship and were able to share their thoughts and feelings about what was happening. Support also came from their two sons and families, friends and relatives far and near. Describing herself as 'Church of England' – she is the granddaughter of a past rector of a local, rural church – Dorcas relates that her church attendance is now irregular and she is not reliant on the ritual to confirm her faith and gain support.

Explaining why, she said: 'I feel nearer to God walking the hills, working in the garden and seeing and experiencing what God has created for mankind. Churches are places that people built to worship Him; what He created is more important to me. I can pray on my own, and do. I talk to God and know that George is with Him and is no longer suffering. It gives me great strength now and during those last weeks. I often look up to Heaven and say thank you. I am a great believer in fate and He will call you when He is ready to accept you. It has brought me peace and given me strength to understand and manage the situation.

'The chaplain at St Richard's Hospice played an important part in those last weeks, supporting us both. George was not what I would call "a religious man" but he took comfort from time with the chaplain, David, over the last weeks and even received Holy Communion from him at home. He seemed happier and more content after that, and, therefore, so was I. David officiated at his cremation and his ashes are now in the garden with special mementoes from the children and grandchildren nearby and I can, and do, talk to George all the while. St Richard's Hospice has now become a very special place as George's spirit departed from there and some of that spirit still remains.'

Like Janet, Dorcas has found strength and support in her faith, and its importance must not be denied in her journey towards healing for herself during her bereavement. I feel very privileged to have been able to record the words of these two generous women.

Talking to carers and exploring with them this part of themselves, I am made acutely aware of how important and integral part of their emotional and coping methods their spirituality is. Good practice starts from the place of the carer – spirituality, faith and religion need to have a place in our assessments with a clear recognition of their healing power.

Don't be afraid to ask the questions and always honour their answers.

My sincere thanks to Janet and Dorcas.

Chapter 12:

A formal carer's story: a reflective account from a spiritual care team volunteer

Alison Wooding

Introduction

'Yea though I walk through the valley of the Shadow of Death, I will fear no Evil.' (Psalm 23)

When I began the first draft of this chapter, I became aware of writing from a 'safe' distance – talking about dying and spiritual care as a discipline, rather than from actual experience. When I realised that I would have to share these personal aspects, a wave of resistance arose. To do this meant making visible something very precious and often intimate, as well as being more deeply in touch with the depth of passion I experience in working with death. And yet it would be impossible to withhold this in writing about work I truly love.

I have therefore taken up the challenge to write from the heart of my practice as a spiritual caregiver in a local hospice, to share how it has changed me and what I have learnt about what helps contribute to a good death. I will describe how death is slowly transforming my perception and understanding, bringing me into direct awareness of the dying process in my own consciousness. I also include references at the end to some sources that have informed and inspired me along the way.

A personal reflection: the power of death

I was born into a Jewish family whose historic circumstances included trauma and emotional pain. Born in 1939, my father spent his childhood in wartime London with the Blitz raging. My mother was born in 1945 and by the age of seven both her parents had died of illnesses that are more preventable today. Both maternal and paternal lineages were also shaped by the Russian pogroms and the Holocaust.

I was about eight years old, in a Hebrew class about the Shoah[1], when I was shown a photograph of emaciated dead bodies being pushed into a pit full of other decomposing bodies. The message was quite clear. Hitler said that Jews were evil and the source of the ills befalling the world, so they needed to be exterminated forever.

'I should not be here', my child mind thought, 'and it could happen again'. In that moment, I knew I was on the run, unconsciously pitted against life in attempts to evade the shadow of death.

At the age of 27, a friend took me to a workshop with Brandon Bays, a woman who appears to have cured her own cancer and then developed an approach to working with body consciousness. In an extraordinary guided inner journey, I found myself standing in the long, dark shadow of an enormous edifice: a tombstone the size of a tower. A wise guide handed me a hammer and invited me to smash and dismantle it, placing each piece into a fire nearby, to be transformed in flames of love.

At that moment, I realised the true depth of loyalty I felt towards the dead of the Shoah and others. *Who will remember them and keep their memory sacred?*

I howled.

When I eventually agreed to the task, it took time and was not easy. When the flames had consumed every piece, time and space slowed down and stopped as unearthly light raised me into an ecstatic vision. When I returned to normal awareness, I was my usual limited self, but changed and now aware of a vision for human potential and a grace beyond description.

---

1 Shoah: The Hebrew word meaning 'catastrophe' denotes the catastrophic destruction of European Jewry during World War II.

Through full awareness, care flows

With this vision in mind, and through the study and practice of meditation, prayer and systemic constellations, I have come to realise that the nature of our mind and its needs are quite distinct from our *being* dimension. Sitting with a person, I see a physical body and a personality with beliefs, values, memories and self-images, but I also consciously recognise and acknowledge the *being aspect* of that person, often called a 'soul', or sometimes 'spirit'.

Providing spiritual care to a dying person is enhanced by being simultaneously aware of the physical, emotional and spiritual aspects of the process, all present and shifting from moment to moment. I was once sitting with a woman whose neck oozed fluids throughout our encounter. Part of me contracted in a natural, visceral response, but instead of avoiding it, I allowed myself to fully include the weeping wound in my field of awareness. And so I was able to include and communicate full acceptance of everything going on in the room to her, which had a deeply settling affect.

The practice of self-awareness and creating spaciousness is vital when working with the soul. Like therapists, our stance must allow awareness of our own inner world. Then we can contain and witness any tension, conflict or belief being triggered in us, so that it doesn't influence the encounter. Once this practice is established, it is possible to hold inner awareness together with awareness of what is happening 'outside'.

Through the practice of systemic constellations, I have learned to open my awareness in a particular way, to widen and hold different thoughts and possibilities in dynamic tension. I consciously refrain from analysing, judging or preferring any one idea over another. In this way, *something gradually emerges in awareness,* which we might then explore or follow. It is about allowing a *movement* – that is, an impulse that occurs in the soul realm, and which is restorative: re-establishing contact between people and the natural flow of love.

Case study: Working with intense emotions

I was once with a big family sitting with a loved one who was taking a very long time to leave. Emotional strains could be felt in the room after eight long days and nights of sitting with the elderly woman: a wife, mother and grandmother.

The family was exhausted and tense from waiting, expressing their ambivalence in wanting her to both stay and go. I tracked the situation in my body and waited for any cue that might come. I inquired gently as to what might be useful. When the husband asked after the chaplain with a certain intensity in his eyes, I sensed an opening.

I responded, saying that the chaplain could certainly come and be with them, venturing that they might perhaps like a blessing. The husband burst out, 'No, no, no, she's not dead!' and I felt the expanding heat of anger and frustration pass through me, wondering if I'd spoken out of turn and simultaneously aware that this is not about me.

I stayed with the physical and emotional discomfort, both my own and the family's. When the husband then said 'It's too hot, I need air', I accompanied him outside and put a gentle hand on his arm. He began to weep as he released a good deal of emotional pain. I realised the rightness of staying, and of not withdrawing apologetically, as may have provided temporary relief. Instead it was possible to remain and witness the full force of what needed to make itself known.

The explosive out-surge had brought something to a head and the relief that followed for the family was palpable afterwards. They continued sitting with their loved one with our informal support. I too made sure I was not left carrying any after-affects and debriefed the story carefully in supervision, so that I could leave the energy where it belonged.

The subtle skills of a practitioner

Our role is to help alleviate suffering by allowing each person we serve to discover their own truth, and sometimes a strengthened sense of well-being and acceptance about what is happening.

I remind myself that every person has access to the same source of wisdom that nourishes me, and that they may also find guidance through contemplation, prayer and visionary dreams. That way, we can discover together surprising resources and gifts hidden within even the most difficult situations.

By holding spacious awareness and using our *whole self*, we can perceive subtle phenomena happening now. This means staying present and paying attention to sensations without retreating into thought-processes and ideas.

Responding to the presence of death requires creative responses, as well as protocols and procedures. For example, on one occasion with a woman of faith in the last stages of her illness, I felt myself in the presence of an extraordinary lightness. She said: 'When I close my eyes I have huge, beautiful wings. But I'm scared to fly. Can I go on your back instead?' We wondered together if she might gently test out her beautiful wings and whenever she felt ready, she would know when it was the perfect moment to fly.

In these 'threshold places' we cannot know (in the ordinary sense) what is called for. But we can remain open and be of service to this unknowable process by listening and attuning to what is happening – even more in the silence than in the spoken word. We can use our many capacities for sensing, feeling and intuiting, as well as thinking, while we align to a greater will and open ourselves to guidance.

It is also very important to tread very carefully, especially on first contact. We must ensure that we are not intruding into a person's space, or indeed holding any of our own judgments, or desire for something to happen for a person. This form of subtle self-discipline is needed when responding to spiritual distress and giving space to existential questions that go right to the heart of things.

One of the hardest things in my experience is to truly do nothing and let a process fully take its course. This means confronting our own discomfort with a person's suffering, and not falling prey to the idea that our skills in midwifery of the dying could – or should – precipitate a faster or different death. A man in his late 30s (described in **Case study: None of your business!**) was a great teacher to me in this.

> ### Case study: None of your business!
>
> With a wife and two pre-teen children, there was a young man whose active dying went on for many months. He had become noteworthy to all the staff. We marveled how he remained alive against all the odds.
>
> I had shared many moving and searching conversations with him and it amazed me each time he went home, seemingly to die, that he returned again to the hospice. After every encounter I reconciled myself to the likelihood it would be the last. But he kept on living. In the latter stages, when he went onto the Liverpool Care Pathway, he'd return again from unconscious states and we'd find him sitting up in bed very engaged with us and eating heartily.
>
> One day I came in and he was unconscious, but the interior work was very visible. I sat by the bed and attuned to his process. Part of me so wanted to be of use and assist in the completion. I approached his soul with inner-seeing and received an image of him surrounded by people. There was great busyness within the barrier of people. Trying to see what was happening, I asked what I might do. I was put in my place by a direct instruction, which I experienced both as a felt sense of being pushed away and clearly audible words: 'Please back off. This is none of your business!'

Learning about letting go

When I began hospice work I was curious about the process of 'letting go'. It often featured in coaching, where outdated beliefs and habits were holding clients back from moving on or creating change. If letting go served growth so strongly, how might it serve dying?

Faced with the imminent reality of death, many people who say they are 'feeling ready' and 'everything is sorted' actually exhibit signs of numbness, detachment and dissociative trances. I've learnt to be very cautious even in using the word 'death' in conversation. It can jolt a person with that reality, even when they themselves are describing how they are preparing for it. The mind appears not to be able to cope with this directly.

As the mind can't apprehend death, it is even more important to connect to the being aspect of a person and to the ground of their faith if they believe in an existence beyond the body. This is where holistic care – including complementary therapies, relaxation, ritual and blessing – can soothe and soften the difficulties around dying.

As a person of faith, I actively inquire into selfhood, to experience a deeper connectedness to life, others and the source of everything. So I work intensely with my own inner attitude and resistance to dying. Having studied how my body stores fear and trauma patterns in cellular memory, I observe how these are re-activated by my psyche in moments of great change and instability.

As a mirror of life, death is an empty dark space into which we naturally project our fears. I've gradually learned to meet the darkness of the unknown differently – choosing work that requires me to stay right at the edge of my skills where my knowledge becomes redundant, where I am at the limit of everything I know and understand. I've learnt to stay there long enough, with the intense discomfort, until I have truly surrendered my limited self and let go of my need to know.

Allowing death close has meant experiencing its effect on my instincts, emotions and identity. Sometimes I discover I am holding on too tightly to a desire or outcome, so it's a very practical means of confronting immediate loss and dissolving attachment. Sometimes the process stimulates a primary fear, activating a deep personal pain and threatening the link that binds me to a familial and ancestral source.

Like many, I have feared death as a murderer of potential, hope and life – the Grim Reaper. But in working with the dying, I experience death more as a transformer and healer, and this is reflected deeply in my dreams and meditation. In meditation, I now see a beautiful and hopeful archetype – for death has become a feminine figure absorbed in separating many fine threads as she gently releases the soul from the body.

Case study: A personal dream about death

Reproduced without interpretation to allow us to wonder about its message and the different levels of meaning that it contains.

I dreamt that I was working at the hospice with an elderly Indian man. He arrived already unconscious and I was sitting by his bed speaking gently and occasionally putting a reassuring hand on his arm. He slipped away at some point and I found myself continuing to sit with his dead body.

Doctors and nurses came and went and he just stayed there in the bed. Nobody moved him, so I continued to sit and this appeared to be treated as quite normal. This continued for two days and I began to wonder why he'd been left and become concerned about decomposition, even though there was no smell, or outward signs of decay.

A few hours later a nurse came in to do something and the man started stirring very gently. Incredibly he started to move and speak and it was clear that he wasn't dead. I tried to move towards him to speak to him, but he was really disoriented and startled by me, so I stood back while the professional staff moved in and did various things efficiently and beautifully.

The next thing that happened was astounding. All the doctors and nurses came in and formed a circle with the man. Arm in arm they sang and turned, somehow singing his return to life with joy. I asked someone what was happening and they said that this was what always happened. There was a tall man in the room who I thought was another chaplain. He looked at me and I was obviously bewildered. He asked if I was OK. I was full of tears on the inside and shocked at what had happened, but I held it all back because everyone else seemed so joyous at this event.

After that, I was in the locker room getting changed and a large, motherly-looking matron came in. She spotted my true state and I just started sobbing, so she took me in her strong arms with a big hug. I said to her, 'I understood and dealt with things knowing that the dead were dead and the living were living'. She smiled at me and understood the change within me.

Where do we go from here?

Through encounters with the dying and their family members, I am aware of a whole *phenomenology of connection* that extends well beyond 'me' and my conscious abilities. For example, whenever words of blessing are spoken in language that I wouldn't ordinarily use. I become aware of the unique connection at that moment in time and space, and of a timeless presence that contains the moment as it communicates through me.

Through dreams, meditation and a growing awareness of shared 'fields' of connection, I glimpse consciousness beyond physical death. I am seeing that what separates the living from the dead is much less than we imagine from our material perspective.

In conversation and collaboration with others, I am exploring the frontiers of selfhood and consciousness – mapping my direct experience to research from neuroscience, quantum field theory and psychology. Their findings indicate that human beings share in and participate in a single, continuous reality now being referred to as *the field*. We might call this Source, Oneness or the *unity of God* in spiritual language.

I am very aware of being at a sacred threshold with another human being on the dying journey, particularly in the final moments. The unknowability of this transcendent 'space between', where inner subjective experience and outer observable reality meet, brings me into a quiet loving presence. In this place I feel most whole, most connected and most free, as my own deep fear and pain slowly transform into a gift that serves life.

With new knowledge from science and practices from faith traditions, I believe we can do even more to help lessen the fear of death and support people to further open to the dying experience. This inspires me to continue developing my own learning and understanding, so we can further realise Cicely Saunders' founding vision for high quality palliative care to: *'aid in the spiritual search for meaning, sense of self and the possibility of growth through loss'* (Saunders, 2013).

Acknowledgements

I want to acknowledge and give thanks to the chaplain Louise, as well as the leaders and staff of the hospice who affirm the value and preciousness of every life. I am also deeply grateful for having had the privilege of learning from others in the field of death and dying, including Martin Nathanael, Felicity Warner and Dr William Bloom.

References

Saunders C (2013) Cicely Saunder's website [online]. Available at: www.cicelysaundersfoundation.org/about-us (accessed March 2013).

Further reading

Here are just five of the publications that have touched and inspired me.

Bryson T & U Franke-Bryson (2012) *Encounters with Death.* Germany: Night Sky Productions.

de Hennezel M (1997) *Intimate Death: How the dying teach us to live.* London: Little, Brown.

Levine S (1989) *Who Dies?: An investigation of conscious living and conscious dying.* New York: Anchor Books.

Peake A (2006) *Is There Life After Death?: The extraordinary science of what happens when we die.* London: Arcturus.

Warner F (2011) *A Safe Journey Home: A simple guide to achieving a peaceful death.* London: Hay House.

For more information on systemic constellations, visit the Centre for Systemic Constellations website (primary UK training body since 2001) at: www.centreforsystemicconstellations.com

Part 4:

Death as a gateway?
A belief system

Chapter 13:

The changing spirituality of Muslims dying in the UK: A personal and communal journey

Hifsa Haroon-Iqbal and Peter Kevern

The forms of Islam that are most widely encountered in the UK are distinguished by two key characteristics. First, they are intensely family-centred: the family is considered to be the proper unit to provide both practical and religious care for the individual. The imam or religious leader is consulted about the teachings of the Quran and the proper way to behave, but is not usually thought of as a 'spiritual minister'. Second, in these forms of Islam, 'spirituality' is more to do with public, moral behaviour in obedience to the demands of the Quran and the teachings (Sunnah) of the Prophet Muhammed rather than with spiritual experiences, mysticism or inner sentiment.

Because of these basic features, a form of 'spiritual care' that focuses on the individual patient's emotional and psychological needs may be doubly inappropriate for British Muslims. It may misunderstand the people involved in giving and receiving care (the whole family, not the professional carer, patient and religious minister); and it may be offering the wrong support (for personal well-being rather than for practical religious duties). At the end of life, the focus both of the individual and their family will be on their practical religious duties, expressing what Sheikh and Gatrad (2000, p.104) term an 'activist model' of spirituality around the end of life.

There is one other important feature of Muslim spiritual practice in the UK: almost all Muslims in the UK belong to ethnic communities that began with the arrival of immigrants within the last 60 years. In common with other communities of this type throughout the world, they are therefore in the process of actively negotiating their relationship with the majority culture and their 'identity' within it. In particular, older members of the community and first-generation immigrants will have a different relationship to the majority culture than younger members and those who have been born and raised in the UK. What holds true for some sectors of the community may not hold true for them all. Consequently, it is important to continue to liaise with chaplaincy services, especially as communities develop (see Chapters 5 and 16)

Based on these initial observations, we may make three important general statements about what constitutes good spiritual care for Muslims at the end of life.

1. It will recognise the primary claims and concerns of family members both before and after death. Within this context, truly 'patient-centred' care needs to be 'family-centred', and as far as possible close family members should be involved in all major decisions affecting the patient.

2. It will adopt an 'activist' rather than a 'counselling' model of spiritual care, ensuring that practical details (such as the orientation of the patient in their final illness and the correct handling of the body after death) are attended to rather than expending energy on the psychological and emotional state of the patient and their family.

3. It will acknowledge the specific concerns of ethnic groups and individuals, negotiating with members of the family (who may in turn need to negotiate among themselves!) about how to provide for the dying process. As individuals may have different needs for spiritual care, so may families and ethnic groups; furthermore, younger generations may have different needs to older ones, and first-generation immigrants from British-born Muslims.

In what follows, we will explore these abstract points about spiritual care with particular reference to the Muslim population of the UK which traces its origins to Pakistan. This is by no means the only UK Muslim population; and not all Pakistanis are Muslim. But Muslims of Pakistani origin constitute the largest proportion of the UK Muslim population (ONS, 2012), and provide a fairly coherently-bounded community for the purposes of discussion. (This chapter will refer to this group as 'Pakistani Muslims'.)

The core of the chapter will be an 'insider view' by the first author, herself a Muslim whose family traces its origins to Pakistan and post-1947 India. Although, as she stresses, this perspective is that of a single person and may not be generalisable, it does provide an invaluable insight into both the broad narrative and the particular issues which inform the spirituality of Muslims around the end of life.

Background: Muslim communities in the UK

The UK has had a steadily rising population of Pakistani Muslims over the last 60 years. The table below illustrates how the population has grown from around 10,000 in 1951 to over 1.1 million in the 2011 census. The number in 1951 and 1961 can be largely accounted for by new immigrants, whereas between 2001 and 2011 there is clearly a large proportion of British-born Muslims.

Table 13.1: British Pakistanis in the UK	
Year	Population (rounded to nearest 1,000)
1951 (estimate)	10,000
1961 (estimate	25,000
1971 (estimate)	119,000
1981 (estimate)	296,000
1991 (estimate)	477,000
2001 (actual)	747,000
2011 (actual)	1,125,000 (Wales and England only)
Abbas (2005 p.18–30) and BRAP (2011)	

From these figures, and from common experience, it is clear that there is a change taking place in UK society which affects new migrants and established communities alike. Muslim individuals and communities from countries where they are in a majority are having to adapt to life as a religious minority, albeit a relatively large one; conversely, UK society as a whole is still adapting to the realisation that a substantial proportion of its citizens, and an even larger proportion of its residents, structure their lives and values on a premise that is neither Christian nor secular.

By far the largest proportion of these Muslims can trace their ethnic origins to Pakistan, although among second, third and even fourth generation immigrants the claims of the country of their family's origin may be differently constructed. This is reflected in the responses to the 2011 census. Thus, some may refute it altogether and claim to be simply 'British'; others may separate the claims of nationhood and ethnicity (British Asian); others again may hold dual Pakistan/UK nationality; and there may remain a proportion of the community that have not yet nor intend to acquire UK nationality at all.

To be a Pakistani Muslim in the UK is therefore to be caught between two currents which interact in unexpected ways: to be part of an expression and understanding of Islam that is changing and adapting to a new context; and to share a sense of 'communal identity' which is evolving as the community itself evolves from 'immigrant' to 'indigenous' status.

Since it is considered to be almost impossible to be a faithful Muslim without being a faithful member of one's family and society, these shifting currents have immediate significance for Muslim spirituality and practice. Not surprisingly, they interact most strongly around landmarks that define human individual and communal life: birth, marriage, and death.

The Pakistani Muslim way of death

As in any other community of belief and practice, belief and behaviour among Pakistani Muslims can vary widely, and it is dangerous to generalise. Nevertheless, there are values and practices that are widely accepted, and which provide the basis for this account by the author (see Hussein, 2010).

Among Muslims generally, there is emphasis upon dying well, and upon reverent and devout treatment of the dead body. It is normal for the whole family to gather around the bed of somebody who is dying, praying for them as they die, as well as encouraging the dying person where possible to reaffirm his or her belief in the one God and His Messenger. It is the responsibility of the family members to conduct the relevant prayers and readings and to prepare the body for burial. If there are no family members present, then the responsibility for this falls onto the local Muslim community. In principle, any practising Muslim can perform the prayers and readings, but this is a poor substitute and it is very important for Muslims to be with their family at the point of death. The family's duties continue after death also, often with a formal period of mourning (typically for no more than three days) with the close family usually staying at home entirely during this time and receiving friends and relatives who come to offer condolences. A common practice is for the grave to be visited on Fridays for 40 days. A widow is expected to stay indoors for a period of four months and 10 days. During this period of *iddah* (waiting) the widow is not allowed to remarry. Thus, the Muslim way of death requires commitment of the *family* in terms of time, geographical propinquity and practical involvement.

In Islam, a life well-lived is one lived in obedience to the Quran and the teachings of the Prophet Muhammed. The rituals and practices surrounding death are understood to be (at least) an application and expression of that obedience. Rules of purity govern such issues as who may touch the body, how it should be laid out, the direction it should face and how it should be shrouded. According to traditional Muslim practice, the body should be buried as soon as possible (and wherever possible within 24 hours), in an unmarked grave and without a coffin. Some of these practices are at variance with UK law and practice, and there is potential for a damaging clash of values if the difficulties are not negotiated sensitively and with forethought on both sides. Thus, the Muslim way of death requires some accommodation from and to the surrounding *society* in order for the individuals to reverently discharge their religious duties.

From these general observations it is possible to derive a general list of good and bad practices which will apply to most Muslims, most of the time, as they approach the end of life (eg. Sheikh & Gatrad, 2000; Neuberger, 2004; Koenig, 2007). Some of these have been incorporated into general NHS advice and policy (eg. DH, 2009). However, a fixed and general list of advice does not capture the complexity that may attend death when many members of the family may be involved, and when they may have different perspectives or priorities. In order to gain a better sense of this complexity, it is necessary to explore the dynamics of the Pakistani Muslim community in more detail.

A changing landscape – death and dying in Pakistani Muslim communities in the UK

This is not an abstract overview of the way in which the Pakistani community is negotiating issues around death and dying, but more an engaged and personal account. It draws on a consensus account within the community, but does not claim to be generalisable in the abstract. It serves a different function: to give an account of those negotiations 'from the inside'. It will mix personal perspective with shared perceptions from within the community.

Taken as a whole, it is possible to tell the history of this community in three phases:

1. **New immigration.** There was a large-scale influx of Pakistani migrants to the UK in the 1950s and 1960s. At this stage the overwhelming majority of migrants were young men, who were either unmarried or had left their wives and children in Pakistan. The expressed intention was to spend a limited time working in the UK to make money, and then to return to Pakistan to settle. Their emotional and cultural attachments were all to their country of origin, and they did not initially make much effort to establish a 'home' in the UK.

Death impinged in two ways. First, there was the death of family members, who by definition continued to be in Pakistan. Because of the strong cultural expectation that all members of the family would be present for the three-day mourning period, these first-generation migrants had to be prepared to travel at short notice: to set aside both time and money for expensive last-minute air tickets.

Second, there was the possibility that they themselves might die in the UK, far from their homes and families. For this generation, the unquestioned assumption was that their bodies would be returned to Pakistan for mourning and burial, for 'who is there here to visit the grave and pray for us?' but there were considerable practical difficulties. Without relatives in the UK, a non-relative would need to take charge of the body. Bodies cannot be transported without permission and embalming, both of which take time to arrange; the whole process would probably be too expensive for the resources of the family, even if funds could be obtained from Pakistan. Finally, facilities did not exist to fulfil the Muslim requirements for laying out the body soon after death.

2. **Early establishment.** The pressures for death to be properly acknowledged may well have contributed to the early establishment of house mosques. Certainly, one of their early functions was to provide and administer 'death funds' in order to respond to both of these concerns.

However, with the lapse of time, increasingly Pakistani migrants settled in the UK for the longer-term, and their spouses and children arrived to join them. As one older Pakistani woman put it, 'Britain can best be described as a honey pot, and we are the flies buzzing around it. Once we have landed in the sweet sticky honey, it is very hard to pull yourself out and leave'. With an increasingly stable community presence in the UK, mosques began to be more visible – as conversions of older buildings, or as new constructions. In many cases, these mosques included community rooms, which could be used for washing and laying out the bodies and for mourning.

Nevertheless, the assumption remained that burial would normally take place in Pakistan, among the relatives. Since it was unacceptable to many Muslims to be buried in a municipal cemetery, there was little incentive to seek alternatives.

3. **Second and third generation British Asian Muslims.** Much of the change that has taken place in the last 30 years or so may be ascribed to a simple combination of lapse of time and demographics. It is now rare to encounter a Pakistani resident in the UK who has no close family in this country; and as the community is increasingly made up of those who have lived in the UK for decades as well as those who were born here, the emotional attachment is more likely to be to the UK than to Pakistan. In particular, the answer to the question of 'who will visit my grave and pray for me?' is now more likely to be the relatives resident in the UK than more distant ones in Pakistan.

The situation continues to be one for active debate and negotiation. It is not uncommon to find older Pakistani Muslims who would still prefer to be buried in Pakistan, and whose siblings support them; yet their children and grandchildren wish for them to be buried in the UK, where they are resident. It is necessary to remember that the solution to this dilemma is as much to do with spirituality and religion as with sentiment: the desire of the dying individual to respond faithfully to the requirements of the Quran and the teachings of the Prophet as they understand them is in some tension with the family's desire to fulfil their religious duties in relation to the death.

In other respects, the potential difficulties of a faithful Muslim death in the UK are being addressed. Thus, the community is learning to live with some aspects of death in the UK which it finds challenging, such as the requirement for a coffin in a marked grave, the frequent necessity for a stranger (such as a doctor) to handle the body and the occasional requirement for a post mortem. The community is also developing its own resources, from information sheets to Muslim undertakers and private cemeteries, to explain and supply its needs. On the other hand, national and local authorities have developed a range of practical adjustments to the needs of Muslims: in some areas, dedicated sections for Muslim burials in cemeteries; readiness to shorten the time between death and burial; careful information around the necessity for a post mortem and explanation for delays. In this most sensitive of areas, it has been shown that, with flexibility and imagination, mutually acceptable arrangements can be made.

Conclusions

From the outside, Muslim communities may give the impression of being uniform and slow to adapt. Perhaps for this reason, it is tempting to substitute a 'tick-list' approach to spiritual care for a genuine engagement with the needs of the individual and their family as they approach the end of life, ensuring that local policies on religious observance are followed without dialogue or understanding.

However, as demonstrated in this chapter, the Pakistani Muslim community has undergone great changes over a few short generations, and has responded to challenges with energy and creativity. Faced with the need to adapt to a new culture while remaining faithful to their own spirituality, the community has developed new structures and adapted old ones; in turn, many local authorities have found ways to accommodate the needs and wishes of Pakistani Muslims in their established practices.

This overall picture provides the basis for a more creative response to the needs of Muslims at the end of life and their families. Returning to the three principles outlined at the start of this chapter, it is clear that the general principles of spiritual care might be summed up as follows.

- Establish contact with the family, if at all possible, or with a co-operative imam if not. Then get out of the way: accept that the family will provide the majority of care and, as far as possible, give them the space to do so.

- Be well-informed about the facilities for Muslim ritual observances both before and after death, and be prepared to offer practical help where you are able. Be aware that some important practices (such as the need to read to the dying person even after they have lost consciousness) which may not be familiar or readily recognised.

- Note that different family members may have different ideas about where and when the body should be buried. Therefore, take care to listen to the next of kin rather than assuming that all family members will speak with the same voice.

Finally, despite the differences, it must be stressed that the 'best practice' in spiritual care applies here as elsewhere: be open, be attentive, listen carefully, and seek to respond generously!

References

Abbas T (2005) Britain's Muslim population: an overview. *Muslim Britain: Communities under Pressure*. London: Zed Books.

BRAP (2011) *Census 2011 Religion and ethnicity data overview*. Available from the authors at brap@brap.org.uk.

Department of Health (2009) *Religion or Belief: A practical guide for the NHS* [online]. Available at: http://www.nursingtimes.net/Journals/1/Files/2009/7/1/Religion%20or%20belief.pdf (accessed March 2013).

Hussein al-Azhari M (2010) *The Muslim Funeral Guide*. Nottingham: Karimia Institute.

Koenig H (2007) *Spirituality in Patient Care: Why, how, when and what* (2nd edition). Templeton Press: West Conshohocken PA.

Neuberger J (2004) *Caring for Dying People of Different Faiths* (3rd edition). Abingdon: Radcliffe Medical.

Office for National Statistics (2012) *Religion in England and Wales 2011* [online]. Available at: http://www.ons.gov.uk/ons/dcp171776_290510.pdf (accessed March 2013).

Sheikh A & Gatrad AR (2000) *Caring for Muslim Patients*. Abingdon: Radcliffe Medical.

Part 5:

Spirituality and care workers

Chapter 14:

Burning a light or burning out?: Sources of pressure and support strategies for healthcare professionals in end of life care

Brian Nyatanga

The notion of caring can be viewed as a basic but fundamental phenomenon to being human. Benner and Wrubel (1989) put it succinctly: *'caring is part of what it is to be a human being. Caring is a basic way of being in the world'* (p.x1). The suggestion here is that human beings may not consciously choose to care, but caring is inherent in them, hence caring is ontological in nature. However, when it comes to healthcare professionals like palliative care nurses, in addition to having ontological tendencies, Edwards (2001) argues that there is intentional care, where professionals choose to care for others. The issue of intentionality has several implications for providing care, some of which include healthcare professionals thinking, believing and feeling that, despite any hardship, pressure or stress encountered, they will not let the patient down. They, therefore, continue to care and may ignore any signs of stress and tiredness inherent in caring.

Intentionality may lead healthcare professionals in end of life care to care intensively, even to the extent of 'forgetting' to care for themselves. Although palliative care nurses may find caring for dying patients emotionally taxing and stressful, Nyatanga (2011) found that they also perceive it a privilege to be part of the patient's journey till death. It is this double-edged sword approach to caring that, in one sense, keeps them at the patient's bedside and yet in another sense, can cause them to 'struggle' to cope both emotionally and physically. Such caring behaviour clearly demonstrates a paradox of feelings often experienced while caring for dying patients. The implication is self-neglect by nurses leading to burnout and negative well-being.

It is well documented (Maslach & Jackson, 1982; Bakker *et al*, 2000; Patrick & Lavery, 2007) that caring for others often 'demands' involvement at emotional and physical levels; the impact being compassion fatigue, depersonalised care and a perception of inadequacy of one's competence (Smith, 1992; Maslach *et al*, 2001; Vachon & Benor, 2003). However, health professionals are motivated to care, even to the extent of 'damaging' their own health and well-being leading to the assertion that caring is the basis of stress and, eventually, burnout. This chapter discusses the notion of burnout with a view to finding ways to prevent or minimise its occurrence. However, the important point is to understand how burnout develops and its impact in end of life care.

The development of burnout

Burnout is viewed as a syndrome which, according to Cohen (2007), develops after prolonged and unresolved job-related stress. According to this view, such stress in turn contributes to poor health and weakens the immune system, making carers susceptible to illness. The experience of the burnout syndrome would appear to affect healthcare professionals' performance in providing quality care for dying patients (Vachon & Benor, 2003; Cohen, 2007; Nyatanga, 2011), and therefore makes it a prime focus for discussion here and in finding ways to ameliorate its impact.

Burnout has been popularly conceptualised as a multi-dimensional construct comprising three main dimensions; emotional exhaustion, depersonalisation and low personal accomplishment to achieve goals and competence. This chapter will discuss further these three dimensions highlighting their sequential development before looking at ways to prevent the syndrome from developing.

The nature of burnout

The question about the nature of burnout remains almost unanswered after more than three decades of research and related debates. The modern concept of burnout can be traced to the work of Freudenberger (1974), and Maslach and Jackson (1982), which shows a relationship between work demands and one's inner resources to respond, adjust and cope. While Freudenberger and Maslach were working quite independently, they both provide the initial conception of the burnout syndrome. They independently show that burnout can be a fairly usual occurrence in many aspects of human life where demands outweigh inner resources. What then follows was the scientific desire to operationalise the burnout syndrome so that it can be measured appropriately.

Thus, research undertaken in the United States on burnout, (Greene, 1961; Maslach, 1976; Zellars & Perrewe, 2000) and later around the world (Smith, 1992; Vachon, 2000; Adali & Priami, 2002), continues to show that burnout is a complex construct which is based on subjective relationships people make with their work and general environment. However, what has transpired from all the studies undertaken over time, and in different languages, is a consensus on the three dimensions of burnout, that is, emotional exhaustion, depersonalisation (cynicism) and low personal accomplishment. The general understanding is that development of these dimensions is sequential in nature.

It is now accepted that during work-related stress, emotional exhaustion tends to develop first, when the individual's coping resources are depleted, inadequate or no longer able to resist the demands of the work environment. It is also generally accepted that the development of depersonalisation is the next phase of the body's psychological ploy in its attempt to arrest further emotional exhaustion. Therefore, depersonalisation can be regarded as a psychological defensive mechanism, and often interpreted as distancing oneself from patients. The final dimension to develop is lack of personal accomplishment, which affects perception of competence in a job. At this final stage, individuals perceive themselves as incompetent and not able to accomplish set goals or ambitions.

Emotional exhaustion in burnout

Maslach *et al* (2001) assert that emotional exhaustion is the central and most obvious manifestation of the burnout syndrome. Emotional exhaustion seems to be a widely reported dimension in most research studies (Nyatanga, 2011). In most cases, when study participants describe themselves as experiencing burnout within the job, they are often referring to the emotional exhaustion experience (Maslach *et al*, 2001; Vachon & Benor, 2003). The focus and emphasis on exhaustion should not be taken to suggest, as Shirom (2003) once argued, that the other two: depersonalisation and low personal accomplishment are incidental. However, having said that, the fact that emotional exhaustion is a necessary condition for burnout does not mean it is also a sufficient condition. The following explanation tries to show the link between emotional exhaustion and the other two components.

On its own, emotional exhaustion would not be able to influence critical aspects of the relationship people have with their work and environment

(Zellars & Perrewe, 2000), as it is not something that is simply experienced, rather it prompts the individual to adopt actions or behaviours that distance one (emotionally and cognitively) from the stress-inducing situation. This may be a way of coping with the work demands. Emotional exhaustion is characterised by lack of energy (Zellars & Perrewe, 2000), possibly as a result of intensive emotional interactions with patients at the end of life.

This exhaustion, also known as compassion fatigue, may co-exist with feelings of frustration and tension (Nyatanga, 2011). The implication from this may suggest that people may not continue to give of themselves emotionally to their patients as they have in the past because they feel emotionally 'bankrupt' themselves. This may be the point where healthcare professionals unconsciously adopt ways of protecting themselves, one of which is the psychological mechanism of depersonalisation with their patients.

Depersonalisation (cynicism) in burnout

This dimension is characterised by healthcare professionals' attempts to put distance between themselves and their work by actively sidelining or ignoring aspects that make these individuals unique and effective. Depersonalisation may be a psychological coping mechanism of making the demands seem impersonal as a way of managing them. For example, a healthcare professional caring for dying patients may start to avoid their questions about impending death by changing the topic, because they cannot prevent death or prolong patients' lives. Maslach and Leiter (1996) and Patrick and Lavery (2007) state that depersonalisation occurs when carers develop negative cynical attitudes and feelings about their patients. Distancing or depersonalisation is an immediate reaction following exhaustion as a protective mechanism against further exhaustion. In most burnout research across organisations and occupations, a strong association and developmental sequence from exhaustion to depersonalisation is consistently found over long periods of time (Maslach & Leiter, 1996; Zellars & Perrewe, 2000; Maslach *et al*, 2001). Toon *et al* (2005) confirmed a similar sequential development following a review and two longitudinal tests of the dimensions of burnout.

Low personal accomplishment in burnout

This dimension is probably the most complex of the three. In some instances, it appears to be a function, to some degree, of either exhaustion or cynicism and at other times, a combination of the two. Patrick and Lavery (2007) view low personal accomplishment as a tendency to perceive and evaluate oneself negatively, especially when it comes to meeting one's goal and patient needs. With this in mind, it is logical to argue that any work environment with chronic, overwhelming demands that result in exhaustion and cynicism is likely to erode one's sense of effectiveness. Therefore, it is almost always difficult to have a sense of accomplishment. Furthermore, it becomes plausible to suggest that, in this state of mind, individuals may not continue to care for patients towards whom they are now indifferent.

Although there is no consensus on the development of burnout, evidence so far helps us hypothesise that exhaustion is experienced first, followed by cynicism/depersonalisation, which subsequently leads to a perception of lack of personal accomplishment. Having said that, Maslach *et al* (2001) later state that the sequential link to the perceived lack of accomplishment is less clear, but instead suggest a simultaneous development of this last dimension with depersonalisation. However, following two longitudinal tests on burnout dimensions, Toon *et al* (2005) reported that there was a sequential development, and that lack of personal accomplishment was the last to develop. This sequence seems logical as low personal accomplishment is only distorted after one feels emotionally exhausted and depersonalising behaviours as a coping strategy. If this state continues unabated then the individual is psychologically 'forced' to abandon future aspirations. Psychological abandonment of aspirations suggests inability to perceive possible options to accomplish them, therefore low personal accomplishment is experienced (Maslach *et al*, 2001; Toon *et al*, 2005).

Contrary to the sequential development that suggests each dimension develops fully first before the next one, Nyatanga's (2011) study found evidence of an overlap in the development of these dimensions as illustrated in **Figure 14.1: Development of dimensions of burnout**. The implication of the findings is important for managers, researchers and educationalists in the need to detect early signs of emotional exhaustion. This will enable early intervention before the complications of depersonalisation are evident. This may be most effective in banishing burnout while in its infancy.

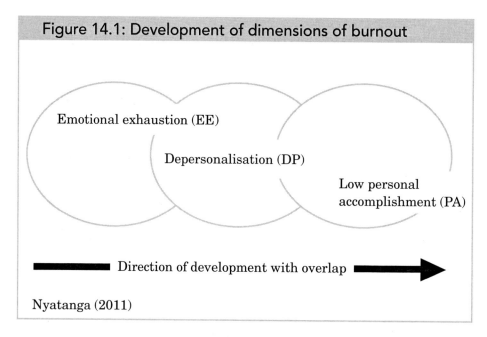

Figure 14.1: Development of dimensions of burnout

Emotional exhaustion (EE)

Depersonalisation (DP)

Low personal accomplishment (PA)

▬▬▬▬▬▬ Direction of development with overlap ▬▬▶

Nyatanga (2011)

In summary, and to show links with other aspects of life, it appears that out of the three dimensions, the emotional exhaustion component of burnout is more predictive of stress-related health problems, both physical and mental. However, the link between burnout and mental health is more complex and Maslach *et al* (2001) claim that burnout is linked to the personality dimension of neuroticism. Neuroticism is also thought to lead to job-related neurasthenia (a condition marked by chronic mental and physical fatigue and depression). The assumption is that burnout precipitates negative feelings (in terms of mental health) like anxiety, reduced perception of self-esteem and depression, and Nyatanga (2011) reported a positive correlation with death anxiety.

Sources of burnout in end of life care

Some of the main sources of burnout are based around expectations palliative nurses bring to work. Some that are idealistic (achieving total pain-free status for all patients) or unrealistic (curing all cancer patients) and both are seen as high-risk factors (Nyatanga, 2011) for the inducement of burnout where these are not achieved. Such expectations may lead nurses to work harder and even do too much additional work to try and achieve these goals. In the event that these expectations are not met, emotional exhaustion may result.

Sources of burnout are well documented (Zellars & Perrewe, 2000; Pines, 2002; Vachon & Benor, 2003) and below, the most common are discussed.

■ Work overload, which can be divided into quantitative and qualitative aspects, is characterised by nurses being over-stretched to provide the type of care they believe is best. It occurs when one is expected to do more than time permits or available resources (Pines, 2002).

■ Palliative caring, once a source of pride in providing plenty of caring time for dying patients (Saunders, 1978; Pines, 2002; Vachon & Benor, 2003), is increasingly restricted with less and less time to interact with patients and their families.

■ Qualitative role overload includes having to do work that is too difficult or without proper training. Palliative care nurses now have extra duties; being on call, visiting patients in their homes, record keeping, managing caseloads and professional leadership expectations (NICE, 2004). Although some of these duties have always existed, the main difference now is that they are being performed with reduced resources, time, inadequate emotional support and training (Nyatanga, 2011).

■ The second common aspect of qualitative role overload is to do with dynamics of healthcare teams, which may create conflict for most palliative care nurses (Vachon, 2000). Although the conflict is associated with teams, it appears the underlying factor is lack of understanding of each other's roles. It is also possible that conflict is due to the old notion of ethnocentric tendencies by in-groups (Foreman & Nyatanga, 1999; Nyatanga, 2002) where group identity is at stake. For example, doctors, nurses and other health care professionals continue to perceive themselves as individuals and not as part of a team.

■ Most nurses in palliative care now appreciate that when nurses care for dying patients, they tend to 'go the extra mile' to ensure that the patient's every need, and in some cases, every want and wish is satisfied, but at what cost?

Impact of burnout on healthcare professionals

There are a number of things that tend to happen when people suffer with burnout.

- **Absenteeism** is a well-known occurrence, where nurses are off work through illness. Absenteeism is a last resort for compassionate and caring professionals. As a result, there is increased shortage of staff which will affect the overall workload demands and quality of care. In some cases, extra costs are incurred by employing agency staff, which affects continuity of care and subsequently, the nurse–patient relationship. In end of life care, these outcomes may affect the dignity of their dying and the experience of those important to the patient.

- A more subtle problem is that of **'presenteeism'** (Nyatanga, 2011), a phenomenon which suggests that, although healthcare professionals may be physically present at work, they are no longer able to function effectively in their roles. Nurses may distance themselves from patients, and it is likely that significant errors and poor clinical judgments occur as a consequence.

- Burnout can be transmitted to others, hence **'contagion'**, (Bakker *et al*, 2005), and happens at emotional and psychological levels, both of which are related to the emotional exhaustion aspect of burnout.

- Emotional contagion occurs at a non-conscious level and is the automatic tendency to mimic and synchronise facial expressions, postures, vocalisations, feelings and movements with those of the burntout person.

- Psychological contagion is where people engage in a conscious cognitive process and 'turn into' and experience the emotions of others as if it were their own. They tend to engage in someone else's negatively-charged world of burnout. The point being that when burnout is experienced by one person it can transmit into other staff working with that individual.

In addition to health, burnout is also a social phenomenon. There is evidence (Hare *et al*, 1988; Maslach *et al*, 2001; Nyatanga, 2011) that burnout has a negative impact on professionals' private and social life due to increased mental and physical fatigue and possible depression. Although detailed exploration of this point is beyond the scope of this chapter, the important point is that it is possible that such impact on social life will eventually cross back over to the professional life, affecting performance and compromising the quality of care being given.

Professionals experiencing burnout have reduced cognitive functioning and an inability to recall experiences (Zellars & Perrewe, 2000), making efforts like reflective practice impossible to attain, since reflection is based on a recall of past experiences. Prolonged exhaustion often leads to individuals' inability to function and provide effective care, which in turn leads to feelings of incompetence or low personal accomplishment. Such feelings could signal the end of careers for nurses and other healthcare professionals, and that would be an unfortunate legacy for palliative caring.

Reducing burnout among palliative care nurses

There are several ways of reducing burnout among the nurses (Weber & Jaekel-Reinhard, 2000; Maslach, 2003; Fearon & Nicol, 2011). Discussion will start by considering strategies that can be used at a micro (personal) level and then move onto organisational input on supporting the workforce. The micro level approach is important as it not only emphasises the need for individual nurses to help themselves first, but recognises the stringent financial cuts currently prevailing, where employers might be forced to cut funding for supportive strategies. The micro level strategies encourage those individuals who may not always feel comfortable expressing difficult personal emotional situations in groups, to learn how to help themselves and overcome their issues.

For individuals, it is important to recognise that the same strategy may work for some and not for others. It is also true that some strategies may require peers to be involved as well so that success is achieved. Some of the individual strategies for minimising burnout are given in **Table 14.1: Micro level approach to preventing burnout,** with key attributes highlighted and which dimension of burnout they help address ie. emotional exhaustion (EE), depersonalisation (DP) and low personal accomplishment (PA).

Table 14.1: Micro level approach to preventing burnout		
Strategy	Key attributes	Dimension of burnout
Setting realistic personal goals	The strategy is to realise that the reality of caring may not always support the ideal, therefore, goals set must be realistic and achievable.	EE & DP
Positive 'selfishness'	We are more likely to 'give' more of ourselves when we feel well – therefore, we have to be 'selfish' in the actions, thinking and choices we make about caring. The 'selfishness' becomes positive because our patients benefit from us through well thought out care being delivered to meet their needs effectively by a caring, dedicated and compassionate professional.	EE & DP
Breaking the continuity	Involves taking 'emotional breathers' to enable time to 'cool off' emotionally from caring. Where possible, professionals can negotiate rotation to different care environments to break the continuity of caring for dying patients.	EE
Resisting the temptation to work harder	With overwhelming workloads, the tendency is to work even harder, accumulate overtime to be in control again. But the reality is you end up doing more of the same, with increasing exhaustion. The strategy is to work smarter, and review the workload, prioritising work and even delegating more. Working smarter also means knowing one's strengths and weaknesses and the best time of day to perform certain activities.	EE, DP

Strategy	Key attributes	Dimension of burnout
Table 14.1: Micro level approach to preventing burnout (continued)		
Investing in education and training – Individual and organisations	With austerity measures in place, it is even more important to ensure workforce education, training and ability to reflect is supported by all organisations. The strategy is also for organisations to encourage more in-house training, preceptorship for new staff, mentorship for all staff and develop closer links with universities to deliver some of the training in the workplace.	EE, DP, PA
Investing in social support	Offers protective intervention to buffer professionals against stressful events in three ways; emotional support which works by reducing distress and at the same time increasing self-esteem; **Informational support** which enhances perceptions of control of situations; **instrumental support** which provides practical assistance to help the other person to regain control over the situation. Also, **clinical supervision** – face to face support with experienced staff.	EE, DP, PA

Interested readers should refer to Nyatanga (2011) for more details on
these strategies, and how they can be implemented into palliative care
settings (also link with **Chapter 17: Spirituality and leadership in
palliative care**).

Conclusion

The understanding gained of how burnout develops is crucial in our
attempts to manage it more effectively. The sequential nature of its
development allows nurses and managers to 'deal' with it in its embryonic
stages of emotional exhaustion. It is clear that dealing with burnout early is
beneficial at many levels; healthcare professionals are still able to care for

patients, and the cost involved may be minimal. However, more importantly, before managers can begin to offer support, healthcare professionals need to start looking after themselves as a basis for self-care and ensure that they can banish burnout for a long time to come. Looking after ourselves may mean being positively 'selfish' and always trying to achieve a work/life balance. It is equally important that employers offer social support for the workforce.

It is important to achieve a balance between 'burning a light' and burning out while caring for patients at the end of their lives. This is a critical point for patients and therefore they deserve the best care possible delivered by the most competent healthy healthcare professionals available. Social support involves numerous strategies that help to relieve pressure and equip healthcare professionals with skills and knowledge to cope and must be a central feature of palliative and end of life care. If we do this well, not only do patients benefit, but those important to them too, as they experience the inevitable stage of life without their loved one.

References

Adali E & Priami M (2002) Burnout among nurses in intensive care units, internal medicine wards and emergency departments in Greek hospitals. *ICUs and Nursing web Journal* **11** 1–19.

Bakker AB, Killmer CH, Siegist J & Schaufeli WB (2000) Effort – reward imbalance and burnout among nurses. *Journal of Advanced Nursing* **31** (4) 884–891.

Bakker AB, Le Blanc PM & Schaufeli WB (2005) Burnout contagion among intensive care nurses. *Journal of Advanced Nursing* **51** (3) 276–287.

Benner P & Wrubel J (1989) *The Primacy of Caring, Stress and Coping in Health and Illness.* Menlo Park, CA: Addison-Wesley.

Cohen S (2007) Psychological stress and disease. *The Journal of American Medical Association* **298** 1658–1687.

Edwards SD (2001) *Philosophy of Nursing: An introduction.* Basingstoke: Palgrave.

Fearon C & Nicol M (2011) Strategies to assist prevention of burnout in nursing staff. *Nursing Standard* **26** (14) 35–39.

Foreman D & Nyatanga L (1999) The evolution of shared learning: some political and professional imperatives. *Medical Teacher* **21** (5) 489–496.

Freudenberger HJ (1974). Staff burn-out. *Journal of Social issues* **30** (1) 159–165.

Greene G (1961) *A Burnt-out Case.* New York: Viking Press.

Hare J, Pratt CC & Andrews D (1988)Predictors of burnout in professional and paraprofessional nurses working in hospitals and nursing homes. *International Journal of Nursing Studies* **25** (2) 105–115.

Maslach C (1976) Burn-out. *Human Behaviour* **5** (9) 16–22.

Maslach C (2003) *Burnout: The cost of caring.* Cambridge, MA: ISHK Publishing.

Maslach C & Leiter MP (1996) *Maslach Burnout Inventory.* California, Palo Alto: Consulting Psychological Press.

Maslach C & Jackson SE (1982) *Maslach Burnout Inventory.* California, Palo: Alto Consulting Psychological Press.

Maslach C, Schaufeli WB & Leiter MP (2001) Job Burnout. *Annual Reviews of Psychology* **52** 397–422.

NICE (2004) *Improving Supportive and Palliative Care for Adults with Cancer: The manual.* London: NHS National Institute for Clinical Excellence.

Nyatanga B (2002) The myth of inter-professional learning. *International Journal of Palliative Nursing* **8** (7) 316.

Nyatanga B (2011) *An Investigation into the Relationship Between Caring, Death Anxiety and Burnout Among Palliative Care Nurses.* Unpublished Doctoral thesis. University of Swansea.

Patrick K & Lavery JF (2007) Burnout in nursing. *Australian Journal of Advanced Nursing* **24** (3) 43–48.

Pines AM (2002) A psychoanalytic existential approach to burnout: Demonstrating in the case of a nurse, a teacher and a manager. *Psychotherapy: Theory / Research / Practice / Training* **39** 103–113.

Saunders CM (1978) *The Management of Terminal Disease.* London: Edward Arnold.

Shirom A (2003) Job-related burnout. In: JC Quick and LE Tetrick (Eds) *Handbook of Occupational Health Psychology* (245–265). Washington DC: American Psychological Association.

Smith P (1992) *Emotional Labour of Nursing.* London: Macmillan.

Toon WT, Le Blanc PM, Schaufeli WB & Schreurs PJG (2005) Are there causal relationships between the dimensions of the Maslach Burnout Inventory? A review of two longitudinal tests. *Work & Stress* **19** (3) 238–255.

Vachon ML (2000) Burnout and symptoms of stress in staff working in palliative care. In: H Chochinov and W Breitbart *Handbook of Psychiatry in Palliative Medicine.* Oxford: Oxford University Press.

Vachon MLS & Benor R (2003) Chapter 11: Staff stress, suffering and compassion in palliative care. In: M Lloyd-Williams (Ed) *Psychosocial Issues in Palliative Care* (165–182). Oxford: Oxford University Press.

Weber A & Jaekel-Reinhard A (2000) Burnout syndrome: a disease of modern societies. *Occupational Medicine* **50** (7) 512–517.

Zellars KL & Perrewe LP (2000) Burnout in health care: the role of five factors of personality. *Journal of Applied Social Psychology* **30** (8) 1570–1598.

Chapter 15:

The caring professions

This chapter brings together a collection of perspectives from those involved in end of life care.

The social worker

Bernard Moss

'End of life care should be an everyday part of practice, not just for palliative care social workers but for every social worker.'
(May-Chahal & Henry, 2012, p.4)

This clarion call from Professor Corinne May-Chahal, the interim chair of The College of Social Work, and Claire Henry, National Director for the National End of Life Care programme, in their introduction to the seminal report *The Route to Success in End of Life Care: Achieving quality for social work* (2012) sets the scene for this important topic. End of life issues, they insist, must not be left to the dedicated few who make this a specialism: they must feature in every social worker's job role. Every social worker needs to be prepared to deal with the challenging, and, at times, emotionally draining, encounters with people – including young people with life-limiting conditions – who are facing the end of their lives. And because social workers are really good at working with families and groups as well as with individuals, they have to be prepared to work with wider networks of people who are deeply affected by the (imminent) loss of someone precious to them.

That this is a personal as well as professional challenge to all social workers is beyond doubt. In some ways the professional challenge is easier to tackle, even if the subject matter and knowledge-base is demanding. *The Route to Success in End of Life Care: Achieving quality for social work* (2012) is an excellent place to start, and builds upon the national framework developed by the End of Life Care Programme in 2010. This framework suggests six main steps that are important for social workers involved in end of life care to bear in mind when planning services and structuring their involvement with the people involved. These steps are: i) discussions as the end of life approaches ii) assessment, care planning and review iii) co-ordination of care iv) delivery of high quality care in different settings v) care in the last days of life, and vi) care after death. These steps – or themes, because they all inter-link and are not neat and tidy self-contained processes – set the scene for any social worker involved in these issues. The report itself is very detailed, practical and sensitively written, and no attempt in this chapter will be made to duplicate material which will have far greater impact when readers look at it for themselves. The point being emphasised here, however, is that this report enables social workers to address these issues as part of their professional role, and guides them through the complexities of this important aspect of their caring role.

Much more difficult to tackle is the personal challenge which this area of work represents to individual social workers and to social work teams. The whole area of loss, which is a fundamental leitmotif for much of social work practice, is difficult to keep at arm's length. It can affect the heart as much as, if not more than, the head. We may intellectualise the impact of loss, and read the many authors whose wisdom and insights have so enriched our understanding of these issues in recent decades, but how do we handle our own emotional responses? We face a young person with a terminal illness, and our legs turn to jelly as we imagine what it must be like to be in that person's shoes, let alone their parents'. We watch the debilitating impact that the onset of Alzheimer's can have upon the individual and their families, and we worry how we would cope in similar circumstances. We hear people at the end of their lives asking the most profound and disturbing questions: *Why? Why me? Why them? Why does God allow this to happen? How can I possibly carry on afterwards? Why, why, why?* And we want to run away, and run fast, because these are questions that frighten us to death as well. So let's leave all of this to the specialist social workers who are good at delivering services like palliative care.

Put thus starkly we can immediately appreciate where the problem lies: it is *our* fear, *our* anxiety, *our* discomfort, *our* grappling with unanswerable questions that is getting in the way. This is not to minimise or dismiss these profound reactions. Rather it is to remind all of us as social workers that at any time, and with anyone on our caseload, we may be faced with these deeply distressing issues. Therefore we owe it to ourselves, and to those whom we seek to help and support in our professional role, to deal with our own personal 'agendas' in such a way that they do not get in the way of our professional responsibilities. And this takes us into the realm of self-care and spirituality.

Spirituality takes us (and also our service users,) into the territory of asking what meaning and purpose we find for our lives; who we are, and how we understand our place in the world. As a 'gateway' word it opens us up to mystery, love, sacrifice, awe and wonder, and invites us to consider whether life as we know it is all there is. For some people spirituality is understood within the religious context of belonging to a faith community, but it is equally powerful and relevant to those who hold to a secular worldview. The questions raised by this tantalising concept 'spirituality', therefore, apply to each and every one of us.

The implications of this for our social work practice are wide ranging. We need to ensure that from the moment a student enters a social work training course and then throughout their career, that they are being prepared to deal with these issues alongside all the practical knowledge and skills training that is also essential. As Margaret Holloway (2012) notes: *'I tell my students that, although they may think it is ageist to talk about the end of life when they are supposed to be enhancing older people's independence and autonomy, actually they are being ageist if they don't talk about it. Quality of life in the dying phase is a vital consideration.'*

Helping each other as fellow professionals to deal with these spiritual, some would say existential, questions is an important dimension to social work practice and supervision. It is also incumbent upon us as social workers to have a heightened self-awareness about our own beliefs, thoughts, doubts and anxieties in this area. This is for two reasons. First, if we have thought about some of these issues for ourselves we will be able to ensure that can be true to our social work values by being open-minded and non-judgmental when working with others. Second, we will avoid the risk of foisting onto others the worldviews we have chose as part of our own spirituality. Just because something works for us it doesn't mean it will work for someone else.

But there is a note of caution to sound here. Our obligation to have thought about these issues does not mean that we necessarily have come to conclusions. Far less will we be experts, people who have *got it all* sorted and can therefore bestow the benefits of our wisdom and insights upon others. The only thing we can remotely become expert in is how all of this affects *us*, and where we are on the confusing, at times disorientating, but sometimes glorious journey towards the end of life. Other people similarly will only be expert in where they have reached on this journey, and the extent to which they are able to articulate how this feels.

This insight about shared expertise – although it could equally be described as shared confusion – brings into sharp focus the role of the social worker. We can perhaps take for granted a thorough knowledge of relevant social work law and guidance; expertise with the benefits system and people's entitlements; good professional commitment to interdisciplinary collaboration and partnership working. All of these are important facets to a social worker's role when dealing with end of life issues or with people with dementia and similar life-limiting conditions. We can perhaps take for granted a communication skills-set that will enable at times distressed and emotionally charged situations to be handled sensitively and with compassion. We can perhaps take for granted a social worker's willingness and ability to work with families and any others caught up in the net of the dying person's life, to help them deal with the many complex and demanding issues that will arise. These after all are what all social workers are trained to do, and are often very good at.

But shared expertise/confusion highlights, perhaps as few other issues in social work practice do, the common shared humanity of social worker and service user. There are no pedestals of expertise on which a social worker can stand (or hide) to dispense wisdom and surefooted guidance. In this area we all stand on an equal playing field, where the most important landmarks are compassion and shared humanity.

This insight lies at the heart of a model for best practice suggested by Margaret Holloway (2010) called the 'fellow traveller'. This model or approach: *'allows the social worker to go with the service user on their spiritual journey for as far as they feel comfortable and competent to assist. The model is one of travelling alongside, rather than carrying a passenger, although it recognises that the person in need may stumble, lose direction or wish to give up at difficult points on the journey ... it is a reciprocal model in which [either] traveller ... might suggest a direction which strengthens the relationship or proves beneficial to either person ... [and] it allows for others to join the travelling party.'* (Holloway & Moss, 2010 p.112).

This 'fellow traveller' approach encapsulates core social work values. It does not for one moment minimise the importance of key knowledge, core skills and a commitment to partnership working. But it does highlight the common shared humanity of everyone involved in the situation, whatever role they may be expected to play. It also recognises that wisdom and resilience may often be found in greater abundance with those who are facing the crisis than those who, for all their professional expertise, may be cast in the role of (active) onlooker. And the experience may turn out to be far more humbling to the social worker as they share this journey than they had ever imagined.

This approach also recognises that spirituality is a common thread to all these encounters. Admittedly, many people – professionals and service users alike – may feel uncomfortable with the word, perhaps because to them it smacks of a worldview to which they do not subscribe. But if it is understood sensitively, and regarded as a 'gateway' word as has been suggested above, then the important range of issues which leap out at us are common to each and every one of us, even if we struggle to articulate them. The 'fellow traveller' approach, therefore, is about having the courage and confidence to raise some of these issues with people who are approaching the end of life, and being able to share and explore with them their responses, however articulate or inchoate they may be.

Maybe – just maybe – the conclusion to all of this is that the role of the social worker in end of life care is captured and expressed not so much by what we do, or what we know, as by who we are, and our willingness to share a common humanity with those whom we are privileged to encounter.

References

Holloway M (2012) Death, dying and the role of social work, interview with Mark Ivory. *Social Work Matters: The College of Social Work e-magazine* **July 2012** 14–17.

Holloway M & Moss B (2010) *Spirituality and Social Work*. Basingstoke: Palgrave Macmillan.

May-Chahal C & Henry C (2012) *The Route to Success in End of Life Care: Achieving quality for social work*. The National End of Life Care Programme: The College of Social Work/NHS.

The nurse

Jo Hockley

There are different levels of nursing experience when it comes to caring for people at the end of life. The majority of generalist nurses, working in settings like care homes where many residents die from comorbidities other than cancer, will have little formal training in palliative care. Nurses working within specialist palliative care – either as a nurse working within an inpatient hospice or advising as a clinical nurse specialist on a hospice home care team – will learn through role modelling and often then go on to do a formal qualification (for further information visit: www.csi.kcl. ac.uk). Finally, there are those working as clinical nurse specialists, who have a formal qualification, working within the generalist setting, such as hospitals, advising on specialist palliative care issues, so as to empower staff in their knowledge and development of palliative care skills alongside different specialties. Within specialist palliative care, each area has its own different challenges: for the nurse working in an inpatient unit it is often the number of deaths they face; for the homecare nurse specialist it is the isolated working; and, for the hospital-based nurse specialist it is the need to be answerable to experienced hospital consultants.

Mary Vachon (2006) has researched the different reasons for nurses taking a career path in specialist palliative care and the associated stress. I was a midwife before I went into palliative care. It was my brother who had done a month's internship at St Christopher's Hospice who suggested I enquire in 1978. It felt a strange career change going from delivering babies to caring for people who were dying. However, through the various positions I have held working within specialist palliative care, from a nurse on the inpatient unit at St Christopher's, to a clinical nurse specialist developing hospital-based palliative care teams, and then to a nurse consultant developing palliative care within care homes, my journey has been challenging and exciting (Dunlop & Hockley, 1998; Hockley & Clark, 2002; Hockley, 2012).

Being able to give spiritual comfort to people facing the end of their lives and their families has always been an important part of my nursing career following my appointment as ward sister at St Christopher's Hospice back in 1978. Having a Christian faith as a ward leader was an important asset for the job – prayers were said morning and evening on a daily basis and especially around the bed after someone had died. The spirituality of caring and compassion underpinned the work within the hospice with people's different religious traditions being celebrated whatever their background.

There are two occasions that I believe laid significant foundations regarding spirituality for me as a nurse. One in relation to the need for good role models as a way of teaching excellence in end of life care; the second, a specific challenge over spiritual anguish in a patient when I was working as a clinical nurse specialist at St Bartholomew's Hospital, London.

The first situation occurred shortly after commencing my job as a staff nurse at St Christopher's. I was in charge of the ward for the first time and had just finished the drug round when matron (Helen Willans – a church army sister) came into the office during her final rounds before going off duty. She told me she thought Mrs Smythe in Room 7 was dying and that her chest was quite wet and rattly. I felt mortified that I hadn't recognised the woman was dying despite having worked for a couple of years as an oncology nurse. Matron returned to the woman's room to sit with Mrs Smythe while I drew up medication to help dry the secretions in her chest. I was just leaving the room having given the injection when matron suggested I sit down at the other side of the bed. It was the first time that someone had role-modelled the importance of 'being with' the dying. There is a danger that one can become so 'tied up' with the tasks of care even within a hospice that the importance of presence-ing oneself with the vulnerable and dying gets lost with the 'doing' (Haraldsdottir, 2011). Mrs Smythe died about 20 minutes later, very peacefully. It was an important learning for me – and was one of the first occasions when I realised the privilege of being with someone who was dying. The skill of recognising imminent dying will become extinguished if we are not careful to keep this alive and take our responsibility in role modelling this important a skill to other more junior staff.

The second situation involved recognising spiritual anguish in a patient within the acute hospital setting and is written up more fully in an article on the concept of hope and the will to live (Hockley, 1993). As a nurse specialist setting up the palliative care team at St Bartholomew's Hospital, I was asked to see a patient who I will call Elizabeth. Her husband had left her following the birth of their son and she had left Scotland to seek work in the east end of London, where she and her son had lived for over 30 years. 10 years' previous to my meeting her, she had been treated for a cervical cancer and now a second primary had occurred in the site of the treated area. She wasn't imminently dying and had palliative surgery with the raising of a colostomy; however, she refused any further cancer treatment. She required 24-hour care. Elizabeth called herself an agnostic and refused point blank to be transferred to St Joseph's Hospice and remained with us in the hospital. She was a dour Scottish woman who didn't say a lot, but gradually over the weeks a trust formed between us. She was desperate to be able to die and asked me on several occasions for euthanasia. If another patient died on the ward she was upset and angry that it wasn't her. After several weeks she had become very thin and was being nursed on a special bed. If anyone should be allowed to die I thought to myself it should be Elizabeth. I met with the nurses on the ward to discuss her anguish and why she was 'hanging on to life' despite her desire for death. We talked through the emotional tie with her only son. The nurses agreed to try and explore this. At the same time I agreed to try to uncover any spiritual issues.

A number of weeks later I was going on holiday. There was an increasing sense that I should be trying to help address Elizabeth's spiritual anguish. I was just finishing our conversation when I asked her if she would like me to pray for her before I went away. To my amazement she said yes. It was visiting time in the open Nightingale ward where we were, so, not wanting to draw attention to us by pulling the curtains around the bed, I gently suggested Elizabeth close her eyes and I would pray. To this day I can remember the exact words: 'Father God, Elizabeth cannot understand how there can be a God of love because of all the things that have happened in her life; but I want you to show your love in Jesus on the cross…' At this point my hands began to shake uncontrollably. It felt as though I was standing on hallowed ground. I opened my eyes to see that Elizabeth had 'cheyne–stokes breathing' – deep irregular breathing that often occurs during the last stages when someone is imminently dying. I was so shocked. Not only was I praying with a patient, but the patient was now going to die without the curtains around the bed! I finished the prayer quickly and sat and watched. After what felt like 10 minutes, but was probably no more than two, Elizabeth's breathing became regular and she turned and opened her eyes to me and said, 'Thank you so much'. If I had had the presence of the moment I would have asked Elizabeth what had happened. However, I didn't. I felt scared. I quickly said my goodbyes adding that I would return in the morning, early before I left for my holiday. I told the staff what had happened. Next morning Elizabeth looked good – she smiled and we chatted. As I said goodbye and was leaving, she asked me to pray for her again like the day before! I did – it was just an ordinary prayer with nothing as powerful as the day before, and I left.

On my return from holiday I checked into the ward to see whether Elizabeth had died while I was away. She had. The day I had left for holiday she had asked one of the nurses to read from the Bible – the nurse told me that she turned to Psalm 23. She struggled with reading out verse 5 'Though I will walk through the shadow of death…' But how comforting for Elizabeth to hear the rest of the verse… 'but I will fear no evil.' Apparently, the following day Elizabeth asked another nurse to read again from the Bible – and that night she died peacefully in her sleep.

I had struggled with the idea of spiritual anguish in Elizabeth and whose responsibility it was to help bring relief. The transformation in Elizabeth as we all tried to do our best for her was a very powerful lesson for me. Euthanasia may seem an appropriate answer, but I believe that we potentially lose the spiritual care/growth if we submit to difficult situations with an answer for euthanasia.

References

Dunlop R & Hockley J (1998) *Hospital-based Palliative Care Teams: The hospital / hospice interface.* Oxford: Oxford University Press.

Haraldsdottir E (2011) The constraints of the ordinary: 'being with' in the context of end-of-life nursing care. *International Journal of Palliative Nursing* **17** (5): 245–250.

Hockley J (1993) The concept of hope and the will to live. *Palliative Medicine,* **7** (3) 181–186.

Hockley J (2012) A day in the life of a nurse consultant. *European Journal of Palliative Care* **19** (3) 141–142.

Hockley J & Clark D (2002) *Palliative Care for Older People in Care Homes.* Buckingham: Open University Press.

Vachon MLS (2006) Staff stress and burnout in palliative care. In: E Bruera, IJ Higginson, C Ripamonti and CF von Gunten (Eds) *Textbook of Palliative Medicine.* London: Hodder Arnold (1002–1010).

The chaplain

Andrew Goodhead

Spiritual care is a key component of end of life. The challenge for staff and volunteers is a willingness and ability to assess and support a patient's spiritual needs as they enter the final phase of life. Religious care is also an important aspect of end of life care and the responsibility to lead on this rests with chaplains. Daaleman & VandeCreek (2000) recognised that faith was a driver in the establishment of the hospice movement.

The NHS recognises that belief is important to patients and has incorporated a requirement for appropriate religious and spiritual care into policy and practice documents. The NICE document, *Holistic Support – Spiritual and religious* (2011), suggested spiritual and religious support should be offered to patients by referrals to chaplains or community faith leaders. The NHS Clinical Knowledge Summaries indicate that discussing spiritual and religious issues is an important aspect of end of life conversations. The NHS End of Life Care (EOLC) Strategy has led to the implementation of pathways enabling discussion of patient preferences. The Gold Standards Framework Register (GSF) created advance care plans (ACP), which ask about a patient's spirituality and belief and whether a referral to a religious leader should be made. Chaplains are part of multi-professional meetings in end of life care settings, and it is at these meetings and informally at other times that referrals should be made. An American study indicated that nurses were more likely to refer a patient to a chaplaincy service than any other professional (Weinberger-Litman *et al*, 2010) perhaps not unsurprisingly as nurses form the largest staff group within a health care setting.

Policy drivers in spiritual and religious care

Capacity, Care Planning and Advance Care Planning in Life Limiting Illness (undated). Available at: www. endoflifecareforadults.nhs.uk/assets/downloads/ACP_booklet_ June_2011__with_links.pdf

Holistic Support – Spiritual and religious (2011). Available at: http://www.nice.org.uk/guidance/qualitystandards/endoflifecare/ HolisticSupportSpiritualAndReligious.jsp

Palliative cancer care – general issues (management) (2012). Available at: http://www.cks.nhs.uk/palliative_cancer_care_general_ issues/management/detailed_answers/view_all_detailed_ answers

What is the Liverpool Care Pathway for the Dying Patient? Information for health care professionals (2010). Available at: http://www.liv.ac.uk/media/livacuk/mcpcil/migrated-files/liverpool- care-pathway/updatedlcppdfs/What_is_the_LCP_-_Healthcare_ Professionals_-_April_2010.pdf

Websites
Gold Standards Framework: www.goldstandardsframework.org.uk/

NHS Improving End of Life Care: www.endoflifecareforadults.nhs.uk/

The role of a chaplain is one which has many facets. A case study will assist in opening up issues and considering what a chaplain does. The chaplain attending a patient does not come to 'do' anything to the patient. It is a unique role and I find myself answering the question 'what have you come to do?' with the response, 'I haven't come to **do** anything; I have come to **be** with you.' This could be seen as a handicap. Isn't it easier to have a reason to call on a patient which can then open up the possibility of more than simply visiting a patient because you are the chaplain? The freedom which being with a patient brings liberates the chaplain to do just that.

The religious care which is offered by a chaplain is usually termed 'pastoral care'. This is different from 'spiritual care', which is broader and addresses how a person relates to the world, others, and themselves. Ainsworth-Smith and Speck (1990) suggest that pastoral care is *'an ability to be present with the dying, providing an opportunity for reconciliation, sustenance, guidance and growth'*. The chaplain's presence with the patient recognises the integrity of the patient's faith. If you like, an added present, but unseen personality in the relationship between patient and chaplain is the patient's deity(s). Peter Gilbert, in **Chapter 1: Rage against the dying of the light, or a new light shining?**, draws attention to the way in which belief supports an individual to cope, find religious meaning in suffering and dying, and through ritual and liturgy experience a connection with their God.

In the article *Hope Beyond (redundant) Hope* (2011), Nolan stated that the chaplain's ability to be with others encourages *'moments through which a chaplain may become a hopeful presence to those with whom they can work.'* This is embodied in ways of being with patients as evocative presence, accompanying presence, comforting presence and, hopeful presence.

Case study: Carole

Carole was a 65-year-old widow. She had two adult daughters who had inherited a neurological condition from their father. Carole was referred to the hospice following a diagnosis of motor neurone disease. She found her diagnosis and the reduction in her mobility and speech difficult to cope with. Carole became depressed and attempted to take her own life with an overdose. Her attempt was unsuccessful and after admission to an acute hospital she was transferred to the hospice as a 'halfway house' before returning home.

> ### Case study: Carole (continued)
>
> On admission, Carole agreed to a referral to the chaplain. She was in a four-bed female bay on one of the hospice wards. There was little information given in the referral form, other than that Carole was willing to see me. On my first visit Carole was sitting in a wheelchair next to her bed facing the wall. Carole agreed I could sit with her. I positioned a chair opposite her, blocking her view of the wall. Carole looked downwards during our conversation, her shoulders were slumped and her speech at times indistinct. Carole was very open about her overdose and her unhappiness at her loss of independence. She believed her present condition was her own fault, caused by her attempt to end her life. Carole also spoke about her changed relationship to her daughters.
>
> After several minutes our conversation slowed to silence and Carole had not looked up once. My impression of our interaction was Carole's sense of hopelessness. After allowing the silence to remain for a few moments longer, I asked her a single question; 'what makes you happy?' The silence persisted full of possibility for a few moments. Carole suddenly and obviously relaxed. Her shoulders fell into a more natural position, her hands loosened on the arms of her wheelchair and she looked up for the first time to look directly at me.
>
> With a smile on her face, she replied 'my grandchildren'. I invited her to tell me about them and with an animation that was previously absent, Carole described young twins about three years of age, who she said loved her because she was their grandmother.
>
> From that day, I visited Carole regularly and she was always more engaged and positive about herself and the possibilities that life held for her. She stopped discussing things negatively and worked with other healthcare professionals to improve her mobility and speech. Carole was discharged home a few weeks after admission.

My engagement with Carole echoes Nolan's description of the chaplain as hopeful presence. Carole's life had lost its quality. Being with Carole and allowing her to speak openly about herself without judging or commenting enabled the 'happiness question' to be responded to with an honesty that changed her own perspective of her life. Reading the case study I cannot help but feel Carole's sense of hopelessness. Everything which gave meaning and purpose to her life had been taken away to be replaced by deteriorating health. My question to her about happiness (see Koffman *et al*, 2012) was a moment of personal realisation that encountering her grandchildren was not only a source of happiness, but a source of quality in life.

Another feature of the chaplain's work is enabling patients to find or make meaning in the midst of their present situation. Making meaning is a vital aspect of spirituality and this requires collaboration between chaplain, patient and other healthcare professionals to explore how meaning is found and understood. Viktor Frankl, an Austrian Jewish psychiatrist, who was confined in German labour camps between 1938 and 1945, wrote a classic text that can help us understand spirituality as a concrete concept. Dame Cicely Saunders was influenced by Frankl's writing *Man's Search for Meaning* (Frankl, 2004) in her description of spiritual pain as a component of total pain.

Frankl stated that people create meaning in three ways; by creating something, by encountering someone or something, or by our attitude in any given set of circumstances. Thus a patient may, even when hope seems lost, be able to find things which make life worthwhile and give future hope, however short. Carole's ability to find joy through her grandchildren gave to her life meaning; using Frankl's descriptors by encountering her grandchildren.

When Carole realised the importance of her grandchildren, she was able to recognise that changing other aspects of her life would improve her relationship with her grandchildren. In his case study of a pastoral encounter with a cancer patient, King noted that the patient *'found meaning in life through work and relationships'* (King, 2012). Spiritual meaning is not found in abstract concepts, but, as Frankl suggested, in ways of doing which make a difference. The chaplain, along with others, has the task of being alongside the patient as he or she makes meaning in their life. The patient does the work of making meaning and others act as accompaniers: This is not our work, it is not our meaning and it is not for a chaplain or anyone else to impose on the patient what an experience does, or does not mean.

At the time of dying, patients who have a belief, or who wish to re-engage with a belief system ask to see a chaplain. In a multi-cultural society, it is important that the particular needs of the patient are met by seeking the assistance of a faith leader from the right grouping within that faith. Simply put, a Shia Muslim would ask for the support of a Shia Imam, and would feel let down if a Sunni Imam called. Similarly, a Vietnamese

Buddhist would want the support of a Vietnamese priest. For a chaplain, it is vital that good links with community faith groups are nurtured and maintained. A paid chaplain should act as a signpost for other healthcare professionals to obtain the services of the correct faith leader.

The Liverpool Care Pathway (LCP) is a tool implemented when a patient nears death and is a means of documenting nursing, medical, emotional and spiritual/religious needs on a regular four-hourly cycle. It requires staff to address issues around religious and spiritual need with all patients and their family members. As death approaches, the need for final rituals from a chaplain or faith leader becomes important for those who have a belief. The LCP enables conversation about what is right for each individual. For a dying Muslim, the bed should be moved to face Mecca and an Imam may be invited to come to say prayers with the patient. Community members will support the patient's family. A Buddhist patient might request minimum sedation so that dying can be experienced with awareness to aid the journey towards death and reincarnation. From the Jewish tradition the recitation by members of the community of the Kaddish around the body after death is the first point in the family and community mourning rituals.

Using the LCP in a palliative care setting enables healthcare staff to discuss with family members what spiritual or religious needs should be observed or fulfilled for the patient. A referral to the in-house chaplain or a faith leader from the community will enable the right pastoral response to be made, improving the holistic care of the dying person and their family. Pugh *et al* (2010), in a report of the use of chaplaincy following the introduction of the LCP in a UK hospital, noted that after the introduction of a reporting protocol to the chaplaincy service for patients placed on the LCP, the chaplains' visits had been well received by families and staff who appreciated the support that they had offered.

Finally, it is important to recognise that a chaplain is a collaborator with others to ensure good spiritual and religious care for patients and those important to them. At times, that collaboration extends to advising staff how to continue and develop their own spiritual support for an individual, at other times it will be in taking a lead in addressing spiritual or religious distress and reporting to a multi-professional team the issues discussed and the action taken. Chaplains and faith leaders are colleagues with healthcare professionals in the delivery of end of life care.

References

Ainsworth-Smith I & Speck P (1990) *Letting Go: Caring for the dying and bereaved.* London: SPCK.

Daaleman TP & VandeCreek L (2000) Placing religion and spirituality in end-of-life care. *Journal of the American Medical Association* **284** (19) 2514–2517.

Frankl V (2004) *Man's Search for Meaning.* London: Rider.

King DW (2012) Facing fears and counting blessings: a case study of a chaplain's faithful companioning of a cancer patient. *Journal of Healthcare Chaplaincy* **18** 3–22.

Koffman J, Morgan M, Edmonds P, Speck P, Siegert R & Higginson JI (2012) The meaning of happiness among two ethnic groups living with advanced cancer in South London: a qualitative study. *Psycho-Oncology* doi: 10.1002/pon.3108.

NICE (2011) Holistic Support – Spiritual and religious. Available at: http://www.nice.org.uk/guidance/qualitystandards/endoflifecare/HolisticSupportSpiritualAndReligious.jsp (accessed April 2013).

Nolan S (2011) Hope beyond (redundant) hope: how chaplains work with dying patients. *Palliative Medicine* **25** (1) 21–25. (See also Nolan S (2012) *Spiritual Care at the End of Life.* 'The Chaplain as a 'Hopeful Presence.' London: Jessica Kingsley.)

Pugh E, Smith S & Salter P (2010) Offering spiritual support to dying patients and their families through a chaplaincy service. *Nursing Times* **106** (28) 18–20.

Weinberger-Litman SL, Muncie MA, Flannelly LT & Flannelly KJ (2010) When do nurses refer patients to professional chaplains? *Holistic Nursing Practice* **24** (1) 44–48.

The doctor

Nicola Wilderspin

'Every man dies – Not every man really lives.'
William Ross Wallace, American poet (1819–1881)

My first experiences of transferring patients from hospital to hospice care were a humbling revelation. Some patients with advanced disease and distress would quickly seem 'better' – sometimes their pain lessened, sometimes they enjoyed their first small meal for days, sometimes those who were withdrawn and 'depressed' found their voice and smiled with their family again. This was humbling for a doctor because these physical improvements often occurred without direct medical intervention. I named this the 'hospice effect' and quickly learnt to resist the temptation to make significant changes in medication on the first day of admission, giving time to see what benefits the 'healing' environment itself would bring. Often it seemed that a patient's spirit was strengthened and restored by the change of setting and approach.

Teasing out the most helpful elements of a patient's 'spiritual care' in these complex situations is challenging. So many factors may play a role in this transformation, without intentionally addressing spirituality – a calmer, less clinical environment, the security of a responsive nursing team that will quickly mitigate distressing or potentially undignified symptoms, and the availability of a specialised multidisciplinary team, to name but a few.

Current definitions of the palliative approach (WHO, 2002), and the UK National End of Life Care Strategy (DH, 2008), place spiritual care as an equal partner alongside physical and psychosocial domains of holistic care in life-threatening illness. Therefore, if the multidisciplinary team truly values spirituality as a core domain, then all members have a practical duty to contribute to the provision of spiritual care, not just the 'specialist' chaplains and religious leaders. Doctors receive little training in this area, but frequently have opportunities to enhance their patients' spiritual well-being, as part of the care they provide to those at the end of life. Research has shown that dying cancer patients who believed that their spiritual care needs had been met by their medical team were more likely to opt for less aggressive medical care at the end of life and to experience better quality of life near death (Balboni *et al*, 2010). Many patients report a desire for their medical caregivers to be involved in their spiritual care, but few doctors see this as their role. The evidence base for the nature of spiritual well-being, and the effectiveness of spiritual care, is in its infancy. It can therefore be difficult to persuade clinicians, who are required to justify their practice with evidence, of the importance of their involvement in spiritual care.

Doctors can help to create an environment where spiritual growth is possible, recognising where specialised spiritual or religious help might be required. Careful, detailed assessment and treatment of distressing symptoms forms the foundation of the medical contribution to care at the end of life. An extra-ordinary doctor, Dame Cicely Saunders, founder of the modern hospice movement, pioneered a new paradigm of whole person (holistic) care in reaction to the unrelieved distress of dying patients (Hinton, 1963) and the doctors who appeared to desert them. She recognised that the dying needed so much more than improved physical comfort. She described a new syndrome of 'total pain', illustrated by a distressed patient for whom 'all of me is wrong' (Clarke, 1999). However, within her holistic framework she exhorted her team to address 'symptoms first'. How can a person concentrate on their spouse's need for closeness when unremitting pain keeps them awake, pacing the house during the night? How can someone find energy to explore their spiritual needs when every small movement or plate of food provokes a new wave of nausea and retching?

Good control of physical symptoms is best achieved through optimal control of the underlying illness and therefore all clinicians have a role in this regard – from the surgeon operating to relieve a cancerous bowel obstruction to the cardiologist using drugs to offload fluid and therefore relieve breathlessness. Effective treatment that controls physical symptoms can create the potential 'space' for spiritual growth and exploration to take place. Specialist doctors often have the privilege of providing the palliative care team's first assessment. This is a crucial time when patients and their families feel at their most vulnerable. They often feel abandoned by their doctors, having heard the one inexcusable message of medicine that 'nothing more can be done'. This sets the stage for hope to be restored, as so much can be done to improve life's quality and to enable them to 'live until they die'.

At their first palliative medicine consultation the agenda is given back to the patient, offering back some of the control lost during illness – what is it that they wish to discuss? As each domain of care is carefully explored, the doctor has opportunities to understand the emotional and spiritual concerns that may underlie or accompany the medical history. Patients may express guilt or shame that they had ignored their early symptoms and continued to smoke. They may share their anger and bitterness over a delayed diagnosis. Palliative medicine assessment includes an exploration of patients' sources of strength and support, and any links to formal religion or faith community. While doctors cannot be expected to answer patients' questions about meaning or purpose, they can be actively involved in encouraging them as they search for their own answers. A number of tools exist to provide generalists with a framework for assessing spiritual care needs, and these may help to provide a more purposeful and effective approach to this domain for 'non-specialist' spiritual care-givers (Kinzbrunner, 2010; McSherry & Eagger, 2011).

The palliative medicine assessment and on-going follow-up give repeated opportunities for the doctor to recognise and respond to spiritual distress. Seldom in my experience are questions of spiritual or religious significance asked directly of doctors, as patients do not see this as our interest or role. And yet, doctors may offer the acceptable face of spiritual support for people who would not usually consider turning to a chaplain or religious leader. Our main role however is to pick up on the unspoken needs. Doctors can begin to learn the 'spiritual language' their patients speak (Stanworth, 2004), where spiritual concerns are expressed through metaphor and symbolism (Southall, 2012). Simple exploration and acknowledgment may be all that is needed, but the offer of referral to a chaplain might be accepted from a trusted clinician.

Often the time the palliative care doctor offers (a first consultation is scheduled for an hour) begins a therapeutic relationship that may lead to articulation of the patient's or family's most important question. At the end of the consultation there is often a long pause as the courage is summoned to ask 'How long have I got, Doctor?'

This fundamental question needs the doctor's acknowledgement and further exploration. A genuine request for information requires that we do our best to respond with honesty. It is helpful to understand the legion of questions that may lie behind 'the question'. Is there a cherished wedding, holiday or anniversary to aim for, or practical plans to be made? From a spiritual perspective a clear answer to the question may catalyse the recognition and expression of spiritual needs. There may be amends to be made with estranged relatives, or a desire for formal religious absolution. Sometimes there is hope that time will in fact be short, when life seems unbearable and death a potential release. Sometimes the question is withdrawn: having tested the waters they realise that their spirit is not ready for truth.

Foreseeing and foretelling a patient's future, or prognostication, is a task of spiritual relevance which is often delegated to doctors, as they are trained in the pattern and behaviour of disease. Doctors may be approached to discuss patients' advance care plans with them for similar reasons, facilitating additional opportunities for patients to reflect on their values, hopes and fears (Watson, 2011). Traditionally, doctors' reputations were based on their ability to prognosticate accurately. However, despite intensive research in this area doctors are remarkably poor at predicting an accurate prognosis (Christakis, 2001) for their individual patients. Much relies on monitoring the progress of an individual's illness over time. In advanced disease, it is often the hands-on nurses and healthcare assistants who doctors turn to as the best judges of the closeness of death.

Doctors often find themselves leading clinical teams, and are therefore responsible to ensure that the team considers appropriate spiritual care. Recently our hospice inpatient unit multidisciplinary team (including doctors, nurses, physiotherapist, chaplain and social worker) struggled to understand the unspoken needs of a man rendered bedbound with advanced cancer. He seemed unusually 'closed' and particularly tense when family were present. Night staff reported his wakeful restlessness.

Different team members intuitively perceived his troubled spirit, but had unsuccessfully tried to help him to 'open up'. All the staff who had approached him, including the chaplaincy team, had been female. As multidisciplinary team lead I requested that an experienced male hospice volunteer try to befriend him. On the first visit, with family present, the volunteer merely offered a 'manly' glass of beer which the patient gladly accepted. On a second visit, without family present, a significant conversation took place. A profound source of guilt was identified and explored within the patient's own religious framework. A simple prayer followed, with a sense of much resolution. The patient died peacefully two days later.

When the volunteer fed back the impact of this remarkable conversation I was struck by how direct this interaction needed to be, given the man's frailty and fatigue. Often there is a sense that our patients have little energy for this spiritual and emotional 'work' by the time they approach their dying phase, as Adrian Plass so eloquently writes in Winter Waking (Plass, 2010):

'the saddest cry
Of men and women taught to stay a step ahead
Who reached the edge
But found that when they fell
They had not learned to fly'

Hospice teams witness significant signs of distress in those who are actively dying, but often the patient does not have the physical or emotional energy left to fully express or explore these. The syndrome of terminal agitation in the dying phase is common, often manifesting as physical restlessness and mental confusion. Biochemical changes of the dying process and side effects of medication are the usual explanation once physical sources of discomfort, such as pain or a full bladder, are addressed. Occasionally the disturbing syndrome of 'terminal anguish' suggests a deeper level of spiritual and emotional pain in the dying phase. Often doses of medication are required to relax the patient and enable them to rest and sleep comfortably through this part of their dying phase. But I wonder, as a prescriber of this medication, whether inducing a restful sleep removes last opportunities of any spiritual work that might bring peace at that late stage. When a patient's distressed, confused mind is beyond the reach of logic or reassurance, doctors have a duty to ensure that appropriate doses of calming medication can be given, consistent with palliative care's principle of 'neither hastening nor prolonging death'. However, I am often left with a sense of regret, and a hope that their spirit remains active even at that stage of their dying. This underlines the need to identify patients' spiritual needs at an earlier stage, before they reach 'the edge'.

Doctors struggle when they cannot produce a solution to heal or ease distress. One of the most challenging expressions of this comes when a patient requests euthanasia. A detailed exploration of requests for euthanasia is beyond the scope of this chapter. However, such desperate requests may bring new opportunities to explore and understand the nature and meaning of a person's suffering and their desire to take control. There may or may not be a spiritual dimension, but this needs to be explored. Dr Sheila Cassidy writes movingly as a palliative care specialist, of the need for doctors who treat the dying to acknowledge their own powerlessness (Cassidy, 1998). This is not a usual part of the medical paradigm. Cassidy's book – *Sharing the Darkness* (1998) – was pivotal in my journey into palliative medicine, when overwhelmed by the hopelessness and despair of dying AIDS patients on African medical wards. I felt so impotent that I was considering a premature return to the UK. This small paragraph, framed within the Christian tradition, spoke into my situation and motivated me to remain:

'Slowly as the years go by I learn about the importance of powerlessness. I experience it in my own life and I live with it in my work. The secret is not to be afraid of it – not to run away. The dying know we are not God… All they ask is that we do not desert them: that we stand our ground at the foot of the cross. At this stage of the journey, of being there, of simply being: it is, in many ways, the hardest part' (Cassidy, 1998 p.64).

It can be the hardest part, and wise doctors find appropriate ways to manage the emotional risks that accompany this approach. However, in my experience the willingness to continue in our humanity when professionally we have done all that can be offered, is one of the most powerful ways that a doctor can identify with the spiritual needs of those who are losing so much.

References

Balboni T, Paulk M, Balboni M, Phelps A, Loggers E, Wright A, Block S, Lewis E, Peteet J & Prigerson (2010) Provision of spiritual care to patients with advanced cancer: associations with medical care and quality of life near death. *Journal of Clinical Oncology* **28 (3)** 445–452.

Cassidy S (1988) *Sharing the Darkness: The spirituality of caring.* London: Darton, Longman & Todd.

Christakis N (2001) *Death Foretold: Prophecy and prognosis in medical care.* Chicago: University of Chicago Press.

Clarke D (1999) Total pain, disciplinary power and the body of work of Cicely Saunders 1958–67. *Social Science and Medicine* **49** (6) 727–736.

Department of Health (2008) *National End of Life Care Strategy.* London: DH.

Hinton J (1963) The physical and mental distress of the dying. *Quarterly Journal of Medicine* **32** 1–20.

Kinzbrunner B (2010) The physician's role in spiritual care. In: B Kinzbrunner & J Policzer (Eds) *End-of-life Care: A practical guide* (2nd edition) (pp379–393). United States: McGraw-Hill.

McSherry W & Eagger S (2011) Assessing a person's spiritual needs in a healthcare setting. In: P Gilbert (Ed) *Spirituality and Mental Health.* Brighton: Pavilion.

Plass A (2010) *Silences and Nonsenses. Collected poetry, doggerel and whimsy.* Milton Keynes: Authentic Media.

Southall D (2012) The patient's use of metaphor within a palliative care setting: Theory, function and efficacy: a narrative literature review. *Palliative Medicine* **27** (4) 304–313.

Stanworth R (2004) *Recognising Spiritual Needs in People Who are Dying.* Oxford: Oxford University Press.

Watson M (2011) Spiritual aspects of advance care planning. In: K Thomas & B Lobo (Eds) *Advance Care Planning in End of Life Care* (pp45–54). Oxford: Oxford University Press.

World Health Organization (2002) *National Cancer Control Programmes: policies and managerial guidelines* (2nd edition). Geneva: World Health Organization.

The physiotherapist in a children's hospice

Alison Bennett

The setting of children's hospices

For the last eight years I have had the privilege of working as a physiotherapist in a hospice for children and young people who present with life-limiting and life-threatening conditions. Having lived through the experience of losing my youngest daughter to cancer some years ago, I'd felt drawn to work with families and children who found themselves on a similar journey to the one that I had taken. What I most enjoy about working in this setting is the emphasis on relationship, as it is through meaningful relationship that spiritual care is most effectively given and received as an integral part of the whole.

Because children's hospice support may be offered to a child or young person from their time of diagnosis onwards, it allows staff the opportunity to get to know the children, young people and their families when their conditions are relatively stable. This is particularly true for those who come in for regular in-house respite stays with us, over the course of what might be several years. Later, when the goal moves on to supporting the child or young person through a 'good death', they will be cared for by staff with whom they have already developed relationships of some depth and trust. This allows them to feel safe and secure at such a significant and vulnerable time.

The spiritual needs of children

We recognise that all children are spiritual beings (Hay, 2003) and those facing life-limiting and life-threatening conditions have unique spiritual needs (Jones & Weisenfluh, 2003). To support these children spiritually we need to respond to their uniqueness with 'companionship at its heart' (Brother Francis OSB, 2006). It has been recognised that it is through relationships that they derive personal value and empowerment and are able to connect with themselves, with others, with nature and with God. (Hart & Schneider, 1997). Recognising and supporting their individuality is reflected in the ethos of the children's hospice movement, which has a child-centred approach at its core.

Keeping links with the familiar to avoid disconnection – a home from home care approach

Keeping their connection with what is familiar, especially in times of illness or crisis, helps a child or young person away from home avoid a sense of isolation, loss of identity and potential 'spiritual distress'. Individual hospice care plans are created which present a detailed picture of the home life of each child or young person who comes to stay with us. Their spiritual assessment will also include the names of their favourite people and those things that are important in bringing them a sense of comfort and strength as well as any faith community details. With such knowledge we can then include their favourite hobbies, television characters, films, celebrities, music or pets in our interaction with them, including their therapy.

Some of the children and young people we care for present with multiple disabilities and are unable to communicate with us verbally, often also experiencing additional sensory impairment. To have knowledge of their individual way of communication and how we can provide meaningful sensory input will also nurture their sense of inclusion, connection and value.

Investing time in building relationships

One of the great pleasures of working in the hospice is its room for flexibility, allowing time to get alongside the children and young people in a non-clinical way. Sometimes this may be spent sitting with a child in the art and craft room, joining an adolescent in a game on the Xbox or assisting a child or young person with profound disability in exploring the textures or sounds they enjoy. Some of my most meaningful conversations with children and young people have taken place at unexpected times such as sitting with them on a minibus on a trip out, getting ready for a pool session or taking part in imaginative play. At such times, they may feel more relaxed in expressing their thoughts and feelings. It is they who choose the time, place and person they wish to open up to and so we must purposefully create opportunities and be thoughtfully listening to what they may be wishing to communicate.

Enabling and empowering

Spiritual care is also about giving an individual the message that their life has meaning and worth. As physiotherapists, we would wish to empower and enable each child and young person to fulfil their potential as creatively as we can through therapy, even if in a situation of ill health or deterioration. We enjoy celebrating their achievements with them in whatever form that takes as they continue to show their desire to engage in life, allowing children options in what they want to achieve and how they would like to achieve it.

Having fun as a means of cultivating well-being

As having fun through play and creativity is a major part of any child or young person's sense of well-being, we like to develop ways to provide therapy in as enjoyable a way as we can, including the use of the hydrotherapy pool, through games, singing with younger children or competition with older ones. Imaginative play for the child or their siblings can also enable feelings and thoughts to be role played.

The human connection of touch

Spiritual care is about the human connection between people and that might include touch. In physiotherapy, much of the assessment and therapy involves touch. We try to give touch sensitively, respectfully and skilfully, with an explanation of what is to be done and why.

Control and choice in being moved and handled

Spiritual care also involves providing individuals with a sense of control and choice. As physiotherapists, our role often requires advising how the less mobile children and young people are moved and handled, including the introduction of specialised equipment. For those who are able to do so, decision making is done through discussion, allowing them to voice their wishes at a time when independency is being lost. For those unable to join in such a discussion, decisions are made so that moving and handling is done sensitively and respectfully with the goal of comfort and safety.

The therapeutic value of immersion in water

Set slightly away from the busyness of the main hospice, we are fortunate to have our own hydrotherapy pool on site. We can set it up as an environment to reflect the different moods of the individual; it can be a place for fun with loud music and noisy activity or as a place of quiet relaxation under the gentle glow of the sensory lights. It has been moving to witness a father gently cradle his young daughter very close to end of life as she floated in his arms in the water when too uncomfortable to be held in his arms elsewhere. Also to see a mother watch her son enjoy the pleasure of water play which she thought he'd never experience again now that he was fully ventilated. Many are the conversations I have shared with children around their views on the meaning of life or the struggles with their situations when we have been in the pool together!

As a tool of enablement, there are those young people who, while totally reliant on the use of wheelchairs on land, can still continue to move themselves independently around the pool; those with physical disabilities find that limited movement can be enhanced by the support of the water and relaxation gained for tight muscles. The sense of floating can be pleasurable to those who spend a lot of the time supported in wheelchairs or postural equipment or experience pain.

The pool can be a venue for quality times of fun sessions with water fights and games between friends and family, while siblings too may come into the pool for an experience of time out when they are surrounded by distraught adults.

The controlling of unpleasant symptoms

Finally, unpleasant symptoms can impact on the sense of well-being and comfort experienced by the children and young people. Addressing their symptoms will require unhurried assessment and sensitive questioning. Working as part of the multidisciplinary team, physiotherapy can provide an adjunct to the specialised medication that is often required. Alongside the use of drugs, pain-relief and comfort can often be achieved through alternate means such as the regular passive movement of a stiff limb, a careful changing of position or the introduction of specialised seating or equipment. Time in the warm water of the hydrotherapy pool can be another means of relaxation and analgesia, as well as an opportunity for gentle movement and a form of diversion. For those children or young people with respiratory problems, the use of chest physiotherapy techniques can help to keep their airways clear, alongside careful positioning to support their breathing.

Reassessing the way the child is moved and handled and advising family or staff on a different approach may also become necessary in times of deterioration. Knowing the child and their condition leading up to their change in symptoms helps in making such decisions.

Accompanying the children and their families

The children, young people and their families are on a journey through ill-health that they take without choice, and we are alongside them as their guests as Brother Francis OSB (2006) reminds us. Our therapy is not purely about 'doing to' but also about 'being with' (Royal College of Nursing, 2011). We keep our eyes open for 'wordless narration' (Coles, 1990) as well as pro-actively creating a safe space for the children and young people to share their feelings and fears. Whatever our interaction, we listen to their experience, affirm their humanity and protect their dignity, self-worth and identity (NICE, 2004). It is an honour, having made the journey myself, to accompany others on theirs.

References

Francis, Brother OSB (2006) The spiritual life. In: A Goldman, R Hain & S Liben (Ed) *Oxford Textbook Of Palliative Care for Children*. Oxford: Oxford University Press (74–83).

Coles R (1990) *The Spiritual Life of Children*. Boston MA: Houghton Mifflin.

Coyle J (2002) Spirituality and health: towards a framework for exploring the relationship between spirituality and health. *Journal of Advanced Nursing* **37** (6) 589–597.

Hart D & Schneider D (1997) Spiritual care for children with cancer. Seminars in Oncology Nursing **13** (4) 263–270.

Hay D (2003) How should we nurture children's spiritual life? *Spirited Scotland* (summer) 4. 222.

Jones B & Weisenfluh S (2003) Paediatric palliative and end-of-life care: spiritual and developmental issues for children. *Smith College Studies in Social Work: Special Edition on End of Life Care* **78** 423.

National Institute of Clinical Excellence Supportive and Palliative Care Guidance (2004) *Spiritual Support Services*. London: NICE.

Royal College of Nursing (2011) *Spirituality in Nursing Care: A pocket guide*. London: RCN.

The occupational therapist

Michaela Morris

Occupational therapists working in people's homes, hospitals, day care and hospices are part of a team to provide supportive end of life care and this chapter will explore the relationship between spiritual care and occupational therapy (OT) as well as descriptions of OT interventions working with people living with life-limiting illness to support them and those journeying with them.

As a search for meaning, spirituality can be more pertinent for people at the end of life where it can be a time of questioning and growth around personal identity. As people prepare for death they often reflect back on their life trying to understand the painful times as well as remember the good. This can lead to spiritual distress and therefore it is important to support people to maintain a sense of self during the dying process where fear can be a major factor. When a person acknowledges this fear and talks about their 'suffering' there can be indicators of spiritual distress and this may include loss of control over physical symptoms, fear of the unknown and changes in relationships as well as issues about their future and those left behind. Expressing spiritual matters can be blocked during illness and/or treatment and can also be affected by socio-cultural and environmental influences. The nearness of death can also raise the bigger existential questions about the meaning and nature of existence, and illness and disability can separate people from activity that has previously given them meaning and purpose.

Spirituality is fundamental to the philosophy and practice of OT because it is concerned with meeting an individual's needs on different levels including, but also beyond, the material and physical. OT intervention is concerned with maintaining and facilitating meaningful activity. Concerns about spirituality can deeply affect people's activities of daily living, for example appetite and motivation. This clearly brings it into the realm of OT where the inclusion of clients' goals in terms of their values as well as their physical and psychosocial needs is fundamental to holistic practice.

We all gain identity, meaning and structure from our everyday occupations, such as relationships, work, hobbies, home tasks, interests and values, and when, through illness or psychological distress, any of these are impaired, limited or compromised, we can experience occupational loss affecting us spiritually, mentally and physically. Most of us know how quickly we can become low or frustrated when suffering something as straightforward and temporary as a bad bout of flu, but escalate that to living with a life-limiting illness and the implications for our home, work, relationships and future are far more profound. OTs work in physical and mental health to support people to deal with and adapt to change and loss incurred through illness, with occupation being the key – even though it may need to be in a very different and adapted way.

During a time of illness or adjustment to change, people can become disconnected and disengaged from their creativity, roles and activities of daily living. Limited occupation can lead to increasing occupational and spiritual loss and reaching out to an individual's spiritual needs through activities can be effective. Meaningful activity or occupation is at the core of OT and can be a tool to enable people to reconnect with themselves and others in addition to fostering a sense of not being alone at a key time. In end of life care, individuals face many emotional and physical challenges, and spiritual care associated with well-being has been increasingly recognised and is expressed in meaningful occupation. To incorporate their desires, hopes and fears and to enable them to express their self-identity and essence, the spiritual dimension will require attention. Also, a change in activity level due to illness can result in activity loss and if the person is both used to and enjoys being active this is of value and could be termed a spiritual need that could be addressed by an OT working alongside them. In this process the individual's freedom of choice is important to preserve dignity and self-esteem through meaningful activity and a sense of control over their environment and choices.

The role of occupational therapy in palliative care

In the majority of clinical situations OT intervention is focused on prevention and treatment to restore and enhance performance and function, clearly this is very different in palliative care. In palliative care the loss of roles and deteriorating health means it doesn't often fit the traditional rehabilitation models and criteria. Working in palliative care, OTs are required to utilise a non-traditional frame of reference where independence and control are encouraged, but the person may have to relinquish these as their condition deteriorates and leads to death.

OTs have an important role in palliative care as part of a multidisciplinary team enabling people to live valued lives until they die and to empower and to engage them in meaningful activity, to affirm life and prepare for death. This can be achieved in a variety of ways including retaining a sense of control, involvement in care planning, and engaging in current and new activities.

Intervention may include facilitating independence, psychosocial concerns including spirituality and loss, fatigue, pain and stress management, the prevention of complications, equipment provision, life review work, and the continuation of meaningful activity. In these areas the OT is there to support, listen, and allow space for the individual to express spiritual pain and feelings as well as being informed about their future care, social and medical situation.

Areas of occupational therapy intervention

Reminiscence and life review work: Living with a life-limiting illness can mean increasing changes in roles and identity adjustment and there can be a pressure to come to terms with loss and a sense of incompleteness. Life review work can help people to evaluate the uniqueness of their lives and maybe to an acceptance of their dying and death. This work in groups or as individuals can facilitate communication, allow people to reflect and share their achievements and express their individuality. It can foster a sense of meaning and provide a sense of fulfilment and validity. It can also be enjoyable, provide a task focusing on them rather than their illness and enable them to create things that can be passed on to important people in their lives. It may include looking together at different times in our shared cultural life, for example, the 60s, the Coronation or the Olympics, or common personal themes such as first jobs, life events and childhood. Putting together memory boxes can be therapeutic both for the individual but also facilitate discussion with children and others close to them.

Carer support: Families and friends may have concerns and experience stress related to their role as a carer. Advice and support is an important aspect of OT work, particularly when a person wants to remain at home. OTs will be involved in training on moving and handling, provision and training on equipment such as hoists and wheelchairs, and also facilitating discussions where there is carer strain and tension within the family.

Comfort and pressure relief: Where people are less mobile and active it is important to reduce the risk of pressure sores, discomfort, unsafe transfers, pain and other complications. OTs provide advice and assessment for seating and positioning as well as the provision of pressure-relieving equipment for chairs, beds and wheelchairs.

Seasonal activity: Autumn, spring and Christmas are examples of times in the year that have associations and spiritual and other meanings – creative activity, shared reflection and discussion can enhance well-being and can be facilitated by an OT. Examples could be bulb planting, creating gifts, card making and creative writing.

Environmental control systems: Assistive technology to aid independence, communication and safety at home.

Meaningful activity: Advice on engaging, even if in a smaller and adapted way, in activities which are of personal importance. For example, table top gardening, cooking and time with family.

Activities of daily living: Advice, assessment and training to maximise independence and safety. Carer support and confidence will be a key part of this.

Group work: OTs run groups which combine education, peer support and skills – for example, carers' groups, fatigue management, breathlessness, creative living and relaxation.

Pain management: Psychological and physical aspects can benefit from non-pharmacological input such as positioning, sleep hygiene, pressure relief, breathing techniques, anxiety management, maintaining meaningful activities, pacing and psychological support as well as complementary therapies and carer support.

Home assessment for daily activities and equipment: Assessing where a person's preferred place of death is, such as wanting to be at home before they deteriorate. An OT will advise on equipment such as adaptations to a bath or shower, sleeping or for seating, and getting around the home. People often resist having equipment at home, but if seen as ways of maintaining independence and safety and essential for staying at home rather than 'hospitalising' their home, they are usually accepted and welcomed and are also a support for family and professional carers at home.

Anxiety management: Anxiety and depression understandably affect many people with a life-limiting illness and can be related to the nature of their illness; uncertainty about their prognosis; fears of pain and other symptoms; fear of helplessness and increasing physical and psychological dependence on others; adapting to changes in body image; confronting issues of dying; financial concerns; changes in roles and changing relationships; difficulties in communicating fears and feelings with partner; children and friends; isolation; loss of confidence and a sense of control in all areas of their life. OTs can support individuals to identify the triggers and thoughts behind their anxiety and look at coping strategies and carer support. Some OTs will be trained in basic cognitive behavioural therapy which enables people to see the links between their anxious thoughts and resulting behaviour, which can leave them feeling 'stuck' and unable to cope. Also, where a person is experiencing panic attacks, the OT can support them to learn techniques to reduce their impact and reoccurrence.

Fatigue management: Fatigue can be an overwhelming symptom of illness and as well as effecting levels of activity, it affects mood, thinking processes, motivation, communication and relationships. Support would include looking at ways of doing daily activities, conserving energy, delegation, pacing, assistive equipment, posture and positioning as well as prioritising and relaxation to focus on what is important and gives the individual meaning.

Breathlessness: Being short of breath naturally affects all daily tasks and activities and can heighten levels of anxiety and fears. OTs can advise on bending, lifting, sleeping, dressing, bathing, communication, sexual activity and mobility. Anxiety around breathing can lead to panic attacks, which can in turn affect our breathing, and therefore relaxation and cognitive behavioural techniques can be of value. In addition, the OT can explore the possible psychosocial issues of being breathless – the impact on relationships and social activity as well as fears around increasing difficulties.

Relaxation: OTs can guide individuals and groups in relaxation sessions and also give them the tools to use the techniques at home. Relaxation skills can benefit people by reducing muscle tension and related pain, can refresh and clear the mind, improve sleep and lessen fatigue. Relaxation encourages well-being, increases confidence and increases a sense of control by aiding a person's ability to cope.

Discharge planning: Home assessment, assessing care needs, discussions with family and other key people, and professionals to maintain safety and appropriate support.

Conclusion

As part of a holistic palliative care team, the OT can enable people to maintain their spiritual self in times of great loss and change, while supporting those around them. To achieve true holistic support, OTs need to engage in their own spiritual journey and have a willingness to address their own issues around death and dying in order to maintain the therapeutic relationship and the therapeutic use of self. By examining the meaning we find in pain and suffering, particularly when working with people who have a life-limiting illness, such a level of change and loss can be draining, and at times overwhelming, but it can be deeply rewarding knowing that dying is a natural part of living and that the OT's role is a privilege in accompanying people at this intimate time of their lives. As Dame Cicely Saunders said: *'We will do all we can, not only to help you die peacefully, but also to live until you die'* (1976).

References

Saunders C (1976) Care of dying – 1. The problem of euthanasia. *Nursing Times* **72** (26) 1003–1005.

Further reading

Armitage K & L Crowther (1999) The role of the OT in palliative care. *European Journal of Palliative Care* **6** (5) 154–157.

Barry E & Gibbens R (2011) Spirituality in practice: using personal reflection to prepare occupational therapy students. *British Journal of OT* **74** (4) 176–180.

Blair S (2000) The centrality of occupation during life transitions. *British Journal of OT* **63** (5) 231–237.

Bye RA (1998) When clients are dying: occupational therapists' perspectives. *OT Journal of Research* **18** (1) 3–24.

Christiansen D (1997) Acknowledging a spiritual dimension in OT practice. *American Journal of OT* **51** 169–172.

Cooper J (2006) *Occupational Therapy in Oncology and Palliative Care*. London: Whurr.

Egan M & Delaat M (1994) Considering spirituality in OT practice. *Canadian Journal of OT* **61** (2) 95–101.

Flanigan K (1982) The art of the possible: OT in terminal care. *British Journal of OT* **45** (8) 274–276.

Howard B & Howard J (1997) Occupation as spiritual activity. *American Journal of OT* **51** (3) 181–185.

Jones K & McIntye M (2002) A multidisciplinary approach to terminal care. *European Journal of Palliative Care* **9** (1) 21–24.

Lyons M, Orozovic N, Davis J & Newman J (2002) Doing-being-becoming: occupational experiences of persons with life-threatening illnesses. *American Journal of Occupational Therapy* **56** (3) 285–295.

Pearson D (2008) Don't die of boredom: enabling occupation at the end of life. *End of Life Care* **2** (2).

Rankin J, Robb K, Murtagh N, Cooper J & Lewis S (2008) *Rehabilitation in Cancer Care*. Chichester: Wiley Blackwell.

Rose A (1999) Spirituality and palliative care: the Attitudes of OTs. *British Journal of OT* **62** (7) 307–312.

Scott H (2007) The psychological distress of a man with end stage MND. *End of Life Care* **1** (2).

The clinical psychologist

Anna Janssen

In today's health system, time required to listen and understand often seems limited. We can become preoccupied with service-based expectations over cost, efficiency and results. Careful clinical judgment is required in balancing priorities. I doubt that service-based expectations around efficiency and improvement can be met without firstly investing time in simply listening to the patient and meeting them where they are emotionally, psychologically and spiritually.

I am a clinical psychologist in my final year of training, with a number of years' experience researching and caring for people living with chronic and terminal illnesses and cognitive change. A belief I continue to hold throughout my experience is that our patients are in many ways our teachers (Janssen & MacLeod, 2010). If we are to genuinely care for a patient, we must get to know them as individuals and understand what good care means to them. In this, learning to care is unending. Valuable insights into the patient's world can often be gained when engaging in creative activity with them (eg. art work, music), observing their behavioural patterns and reactions to environmental stimuli, and including the perspectives of loved ones, for instance.

In interviewing people dying of cancer and their spouses in a study exploring the meaning and experience of care at the end of life, I learned from one participant *'In the nine months of [patient] being sick, that was the very first time anyone said 'tell me about yourself'... You need to have a little chat with them to find out how they explain themselves, what their mode of understanding is ... so when you get to the serious stuff you can pitch the information right ... [then] you've got a sense of who you're dealing with, it actually speeds things up a hell of a lot.'* (13b; Janssen & MacLeod, 2010).

A clinical psychologist working in dementia and palliative care is privileged to work with people during a time of such change and vulnerability. Observing, listening to, validating and containing the individual and their loved ones during a time of loss, confusion, anxiety and reflection is vital. Notably, however, psychological care is not often actively sought or expected by the people who arguably need it most, the patients and their loved ones. To sensitively and effectively support those affected by both cognitive degeneration and terminal illness in making sense of their situation requires a genuine interest and respect for their experiences.

Anger is a principle emotion experienced among informal caregivers of people with dementia (Rudd *et al*, 1999). The limited acceptance of anger in much of society means that this can remain unexpressed and poorly managed. Over the last 10 years I have often heard family members express their confusion, anger, relief and sadness as they came to terms with their loss. It appears that with dementia, the loss of a loved one, *'the person I married'* can come before they die. It highlights the need to support the family, particularly in maintaining a meaningful relationship with their loved one as part of dementia care.

To truly understand and support a person with dementia who is dying, the expertise of the patient and family are crucial. We can draw upon models of family therapy in clinical psychology which regard the resources and strengths of the patient and family members as integral to managing the difficulties experienced. Family engagement in patient care is important; for the person to be well cared for, the carers require support. Research in cognitive change demonstrates the efficacy of including and training carers as co-therapists in cognitive behaviour therapy (CBT) for mood decline (eg. depression and anxiety) in the context of dementia. Carer-led CBT for depression in the context of dementia is shown to be effective in reducing anxiety and depression for both patients and carers (Teri *et al*, 1997; Teri *et al*, 2003).

Caring for another requires the therapist to understand themselves in relation to the patient. As we get to know a person with dementia and accompany them, we witness changes in their cognition, behaviour and personality. Such a process of loss can challenge us as clinicians. Another challenge in getting to know a patient is finding that their wishes and preferred ways of living are unfamiliar or conflict with our own values and experiences. Whatever the challenge, remaining aware of my personal biases, needs and vulnerabilities allows me to be fully present with the patient. Personal self-care and the professional development that comes with regular supervision and reflection are vital.

We must support those we care for in participating fully in the therapeutic relationship. As models of psychodynamic therapy uphold, a sense of safety and security is required for the patient to engage in the emotional and challenging process of identifying, understanding and expressing their current sources of distress and needs for care. This involves unconditional positive regard for the patient as they go in search of a greater understanding of who they are and the life they are living. This process can generate difficult emotions. We can help to facilitate healthy expression and management of thoughts and feelings thereby reducing their burden on the carer and patient.

Patients teach us to challenge assumptions about what it means to face death. When interviewing participants in a large study into motor neurone disease (MND) I met a woman whose condition was progressing rapidly. She shared with me her losses and anxieties as well as the protective spiritual resources she drew upon to nourish her in her final days. I also heard of the joyous discoveries made when facing death when interviewing people dying of cancer (Janssen & MacLeod, 2010). One participant explained *'[h]onestly the last four months even though I have been through pain ... they are the best four months of my life ... I didn't know that I had so many friends. It is unbelievable; I am loved by so many people'*. It seemed that powerful resources including hopes and relationships shone through some of the dark realities of pain and loss.

Clinical psychologists are not formally trained to provide spiritual care and we must acknowledge the limits of our expertise. However, recognising that relationships are a vital part of spirituality and spiritual care (Edwards *et al*, 2010) is a promising basis upon which to provide therapy. By focusing on the whole person, clinical psychologists can acknowledge and incorporate the patient's spiritual experience into therapy, just as we recognise physical pain or disability as relevant to a patient's psychological well-being. In my experience, spirituality can arise organically as part of developing an understanding of the person as an individual and their wider context. I enquire about a patient's journey to the present, areas of distress and how these relate to their narrative or identity, values and sources of strength and resilience. As part of this understanding we can invite and respect the exploration of the spiritual self, spiritual distress and spiritual needs. Some people can readily access and communicate about their spiritual practices and needs. For others, this can take time and require careful attention to the building of trust in the therapist before they are ready to acknowledge and share these aspects of themselves.

How a clinical psychologist assesses, makes sense of and provides for a patient's spiritual needs can reflect the therapist's world view, beliefs and experiences as well as the patient's. Spiritual well-being is a protective factor against psychological distress among people who are dying (Rodin *et al*, 2009). Spiritual distress is associated with depression, advancing age and pain. In an effort to alleviate such distress, a clinical psychologist can draw upon their expertise in therapy for depression and understanding and attending to pain-related factors, which often have a psychological component.

Taking care with spirituality

'Spirituality means different things to different people. It may include (a search for): one's ultimate beliefs and values; a sense of meaning and purpose in life; a sense of connectedness; identity and awareness; and for some people, religion' (Egan *et al*, 2011, p.321). How we approach spirituality as health professionals depends on the model within which we work and the assumptions therein (Rumbold, 2007). For example, Phelps *et al* (2012) identified more negative perceptions of spirituality among

physicians than patients and nurses. This may reflect differences in the roles played by nursing and medical staff, their goals in patient care and the place for spirituality in their profession. Spirituality may also be part of what the patient refers to as 'quality of life' or 'hope', religion, formal ritual, or personal relationships (Hui *et al*, 2011; Rumbold, 2007; Running *et al*, 2008). Whether or not we hear or use the term 'spirituality' we can enjoy capturing the essence of it as we work with people and focus on empowering them to identify and draw upon their own resources.

Working with dementia and end of life care as a clinical psychologist: a personal experience

The role of a clinical psychologist working in dementia and palliative care can be described in a variety of ways depending on the context. Variables include the service providing the care (community-based, inpatient, nursing home), the stage of the person's dementia and the purpose of the referral (eg. initial assessment, capacity assessment, follow-up assessment). In brief, a clinical psychologist is part of a team working in collaboration to understand the person, their needs, minimise risk and optimise quality of life.

Clinical psychologists working in dementia and palliative care can contribute meaningfully to patient care through teaching. Preserving hope and respecting the identity and wishes of the patient can be challenging when dementia is poorly understood. Helping team members to understand dementia, its implications and ways in which they can effectively contribute to patient care is a key task. I enjoy combining my experience as clinical psychologist and academic to provide care indirectly and more broadly through teaching and research.

Sharing knowledge within the multidisciplinary team is important. Drawing together expertise from specialists in both dementia care and palliative care can optimise end of life care for people with dementia (Barber & Murphy, 2011).

Research to inform care

My research includes improving our understanding of the cognitive MND and Parkinson's disease that are often regarded as primarily physical.

My experience with patients and families demonstrates that the distress, grief and inadequate care received by patients and families facing these conditions is borne out of a lack of understanding of the non-motor, cognitive and mood changes that can be expected in such an illness. As a researcher and clinical psychologist in training I believe we must help health professionals, patients and carers make sense of and normalise these changes, and provide support in these areas as well as symptom management for physical changes.

My concern for the patient's right to live meaningfully until they die has drawn me to carefully consider their experience of care, what care means to them and what this means for clinical education. As in my clinical practice, my research recognises health professionals as individuals with their own vulnerabilities and care needs. In collaboration with experts in palliative care and bioethics, I have looked closely at how patient care can be optimised by encouraging greater contact between clinicians and patients from an early stage of clinical training and a culture of self-care among health professionals. Moreover, opportunities for continuing professional and personal development through reflection and role modelling by senior colleagues are vital in establishing a culture of care among new generations of professionals, yet are not always available or valued in more traditional modes of clinical education (Janssen *et al*, 2008). I hope the value placed upon reflective practice in clinical psychology may be recognised and mirrored more widely across professions in future.

References

Barber J & Murphy K (2011) Challenges that specialist palliative care nurses encounter when caring for patients with advanced dementia. *International Journal of Palliative Nursing* **17** (12) 587–591.

Edwards, A, Pang N, Shiu V & Chan C (2010) Review: The understanding of spirituality and the potential role of spiritual care in end-of-life and palliative care: a meta-study of qualitative research. *Palliative Medicine* **24** (8) 753–770.

Egan RMM (2010) Spirituality in New Zealand hospice care (Thesis, Doctor of Philosophy). University of Otago. Available at: http://hdl.handle.net/10523/442 (accessed April 2013).

Egan R, MacLeod RD, Jaye C, McGee R, Baxter J & Herbison P (2011) What is spirituality? Evidence from a New Zealand hospice study. *Mortality* **16** (4) 307–324.

Hui D, de la Cruz, M, Thorney S, Parsons HA, Delgado-Guay, M & Bruera E (2011) The frequency and correlates of spiritual distress among patients with advanced cancer admitted to an acute palliative care unit. *American Journal of Hospice and Palliative Medicine* **28** (4) 264–270.

Janssen AL & MacLeod RD (2010) What does care mean? Perceptions of people approaching the end of life. *Palliative and Supportive Care* **8** 433–440.

Janssen AL, MacLeod RD & Walker ST (2008) Recognition, reflection and role models: critical elements in education about care in medicine. *Palliative and Supportive Care* **6** 389–395.

Phelps AC, Lauderdale KE, Alcorn S, Dillinger J, Balboni MT, Van Wert M & Balboni TA (2012) Addressing spirituality within the care of patients at the end of life: perspectives of patients with advanced cancer, oncologists, and oncology nurses. *Journal of Clinical Oncology* **30** (20) 2538–2544.

Rodin G, Lo C, Mikulincer M, Donner A, Gagliese L & Zimmermann C (2009) Pathways to distress: the multiple determinants of depression, hopelessness, and the desire for hastened death in metastatic cancer patients. *Social Science & Medicine* **68** (3) 562–569.

Rudd MG, Viney LL & Preston CA (1999) The grief experienced by spousal caregivers of dementia patients: The role of place of care of patient and gender of caregiver. *The International Journal of Aging and Human Development* **48** (3) 217–240.

Rumbold BD (2007) A review of spiritual assessment in health care practice. *Medical Journal of Australia* **186** (10) 60.

Running A, Girard D & Tolle LW (2008) When there is nothing left to do, there is everything left to do. *American Journal of Hospice and Palliative Medicine* **24** (6) 451–454.

Teri L, Logsdon RG, Uomoto J & McCurry SM (1997) Behavioral treatment of depression in dementia patients: a controlled clinical trial. *The Journals of Gerontology Series B: Psychological Sciences and Social Sciences* **52** (4) pp159.

Teri L, Gibbons LE, McCurry SM, Logsdon RG, Buchner DM, Barlow WE & Larson EB (2003) Exercise plus behavioural management in patients with Alzheimer disease. *JAMA: The journal of the American Medical Association* **290** (15) 2015–2022.

Part 6:

Looking ahead

Chapter 16:

Invisible possibilities: art therapy, healing and spirituality at the end of life

Irene Renzenbrink

'Art is my way of knowing who I am … soul is the place where the messiness of life is tolerated, where feelings animate the narration of life, where story exists.' (Allen, 1995, p.ix)

When the Russian author Fyodor Dostoevsky was sentenced to death in 1849 he wrote to his brother saying: *'Well, goodbye brother! Do not grieve for me … Never until now have such rich and healthy stores of spiritual life throbbed in me.'* (Dostoevsky in Pevear, 2002)

Dostoevsky was reprieved at the last moment, but he had truly believed that he was about to die. His spiritual life was flourishing as he prepared for death. In my work as a social worker and art therapist in end of life care I have met many hundreds of people whose spiritual lives seem to 'throb and grow' in the last days, weeks and months of life. Although dying people often become weaker and more frail physically, they seem to find a new way of living or perhaps *'another way of knowing'* (Allen, 1995) that brings renewed strength and courage. Despite the limitations of the body, there appear to be many opportunities for spiritual growth and the healing of suffering.

In this chapter I will provide examples of art therapy with patients and their families in end of life care to show how art-making in the context of a therapeutic relationship can 'make visible' some of a person's deepest thoughts, feelings and aspirations. I will also discuss the importance of self-awareness, spiritual depth and sensitivity to symbolic language in the therapist, as Levine suggests when he says: *'Good therapists are open to metaphor and symbol; they listen with a third ear that hears what is not said; they see the potential for development in the person and are animated (ensouled) by these invisible possibilities.'* (Levine, 1997, p.4)

Indeed, the chapter takes its title from Levine's notion of 'invisible possibilities'; those creative opportunities that bring healing, comfort, and even joy to patients whose sense of self and self-worth may have been diminished by the debilitating effects of treatment, difficult experiences within the health care system, and the confrontation with their mortality.

The restoration of creative capacity

'You matter because you are you, and you matter until the last moment of your life.' Dame Cicely Saunders (in Clark, 2002)

When medical and nursing staff focus on the physical body and the problems associated with an illness, there is a danger that patients will begin to see themselves as decaying bodies. A woman who was dying of breast cancer told me that she was 'rotting inside'. Other patients have described themselves as 'useless', 'finished' and 'nothing but skin and bone'. Dame Cicely Saunders, founder of the modern hospice and palliative care movement, developed her concept of 'total pain' after one of her patients told her that, *'all of me is wrong'* (Clark, 2002). Given her training as a social worker, nurse and doctor, and with her strong Christian faith, Saunders fully understood that dying people need physical, psychological, social and spiritual care.

When Christopher Hitchens was diagnosed with cancer he described his experience of entering 'Tumortown', taking him from Wellville, *'the country of the well across the stark frontier that marks off the land of malady'* (Hitchens, 2012, p.2). He writes eloquently and graphically about his illness, the brutality of cancer treatment and how he faces his mortality. He described writing as *'not just my living and livelihood but my very life'* (Hitchens, 2012, p.71). Although cure was no longer possible, Hitchen's writing ability and creativity were central to his endurance of suffering and has become a legacy since his death.

One of the goals of art therapy, and other expressive arts therapies such as journalling, poetry and music therapy, in end of life care is to help patients engage or re-discover their creative capacity. Reduced anxiety and depression and an increased sense of hope and self-esteem have been reported as outcomes for oncology and palliative care patients following experiences of art therapy. Music therapy has been well established in palliative care for many years, given its proven benefits for patients in enhancing their quality of life. Sometimes the patient is helped by the therapist to create a song or to compile a collection of music they have enjoyed throughout their life. Music may evoke tears of sadness as well as joy.

For patients engaging in art therapy, art-making is often a new experience and they are truly surprised by the images that emerge. For others, it brings back memories of childhood art activities at home and school. There may be some anxiety about the need to produce something that is beautiful or worthwhile, so I emphasise the importance of simply 'giving it a try', playing with the materials and not feeling pressured. In art therapy, the process is more important than the product and healing is seen as a restoration of a person's imaginative capacity rather than as a cure. Sometimes the patient's artwork also serves as a legacy for the family left behind. I have worked with patients who have created pictures and drawings that trigger memories of home and family life, of pets and favourite holiday places and gardens. A woman who was dying made a simple drawing of raspberries and spoke about the raspberry jam she made every year and gave away to friends and neighbours. It reminded her of the time that she managed a large farm alone after her husband died.

The following example shows how a family member used art-making to make sense of her experience as a caregiver. It is also an example of what is known in the expressive arts field as a 'low skill and high sensitivity' approach (Knill *et al*, 2003, p.150). This means that the emphasis is on the experience and exploration of thoughts and feelings rather than on mastery of methods, techniques and the quality of the art making.

Case example: Alandina's tea cup

While working in a palliative care unit I met Alandina, a woman in her 60s whose mother, aged 96, was dying of cancer. The nurses were concerned about the fact that Alandina hardly ever left her mother's bedside. Since her mother was unable to speak English, Alandina felt it necessary to be with her at all times unless another family member came to relieve her. When she expressed interest in an art therapy session I brought paper, brushes, acrylic paints and soft pastels into her mother's hospital room. We sat across from each other at a small tray table and were aware of the dying woman's gentle breathing as she slept. It felt like a sacred and privileged place, the sort of place that allows those invisible possibilities to emerge.

I asked Alandina about her experience of being at the hospital every day and what it was like spending every waking moment with her mother. She thought carefully before responding with the words: 'I feel broken … I feel like I'm losing myself.'

I then asked her to think about an image that might convey this feeling of brokenness and being lost, and invited her to use the art materials. Almost immediately she began to paint a cup and saucer.

Reproduced with permission from Alandina La Plante

Alandina went on to paint a line across the cup and said, 'It's broken. There's a crack in the cup'. When I asked her whether there was anything in the cup, she answered, 'raspberry tea'. Some pink wavy lines represented the tea and we spoke about the pleasures of tea drinking. I pointed out that the cup was still functioning as a container for the tea despite being cracked and broken. I also admired the colours she had used and the way she had decorated the cup with a flower. There was a small bottle of glue in the art materials basket and I invited Alandina to use it if it 'felt right'. She decided to add a line of glue to the crack on the cup she had painted. It seemed to me that she was also symbolically mending her sense of self. Alandina proudly showed her tea cup picture to the nurses who entered the room and later placed it on the window ledge so everyone could see it. She was eager to do more art-making with me and was grateful for the opportunity. She told me that she had not really known what to expect and was pleasantly surprised by the work we did together.

Alandina was able to care for her mother at home in the end and this decision made it possible for other family members to become more involved and supportive.

While working with Alandina in the presence of her dying mother I was acutely aware of my own mother's frailty and decline and my sadness about not being with her because we were living on two different continents. While acknowledging the strain and sacrifices involved for Alandina, I found myself feeling envious of her opportunity to spend so much time with her mother. I had just returned from a visit to Australia to support my mother following a major heart attack. While waiting for pacemaker surgery she told me that she felt 'like a tree whose leaves were falling off one by one'. Her words inspired me to paint a watercolour which I called the 'Tree of Hearts'. As the leaves were falling off the tree in my painting they seemed to be turning into hearts.

Tree of Hearts by Irene Renzenbrink

I shared the image with my mother and we had a long conversation about her philosophy of life and death and made some plans for her funeral, although hoping that she would have a much improved quality of life for some time to come. The 'Tree of Hearts' seemed to capture the idea expressed by leading bereavement researcher and psychiatrist, Colin Murray Parkes, that love and loss are two sides of the same coin and that *'the pain of grief is just as much part of life as the joy of love; it is perhaps the price we pay for love, the cost of commitment'* (Parkes, 1996, p.6).

My mother died unexpectedly six months after the pacemaker surgery and the image of the 'Tree of Hearts' was included in the order of service at her funeral. The image continues to comfort me and the tree has taken on an angelic quality.

Welcoming the image

'Images take me apart; images put me back together again, new, enlarged, with breathing room.' (Allen, 1995)

In his book *Art Heals* (2004a), Shaun McNiff explains that healing occurs when we are open to the expression of an image and do our best *'to be present with it, understand it, and accept it, rather than attempting to fix it, resolve or eradicate it'* (McNiff, 2004, p.98). Rather than 'interrogating' images and trying to decipher what they mean he suggests welcoming them and simply reflecting on their expressive qualities, saying something about what we see and how we feel in their presence. One of the founders of the expressive arts therapy movement, Paolo Knill (2003) refers to the pitfalls of 'problem saturation', the tendency to focus on the *'problem-bound narrow logic of thinking and acting'*, which often means more of the same.

He and his colleagues have pioneered an alternative way of helping people in pain and turmoil to move away from the presenting problem into an imaginative realm from which new possibilities can emerge in surprising ways. This process of moving away is referred to in the field of expressive arts therapy as *'decentering'* or an *'expansion of the range of play'* (Knill *et al*, 2003). Whether it is through visual art, creative writing, dance, movement, performance or music, or a combination of these modalities, it is often through creative activities that people in crisis find respite from their difficulties as well as inspiration and meaning. Words alone cannot always convey the richness and complexity of the inner world. For dying people who may lack the physical strength and ability to engage in strenuous activity there are many gentle alternatives.

The therapeutic alliance

'The soul finds its form in art.' (Levine, 1997)

Leading psychotherapist Carl Rogers (1961) believed that successful helping encounters required the therapist to demonstrate genuineness and a warm, unconditional positive regard towards anyone who is vulnerable, but especially when someone is facing their own death. In the context of art therapy, Moon (2007) emphasises the need for *'reciprocal self-disclosure, the sharing of vulnerabilities, the shared journey and the therapist and client coming to know each other in the mutual art making process'* (Moon, 2007, p.viii). It is a therapeutic and creative alliance that requires self-knowledge, compassion and an imaginative capacity in the therapist.

Helping professionals often deny their need for comfort and support when they themselves are grief stricken. Henri Nouwen's concept of the' wounded healer' provides us with a valuable model for acknowledging our own needs as caregivers (Nouwen, 1972). He urges us to use our woundedness constructively and in the service of others. Knill (2003, p.124) believes that *'a therapeutic presence is characterised first of all by a clarity and awareness of one's own psychic state'*. In recent years I have conducted many art therapy sessions with hospice staff and volunteers. These creative opportunities for reflection about both the stressors and rewards of their caring roles often result in greater self-awareness and a renewed commitment to the work. Kearney *et al* (2009, p.158) found that *'experienced palliative care providers describe feelings of satisfaction and gratitude and enhanced appreciation of spiritual and existential domains of life as a result of their work with dying persons'*.

One of the themes that I have presented to patients, staff and volunteers in end of life care is the idea that Leonard Cohen presents in his song Anthem, with the following words:

'Forget your perfect offering
There is a crack in everything
That's how the light gets in.'

As Cohen himself explains (Simmons, 2012, p.169): *'The light is the capacity to reconcile your experience, your sorrow, with every day that dawns. It is that understanding, which is beyond significance or meaning that allows you to live a life and embrace the disasters and sorrows and joys that are our common lot. But it's only with the recognition that there is a crack in everything. I think all other visions are doomed to irretrievable gloom.'*

Awareness of our imperfections as human beings in whatever role we play in life is an important part of self-acceptance and self-compassion. The growth that comes from challenging life experiences is not always immediately apparent and requires time, patience and the support of others. As a social worker, bereavement counsellor and art therapist I have found that sharing some of my own struggles and their ensuing lessons is a more authentic style that encourages clients to feel safe in exposing their vulnerability. Expecting clients to share their innermost secrets while the therapist remains mute has always seemed rather hypocritical to me. Experiences of dying people at the end of life and of those who mourn after a death are not pathological conditions, but rather times of existential crisis that will come to us all. Support is everything. As Hitchens writes: *'My chief consolation in this year of living dyingly has been the presence of friends'* (2012, p.54).

Living dyingly

Hitchens' notion of 'living dyingly' is one that reminds us to live fully in the knowledge that we are mortal and that nothing is permanent nor constant. While this awareness is not always comfortable, it does point us to what really matters in relationships and in the way we live our life. Our priorities change in accordance with the time we have left to live. Perhaps we start to take more risks, live more dangerously, say the things that need to be said to the people we care about and finish our 'unfinished business' as best we can. The Canadian author Gabrielle Roy (1962) once wrote: *'Could we ever know each other in the slightest without the arts?'*

Art therapy in end of life care acknowledges the healing power of the arts and the creative potential that is present in all people at every stage of life. The arts help us to connect deeply with one another, to know ourselves and to reveal those mysterious invisible possibilities that characterise a rich spiritual life.

References

Allen P (1995) *Art is a Way of Knowing*. Boston: Shambhala Publications.

Clark D (2002) *Cicely Saunders: Founder of the hospice movement – selected letters.* London: Oxford University Press.

Dostoevsky F/Pevear R (1878/2002) *The Brothers Karamazov, Farrar, Straus and Giroux.* New York: Farrar, Straus and Giroux.

Hitchens C (2012) *Mortality.* Crow's Nest, NSW: Allen and Unwin.

Kearney M, Radhule B, Vachon M, Harrison R, Balfour M & Mount B (2009) Self-care of physicians caring for patients at the end of life: being connected… a key to my survival. *Journal of the American Medical Association* **301** (11) 1155–1164.

Knill, P, Barba, H & Fuchs M (2003) *Minstrels of Soul: Intermodal expressive arts therapy.* Toronto: EGS Press.

Knill P, Levine E & Levine S (2005) *Principles and Practice of Expressive Arts Therapy.* London: Jessica Kingsley Publishers.

Levine SK (1997) Poiesis: *The language of psychology and the speech of the soul.* London: Jessica Kingsley Publishers.

McNiff S (2004a) *Art Heals.* Boston: Shambhala Publications.

McNiff S (2004b) *Art As Medicine.* Boston: Shambhala Press.

Moon B (2007) *The Role of Metaphor in Art Therapy.* Illinois: Charles Thomas Publishers.

Nouwen H (1972) *The Wounded Healer.* New York: Image Books, Doubleday.

Parkes CM (1996) *Bereavement: Studies of grief in adult life.* Philadelphia: Taylor and Francis.

Rogers C (1961/1995) *On Becoming a Person: A therapist's view of psychotherapy.* New York: Houghton Mifflin.

Roy G (1962) *The Hidden Mountain.* Montreal: McClelland and Stewart.

Simmons S (2012) *I'm Your Man: The life of Leonard Cohen.* Jonathan Cape: London.

Chapter 17:

Spirituality and leadership in palliative care

Richard Hayward

Spirituality and leadership have much in common. Both have been described as ephemeral, difficult to define and impossible to measure. They are also the source of much misunderstanding and debate. What is the difference between leadership and management; how is spirituality different from religion?

It is the aim of this chapter to explore the relationship of spirituality to leadership, particularly in a palliative care setting. To do this, spirituality will be defined in a leadership context using two theoretical models to help understand some of the underlying dilemmas faced by leaders in palliative care.

Although two models will be explored, it is the practical applications of these theories that is important for both the day-to-day delivery of services and the strategic direction that the services should take.

The chapter will also explore some of the inherent difficulties in measuring spirituality. While this has been explored in some detail looking at spirituality from the client's perspective, particularly using quality of life indices, there is much less research on the impact of spirituality on the staff that have to care for a particularly vulnerable group of clients.

Definitions of spirituality

In the first chapter of this book, five elements of spirituality were articulated. These were:

1. meaning
2. value
3. transcendence
4. connecting
5. becoming.

While all of these are important in terms of leadership, meaning, value and connecting, they are particularly worthy of further exploration since they underpin the compassionate nature of leadership in healthcare settings.

What defines what is important to employees can be described as meaning, a concept that is related to values, but is greater. It seeks to explore the rationale for behaviours; the Why question in life. There is seldom a single purpose in life, and the interconnectedness of multiple purposes is underpinned by spirituality. Another vital aspect of this connectedness is the ability to articulate these values to other colleagues as misunderstandings of others' worldview can often lead to poor communication and conflict.

What provides meaning to a group of staff differs depending on their professional background, personal beliefs, and the cultures in which they grew up and now live. All of these elements are equally important and will have a different impact at different stages of people's working life.

Leadership is about influencing context. The environment in which people have to work is absolutely vital to their effectiveness. For many years, academics have discussed the difference between leadership and management (Gilbert, 2005; Storey, 2010; Northouse, 2012), an argument that I always felt to be slightly spurious. Leaders create context; managers maintain it. There will be times when the environment needs developing to support new initiatives and other times when maintaining the status quo is more important because of the turbulent nature of the environment in which care is being delivered.

Much has been made since the turn of the century of the value of a good work–life balance. Indeed, Glassdoor.com, an American social jobs and careers community, publishes an annual survey of the top 25 (American) companies for the best work–life balance. There has been a feeling from both employers and employees that the quality of life of staff at work should be equal to that of the quality of life at home. It is a sad reflection that sometimes people's home life is more turbulent and stressful and that those people go to work to find a little bit of quiet relief. It is surely the aim of a good leader to ensure that as far as practicable, employees have meaningfulness in and value the time they spend at work as much as they do their time at home with family and loved ones.

Reflection points

Do you know what is valuable in your life? Have you ever stopped to consider what is most important to you? Make a list of the five most important values and then rank them in order of importance.

Ask the question –'Is this value mine, or is it inherited from my culture, my family, or a religious faith?' If it is inherited, does it still hold true?

A commonly held value is that friends and family are important. If this is true, then ask yourself the question 'When did I last see my friends?' You will often hear it said that people mean to get in touch, but work gets in the way and suddenly six months has passed with only a Christmas card...

Is this a true value, or an aspiration?

One of the reasons for this tension is often that there is a conflict between an individual's and an organisation's values, and the values that employees consider necessary for a successful organisation (Barrett, 2003). What your personal value system is will have a profound effect on all aspects of your life and is something worthy of deeper consideration.

There are two definitions of spirituality that resonate with leadership function.

'The majority [of those questioned] defined spirituality as a search for meaning, reflection, inner connectedness, creativity, transformation, sacredness, and energy.' (Dent *et al*, 2005, p.633).

'Spirituality is a state or experience that can provide individuals with direction or meaning, or provide feelings of understanding, support, inner wholeness or connectedness. Connectedness can be to themselves, other people, nature, the universe, God, or some other supernatural power.' (Rayment & Smith, 2010, p.59)

The critical aspects of both of these definitions for leaders in palliative care are the ideas of interconnectedness and providing meaning to the work that is undertaken.

The Global Fitness Framework and palliative care

One way of exploring the leadership function in palliative care is to look at the Global Fitness Framework model developed by Smith and Rayment (2007). This is a three-dimensional representation of an approach to leadership that tries to ensure fundamental aspects are not overlooked. The 'Organic level' in **Figure 17.1: Global Fitness Framework** relates to whether an individual, group, or society is being considered, 'Holistic depth' considers physical, mental and spiritual aspects, and the 'Fitness plane' examines strength, stamina and suppleness. Thus, each of the three aspects has three elements, giving a total of 27 individual cells.

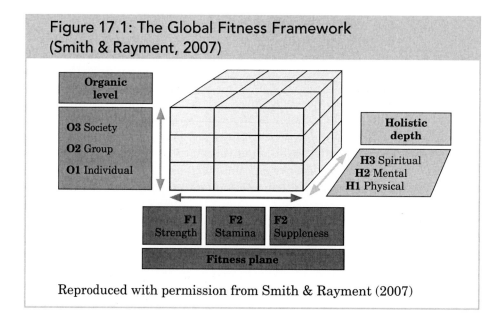

Figure 17.1: The Global Fitness Framework (Smith & Rayment, 2007)

Reproduced with permission from Smith & Rayment (2007)

According to this model, there are three elements that make up an individual's, an organisation's and society's infrastructure. These are physical, mental and spiritual constructs.

Physical dimension

The physical aspects are the material trappings that make up our world – for an individual it might be our clothes, our car and our house. It looks at our health and ability to function in the multifaceted environments where we live our daily lives. For organisations, it is the estate, financial reserves, equipment and buildings that enable them to perform the business that they are engaged with. For society, it is the infrastructure of transport, health care, justice, and financial rules and regulations that keep us from anarchy.

Mental dimension

The mental aspect of the Global Fitness Framework considers how decisions are made. For individuals, this might be conscious or unconscious, deliberate or unconsidered. The route which we take to work is often unconscious until there is a traffic jam. It is also important to remember that no action is still a decision. This again may be unconscious, but it is still a decision nonetheless.

Mental suppleness explores our capacity to examine issues from different perspectives. This is closely linked into our worldview and the values that we espouse. If we always provide the same solution to a problem, then we shouldn't be surprised if we get the same results. It is important, sometimes, to reconsider our approach to familiar problems and acknowledge that other members of the team could have a significant contribution to make. It is also vital that these members of the team are given permission to be innovative. Too often the culture is so risk averse that failure is not permitted so risk avoidance is the dominant leadership style. Risk needs to be managed, not avoided, and potential harmful consequences minimised. For innovation and change to be successful, there must be the risk of failure.

Society's decision-making is often based on policy, culture and tradition. The future direction that society takes will be based on the political will of the ruling coalition. This often involves compromise, negotiating and bargaining. This could equally well be applied to organisations and individuals – the classic win-win scenario.

An important question to ask when looking at the decision-making process is where we want to be in one year, two years or five years' time. Using the Global Fitness Framework ensures that fundamental aspects are not overlooked.

Spiritual dimension

The spiritual aspect of the Global Fitness Framework is the least understood, but possibly most important aspect of the model.

The idea of interconnectedness is very important in spirituality. Ultimately, organisations and society are made up of individuals and it is their actions which determine the spiritual nature that makes up both groups and the wider environment. One of the difficulties in assessing spirituality is the discomfort we have in expressing the ideas and the language used to explore these complex and sometimes contentious ideas.

Spiritual fitness of an individual considers the clarity of their worldview and belief system and the ability to withstand questioning from those who have different worldviews. It is important however that leaders are not rigid, but are prepared to accept others' points of view.

Spiritual suppleness explores the ability to listen to others, accept that they have a valid viewpoint and on occasion to adopt aspects of their viewpoint as being more applicable than their own. While knowledge of the situation and environment is important, sometimes our cultural and personal circumstances influence this worldview, and therefore our interactions with others.

Spiritual strength identifies the clarity, depth and breadth of conviction and the ability to resist an attack from outside. This is also linked to the values, as discussed earlier.

For leaders in a palliative care setting, it is important to consider all aspects of the physical, mental, and spiritual dimensions, and the interaction and connectedness between them as ignoring any one of them leads to less effective leadership.

While it is easy to assess somebody's physical stamina, for example, measuring societies' spiritual suppleness is a much more difficult task and therefore one that might be avoided. It might be argued that if an organisation doesn't have a robust occupational health department, then the individual's physical well-being might be overlooked. It is also argued that the role of the occupational health department should also look beyond the physical to the mental and spiritual well-being. Just because someone is physically able does not ensure that they have the mental or spiritual strength that enables them to function appropriately.

Definition of spiritual intelligence

Spiritual intelligence is the ability to behave with wisdom and compassion while maintaining inner and outer peace (equanimity) regardless of the situation. It reflects an increasingly stable connection to something bigger than us that is translated into the world of behaviours, habits and attitudes (Wigglesworth, 2012).

> ## Reflection point
>
> Name some people you admire who you considered to be spiritual leaders. They can be alive or dead, fictional or real, and you don't have to have met them.
>
> List the traits of the spiritual leaders that cause you to admire them.
>
> (Some examples of spiritual leaders and their traits are given in Box 17.1.)

Gardner (1999) has written extensively about different types of intelligence:

'I now conceptualise an intelligence as a bio-psychological potential to process information that can be activated in the cultural setting to solve problems or create products that are of value in a culture.'
(Gardner, 1999, p.33)

Multiple intelligences have been identified, and their importance recognised at different stages of development. As a baby, developing into a toddler, the physical development is one of the most extraordinary journeys that we make. As we go to school, cognitive intelligence and the ability to read and comprehend the world around us becomes more pronounced, although the physical maturing still occurs, particularly in puberty. Emotional intelligence develops, and instead of reacting to our emotions, we begin to recognise how our behaviour impacts on other people. This close relationship between emotional and spiritual intelligence is reflected in the spiritual dimensions of the Global Fitness Framework and according to Wigglesworth (2012) is the capstone of intelligence where our worldview and values become more pronounced.

Box 17.1: Examples of spiritual leaders

Major religious figures: Jesus, Buddha, Mohammed, Moses, Abraham, Mother Teresa, Dalai Lama

Political leaders: Mahatma Gandhi, Nelson Mandela, Martin Luther King

Other: Relatives or friends, neighbours, clients

Common traits of spiritual leaders: Loving and compassionate, humble, honest, wise, courageous, faithful, forgiving, accepting, calm, peaceful, visionary, outstanding teacher, ability to inspire others, persistent, good at developing others.

Figure 17.2: The relationship between multiple intelligences

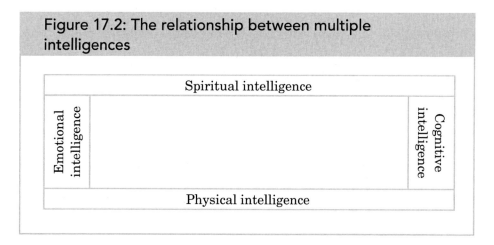

In America, Cindy Wigglesworth has spent many years developing a tool to measure spiritual intelligence. This is a competency-based framework that explores 21 aspects of spiritual intelligence, which is closely intertwined with the development of emotional intelligence. Her definition of spiritual intelligence is: *'The ability to behave with wisdom and compassion, while maintaining inner and outer peace, regardless of the circumstances.'* (Wigglesworth, 2012, p.8)

The competencies identified in the SQ 21 are beyond the scope of this book, but have been explored in some detail. The four quadrants and 21 skills of spiritual intelligence are shown in **Figure 17.3: Spiritual Intelligence Skills**.

Figure 17.3: Spiritual Intelligence (SQ) Skills (Wigglesworth, 2011, p.9)

Higher self/ego self-awareness	Universal awareness
1. Awareness of own worldview 2. Awareness of life purpose (mission) 3. Awareness of values hierarchy 4. Complexity of inner thought 5. Awareness of ego self/higher self	6. Awareness of interconnectedness of a life 7. Awareness of worldviews of others 8. Breadth of time perception 9. Awareness of limitations/power of human perception 10. Awareness of spiritual laws 11. Experience of transcendent oneness
Higher self/ego self-mastering	**Social mastery/spiritual presence**
12. Commitment to spiritual growth 13. Keeping higher self in charge 14. Living your purpose and values 15. Sustaining your faith 16. Seeking guidance from spirit	17. A wise and effective spiritual teacher/mentor 18. A wise and effective change agent 19. Takes compassionate and wise decisions 20. A calming, healing presence 21. Being aligned with the ebb and flow of life

Reproduced with kind permission from Cindy Wigglesworth

It can be seen that there are echoes and interrelationships between spiritual intelligence and emotional intelligence. A degree of self-awareness, realistic confidence in your own abilities and insight as to the effect that you have on others around you are all aspects of both spiritual and emotional intelligence. You cannot have one without the other, but as spiritual intelligence grows so will emotional intelligence and vice versa.

Given the nature of palliative care, it can be seen that leaders with a well-developed sense of emotional and spiritual intelligence will be more effective than those with a less developed one.

Thoughts on leadership by Mark Jackson, chief executive, St Richard's Hospice, Worcester

The ability of an individual to lead and the willingness of others to be led is a deeply spiritual relationship in any environment, but leadership within the context of end of life introduces additional dimensions and complexities. Imminent death will be desperately unwelcome to patients, many of whom will be frightened, hesitant and unsure of something that is completely alien to them. Carers, family members and friends will be suffering the same emotions with the added complication of grief and bereavement. They will all need to be led by doctors, nurses, chaplains and other health and social care professionals so that the patient's dignity is maintained and all physical, social, psychological and spiritual needs are met. That leadership will not be simple because every individual is different and the emotional intelligence of the professionals needs to be very finely tuned to act and react in accordance with the wishes of the individual, as well as their needs, which may not be the same. The professionals will benefit from the multidisciplinary team meetings at which each patient is discussed in depth and decisions on care reached. These require a leadership style that is gentle but firm in order that treatment and care can move on, and so that all know exactly what is required of them in relationship to the patient who will be reassured that they are in the hands of a team that knows exactly what is best for them.

Working in palliative and end of life care is traumatic for all the staff and volunteers concerned. As they are confronted with death and bereavement on a daily basis they themselves are subject to cumulative grief whose impact must be understood by leaders at all levels. They will need to monitor team members and ensure that the direction and guidance given is suited to each individual. Some will need comfort, some cajoling, some firm direction, but all will need to understood how deeply valued they are as individuals. The extraordinary joy of working in a hospice is the realisation that you are sharing your life with people who are all united by one particular mission that drives their compassion. They are hugely professional and in most cases need very little active leadership. It is the role of hospice leaders to provide the framework within which they feel secure to focus 100% upon their patients and their families.

The comments on leadership in palliative care made by Mark Jackson resonate with the theoretical constructs and re-emphasise the importance of the Global Fitness Framework and multiple intelligence in the successful leading of what are complex organisations. It is an interesting thought that Mark emphasises the role of emotional intelligence, compassion and professionalism in leadership in palliative care, and his assertion that the professionals involved need very little active leadership, I would contend, manifests itself in one aspect of leadership: ensuring that they have the environment in which they can work effectively is a hidden tenet of leadership which, if done correctly, enhances care provided.

Geraldine Walters, the executive director of nursing and midwifery at King's College Hospital, London, was appointed as a trustee at Trinity Hospice in June 2011. In an article in *Nursing Management* (January 2013), Walters reflects on the leadership role that trustees have and how multifaceted this role has become:

'Trinity, like many other hospices is a charity and receives one-third of its funding from the NHS; the rest comes from fundraising and Trinity's 21 shops. Together, these must raise in excess of £6 million a year to support the hospice's services.' (Walters, 2013, p.37).

It is interesting to reflect that managing 21 shops could be considered a full-time role for any organisation – the fact that it is there purely to support the care provided by a hospice illustrates the multifaceted leadership role required in palliative care.

Conclusion

In December 2012, the chief nurse for England, Jane Cummings, produced a vision paper on compassion in practice. This emphasised a 6C framework, and elements of which are care, communication, compassion, courage, competence and commitment.

'The values and behaviours covered by the 6Cs are not, in themselves, a new concept. However, putting them together in this way to define a vision is an opportunity to reinforce the enduring values and beliefs that underpin care wherever it takes place. It gives us an easily understood and consistent way to explain our values as professionals and care staff and to hold ourselves to account for the care and services that we provide.

Each of these values and behaviours carry equal weight. Not one of the 6Cs is more important than the other five. The 6Cs naturally focus on putting the person being cared for at the heart of the care they are given.'
(Cummings & Bennett, 2012, p.13).

While the necessity to say this is unfortunate, the underlying vision for palliative care can only be supported by determined leadership which is underpinned by spiritual values. Leaders create context and can only be effective if they are seen to be as passionate about care as those clients and relatives who are receiving that care. Leadership must be exhibited by all levels and professions delivering care. Without it, the contribution of a highly skilled and dedicated workforce may be blunted and the compassion and professionalism expected by the clients and their families could be compromised. A positive culture of care and compassion must be supported by spiritually intelligent leadership.

References

Anon (2012) *Top 25 Companies for Work-Life Balance* [online]. Available at http://www. glassdoor.com/Top-Companies-for-Work-Life-Balance-LST_KQ0,35.htm (accessed April 2013).

Barrett R (2003) Culture and consciousness. Measuring spirituality in the workplace by mapping values. In: R Giacalone & C Jurkiewicz (Eds) *Handbook of Workplace Spirituality and Organizational Performance.* Armonk NY: ME Sharpe.

Cummings J & Bennett V (2012) *Compassion in Practice Nursing, Midwifery and Care Staff Our Vision and Strategy* [online]. Available at http://www.commissioningboard.nhs.uk/ files/2012/12/compassion-in-practice.pdf (accessed April 2013).

Dent E, Higgins M & Wharff D (2005) Spirituality and leadership: an empirical review of definitions, distinctions, and embedded assumptions. *The Leadership Quarterly* 16 (5) 625–653.

Gardner H (1999) *Intelligence Reframed: Multiple intelligences for the 21st century.* New York: BasicBooks.

Gilbert P (2005) *Leadership: Being effective and remaining human.* Lyme Regis: Russell House.

Northouse P (2012) *Leadership: Theory and practice* (6th edition). London: Sage.

Smith J & Rayment J (2007) The Global SMP Fitness Framework: a guide for leaders exploring the relevance of spirituality in the workplace. *Management Decision* 45 (2) 217–234.

Rayment J & Smith J (2010) *MisLeadership: Prevalence, causes and consequences* (1st edition). London: Gower.

Storey J (2010) *Leadership in Organizations: Current issues and key trends* (2nd edition). London: Routledge.

Walters G (2013) Quality comes first. *Nursing Management* 19 (9) 37.

Wigglesworth C (2011) *Integral Spiritual Intelligence 2011* [Online]. Available at http://www. deepchange.com/system/docs/10/original/Integral%20Spiritual%20Intelligence%202011. pdf?1311106184. (accessed April 2013).

Wigglesworth C (2012) *SQ21: The 21 Skills of Spiritual Intelligence.* New York: Select Books.

Further reading

DeepChange.com (2013) at www.DeepChange.com gives many resources and a link to the SQ21 assessment tool.

Goleman D, Boyatzis R & McKee A (2004) *Primal Leadership: Learning to lead with emotional intelligence.* Boston: Harvard Business School.

Malloch K & Porter O'Grady T (2009) *The Quantum Leader: Applications for the new world of work* (2nd edition). London: Jones and Bartlett.

Robinson S & Smith J (2013) *Managing the Spirit: Spirituality, values and leadership.* Oxford: Peter Lang Academic Publishers.

Part 7:
Conclusions

Chapter 18:

Between life and death

Peter Gilbert

'Men (sic) fear death as children fear to go into the dark.' (Sir Francis Bacon)

'I am not afraid and would be more than willing to die. But I have an irrepressible desire to live till I can be assured that the world is little better for my having lived in it.' (President Abraham Lincoln)

'The communication of the dead is tongued with fire beyond the language of the living.' (TS Eliot in Little Gidding, *The Four Quartets*)

'In so many ways I am not "me" anymore.' (The late Rev Philip Wetherell, 2011, p.17)

'...Love is not changed by Death, And nothing is lost, and all in the end is harvest.' (Edith Sitwell, *Eurydice*)

Late one evening a hospital chaplain was called by a ward sister in the acute hospital he served. The sister had a good appreciation of people's spiritual needs when they reached a life crisis, and the chaplain very much trusted her judgment. When he arrived this sister talked to him about a patient facing likely death in a few days. In his notes, the box for 'Religion' had a cross in it, not a tick, but recently the ward staff, who were good listeners, had picked up intimations that the patient wished to discuss issues around the meaning of life and death with the imminent final journey he faced. 'I know these situations are tricky, when there is no designated religious or spiritual belief set out in the notes', said the sister to the chaplain. With this complex task the chaplain went and sat by the patient's bed and, having introduced himself, listened carefully. Two days later the man died, and his son drew the chaplain to one side, and said: 'I'd like to thank you and the staff here. My father lost his faith some time ago due to difficult life experiences, but I was concerned that he was missing that sense of purpose at this time, and I am grateful to you for listening so well, that he took the decision himself to come back onto the path of our faith. He died with a great sense of peace.'

The Department of Health (2008) *End of Life Care Strategy* states that: '*As a society we do not talk openly about death and dying*' (para 1.4). One of the obvious problems with this is that we ourselves may not be open to what we want in terms of care and our route 'across the river'. Because we usually come to life decisions through using our family and friends as sounding boards, those closest to us may not have any idea what our wishes would be; and the same would go for professional carers such as our general practitioner. All this is even more complex in the care of children, as set out in **Chapter 6: Birmingham Children's Hospital: Paediatric end of life care and the bereavement care pathway**, and values-based practice assists professionals in thinking through aspects of good care with those they serve. As the Department of Health guidance puts it, services need '*to ensure that all those approaching the end of life have access to physical, psychological, social and spiritual care*' (para 1.34).

We see clearly from the contributions in this book how human beings are meaning-seeking creatures. Dick Beath's story (**Box 18.1: A journey home**) demonstrates how the search for meaning takes many twists and turns throughout our lives and our relationship with our family and close friends as they too try to work out what life is all about.

Box 18.1: A journey home by Dick Beath

I joined the Army because I thought it might be an answer to my life, giving me structure, position, status and respect. After nine months in the ranks I went to Sandhurst and was commissioned into the Light Infantry as an officer. Within months I was a platoon commander in a combat zone. I called upon God (who I was unsure existed at all) for the first time after we got ambushed and a soldier was shot in the back. Remarkably things went a lot better the next day, with us developing a new way of safe patrolling, which was eventually taken on by the whole British Army a year later. I still felt that God was miles away.

After two more tours I found myself at university and went to some Christian meetings. I really felt that I did not know who I was nor where I was going in life. I also knew very little about keeping successful relationships. In my logic it was pointless going through life, coming to its end and meeting God and yet not being sure about whether one had lived

(continues)

Box 18.1: A journey home by Dick Beath (continued)

correctly or not. In this frame of mind, one evening in a quiet Bible study meeting, I was suddenly aware of being flooded with peace and an intense sense that God loved me deep down and had for some reason accepted me. I could speak to Him as though He was sitting next to me. I later sat on my bed truly amazed at the experience and just thanked God for what He had done.

My stutter, with me from childhood, went immediately and a deep peace remained with me. I knew now that I would have to live my life differently as I was now on God's map and wanted to ensure everything I did was related to who He was and what He had done. I had a strong sense of being rescued and found, and that this was to do with my faith in Jesus Christ.

My faith journey continued and I eventually found myself being medically discharged from the Army. I felt I should stay with my elderly and alone father and not worry about money. He had been married three times and my mother had left him when I was 18. He had an accident in the Second World War and had some mental problems. He was seen as difficult and I had hardly had any kind of relationship with him in the past. What I learnt was a deeply practical form of God's love towards him. I found that as long as I treated him with respect and put myself alongside and listened to him, all was well. We actually started to have fun together, which was a little bit of a miracle as he suffered from depression and was used to just sitting around and not doing very much. I also used the time to do up the house, which had not been touched for 60 years.

Eventually my father developed prostate and secondary bone cancer and he needed close care – it was diagnosed late and was therefore terminal – which I was able to provide. During this period it dawned on him that he was dying. When he was within two weeks of his death, one evening he asked me seriously what would happen to him when he died. Almost reluctantly and in a very tired state I knew I needed to treat this very seriously. I went through some of the key Christian scriptures and prayed with him to receive Jesus Christ as his Lord. I did not really know what would happen next or even that what I had done was real or not. A day or so later my father asked me for the first time, how I was. And later said

(continues)

> ### Box 18.1: A journey home by Dick Beath (continued)
>
> he felt like a new person, which was all the more extraordinary as he was by this point taking 100 milligrams of morphine regularly throughout the day for the pain and could not move without help. A few days later we transferred him to the Dorothy House hospice for two days only, while I had to accompany a friend on a court case in which they were a witness. On returning, he died later that evening. God had rescued him in the nick of time. All his life he had seen God as distant, just like his Victorian father, but now God had made himself known to him, personally to take him home.

Some people, perhaps not many, tread a straight and simple path, but for most it is complex with many twists and turns, choices of route and blind alleys, as Michael Ondaatje describes in *The English Patient* (1992):

'We die containing a richness of lovers and tribes, tastes we have swallowed, bodies we have plunged into and swum up as if rivers of wisdom, characters we have climbed into as if trees, fears we have hidden in as if caves. I wish for all this to be marked on my body when I am dead. I believe in such cartography – to be marked by nature, not just to label ourselves on a map like the names of rich men and women on buildings. We are communal histories, communal books ... All I desire is to walk upon such earth that has no maps.' (Ondaatje, 1992, p.261)

Where and how people die is of vital importance not only to them but to those they leave behind. As the Department of Health strategy points out, the demographics of death in relation to age profile, cause of death and place of death have changed radically over the course of the past century. Around 1900 the majority of people died in their own homes, many succumbing to virulent infectious diseases, and the incidence of death in childhood and adolescence was very much higher than it is today. Nowadays, about half a million people die in England each year, and almost two-thirds of these are aged over 75. Most people die of chronic illnesses: cancer, heart disease, neurological conditions, dementia, respiratory disease and strokes. Most people (58%) die in NHS hospitals; whereas most of us wish to die in a homely environment (as per DH, 2008). Hospitals are not where most people would prefer to end their lives. Modern hospitals are increasingly focused on acute medical care and a quick turnaround of inpatients. The staffing levels, training and gradings of care staff are not all appropriate for the care of frail older people, who will needclose attention to all aspects of care for their

Figure 18.1: A sense of something 'other'

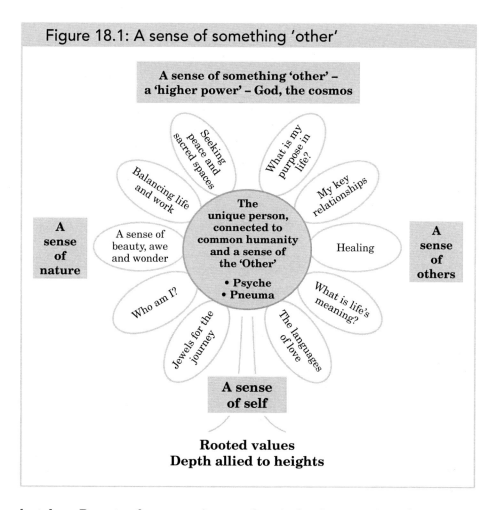

A sense of something 'other' –
a 'higher power' – God, the cosmos

Seeking peace and sacred spaces

What is my purpose in life?

Balancing life and work

My key relationships

A sense of nature

A sense of beauty, awe and wonder

The unique person, connected to common humanity and a sense of the 'Other'
• Psyche
• Pneuma

Healing

A sense of others

Who am I?

What is life's meaning?

Jewels for the journey

The languages of love

A sense of self

Rooted values
Depth allied to heights

last days. Reports of poor care in acute hospitals often mentions the shocking details around the denial of water, and people being left in soiled bedclothes. As Cambridge University researcher Guy Brown said in a forward thinking article: *'Death has been banished to hospitals, the worst possible place to end life'*, and again *'Hospices ought to be as ubiquitous and well-funded as maternity hospitals. The ageing should be able to choose how they die'* (Brown, 2007, p.6).

Most people wish to remain in a familiar setting with familiar faces for as long as possible. This may well be in their own home but may also be in the nursing home or care home that they have provided for themselves in their last years. I recall, as a senior manager in Staffordshire, some years ago, talking with a woman in one of our council residential homes, who was dying of cancer. She did not wish to move, because she had lived there for several years and saw it not as a home but as 'her' 'Home'. The manager of the care home, backed by support from the GP and Macmillan nurses, was able to ensure that she did remain where she felt at home with the best care available to her. She died pain-free and peacefully in her own bed. Human beings need to feel an element of control and choice in their lives, and in the manner of their death, for dignity to be maintained. In this respect advance care planning (Thomas & Lobo, 2011) is of increasing importance.

Recent scandals in hospitals and care homes have led to a reiteration of the basic values for care. In December 2012 the chief nursing officer for the Department of Health in England, Jane Cummings, stressed that there should be 6Cs for excellence in nursing: care, compassion, competence, communication, courage and commitment (Cummings & Bennett, 2012), and clearly these six Cs must be essential for all of the caring professions. Of course it would be naïve to think that this is in any way easy. Time pressures are a major factor, and also staff are often nervous about moving over the boundary lines in care. **Figure 18.2** looks at the 'Languages of love' and suggests that they really are languages in a broad sense. Just as, when we go abroad, we may find it difficult even to say 'good morning' in the language of the country we are staying in, each of these six languages will contain different messages for each individual. For example, touch may be very important for somebody who is slipping away from life and needs to feel someone at the end of their rope, holding that line of strength for them as they move on, but in other cases touch may be seen to be invasive. 'Words' can be very affirming, but many people find affirmation difficult to accept because of their innate lack of self-confidence. We need to work out carefully what language people speak and what will help. Alison Wooding, in **Chapter 13: A formal carer's story: a reflective account from a spiritual care team volunteer** talks about some of the issues she has experienced as a professional carer (see also Cassidy, 1988).

As a society we should be proud of the medical advances made in recent years. One of the downsides, however, is that, following intervention, someone may live on for a number of years in a state where they feel they are living, but in pain, or as only a shadow of their former self. Tony Nicklinson brought much of this into sharp focus when he talked of himself as 'already dead', meaning that his 'real self' had died at the time of his original stroke. And in many ways this is the crucial pinhead that we now balance on, because it is important that, as doctor and philosopher, Professor Robert Winston puts it: *the central tenet of our morality is that human life is sacred'* (Winston, 2006, p.330). It is to be profoundly hoped that we are saying to people at the end of their life, whatever state they are in physically and mentally, that we still value them as human beings, from the point of view of a common humanity and/or as fellow creatures of a divine force. But most of us have a view of ourselves as an autonomous Homo sapiens and/or a created being, with an individuality and a concept of who we essentially are, and what constitutes our sense of dignity and humanity. The late Rev Philip Wetherell, who died from motor neurone disease, wrote movingly of how he felt he had lost his 'real self', and his chapter on assisted dying is worth reading for a balanced view from someone facing the reality of decline and demise (Wetherell, 2011).

Two prominent television personalities, John Humphrys, the BBC Radio 4 newscaster, and John Simpson, the BBC's chief foreign correspondent, have both explored the moral issue about whether we should be allowed to choose how and when we die. Humphrys speaks about the sadness of watching his father lose the will to live and his cries of 'Help! Help!' (see Humphrys, 2009; Humphrys & Jarvis, 2009). John Simpson has everything to look forward to with strong family ties and a successful career which still sees him reporting from troubled spots across the world. He writes that he *'Loathes the idea that Rafe, my grandchildren, my wife, my close relatives and friends, should remember me as a drooling ancient who does not even know who they are'* (Simpson, 2012). Simpson upholds the right to life, but he thinks that a *'decent society should also allow people to be in charge of their lives'* (Simpson, 2012). A bill will be going to the House of Lords in 2013 on this issue. There are always the concerns about the slippery slope (see **Chapters 1** and **2**), but perhaps a change in the law to allow assisted dying would actually put UK society on its mettle to do its very best to promote palliative care in settings other than in hospitals.

Figure 18.2: Languages of love

Six languages of love

LANGUAGE:

'The method of human communication, either spoken or written, consisting of the use of words in an agreed way'

It is said that there are six languages of love:

TIME

WORDS

PRESENCE

TOUCH

GIFTS

ACTS OF SERVICE

But language is sometimes difficult, country to country, or even the use and understanding of language from region to region within the same country.

What is precious, valuable, acceptable, difficult to appreciate or accept in one language might be quite different in another.

Many people find it hard to accept verbal compliments, but many find a small gift an affirmation which they can accept without problems.

Some professions may use different languages eg. nurses, especially in physical care, may be using a great deal of touch. Social workers and psychiatrists may be using words more often. Care workers, acts of service.

How do we understand and use these different languages?

Recent research by Bangor University considered an extensive international literature review and found that two-thirds of people studied across these surveys wish to see assisted dying as an option in their country. Issues such as unbearable suffering, the loss of dignity and the wish to have some control over one's life, were among the issues mentioned (Hendry *et al*, 2013). I have found a number of people with religious faith also wishing to, as one put it, 'Go to my God with dignity'. Another quoted the novelist Graham Greene: *'Beware of formulas. If there's a God, he's not a God of formulas'* (Greene, 1958/2001, p.192).

As all the major government documents make clear, a person's spiritual needs at end of life are a crucial dimension of their innate self and of the care they and their carers should receive (see Box 1.2, Chapter 1). As we have seen throughout this book, a person's spirituality may be made up of a number of diverse factors, and their belief systems may ebb and flow when they come to the ultimate life challenge. In a moving novel about the death of a revered educationalist, *Tuesdays with Morrie*, Mitch Albom (Albom, 2007) has his main character say: *'Ted, this disease is knocking at my spirit. But it will not get my spirit. It'll get my body. It will **not** get my spirit'* (p.163).

The picture of belief systems in the UK is now very complex, especially in urban areas (see Woodhead & Catto, 2012; Parkes & Gilbert, 2010; Day, 2011). Although the 2011 census has seen a fall from 73% to 59% of those identifying themselves as Christian, while the 'no religion' rose from 15% to 25%, some Christian churches are growing strongly, and the ethnic diversity of many congregations has changed dramatically. Many other faith communities are flourishing, but even this is not the whole picture. Research by the Theos thinktank (Spencer & Weldin, 2012) shows that a significant percentage of people who had no affiliation to a faith still believe in a soul and a god or higher power, often with the belief in an afterlife. Theos concluded that only nine per cent of British people were consistently non-religious and suggested that 21st century Britain is marked by religious and spiritual pluralism rather than secularism.

People often like some form of connection with a culture of faith on reaching the milestones of life. Commentator Simon Jenkins remarked recently that in many parts of urban Britain the clergy are the ones who remain as the 'public face' of society, a local leader and someone that people turn to when things go wrong (Jenkins, 2012). John Canter describes his sister's funeral after her untimely death of cancer at the age of 61. Although his sister, Rosemary, was an atheist, the funeral that she had described to him that she desired was shot through with religious themes, words and music, so much that the article is entitled: *'My sister wanted a godless funeral. But still invited God'* (Canter, 2011) and he concludes the article by stating: *'We are not a religiously observant nation – except when it really counts'*.

One of Judaism's great historical figures, Moses Maimonides (1138–1204) wrote in his *Guide for the Perplexed: 'Every fool imagines that existence is for his sake ... but if man examines the universe and understands it, he knows how small a part of it he is'* (Winston, 2006, p.350), and we know from the amazing work of the Hadron Collider at Cern, that we probably still only grasp about four per cent of what makes up the universe. Much is still a mystery. As we face the cosmic maze between life and death it might be worth thinking on the wisdom of theologian Karl Rahner: *'And even if this term (God) were ever to be forgotten even then, in the decisive moments of our lives, we should still be constantly encompassed by this nameless mystery of our existence ... Even supposing that those realities which we call religion ... were totally to disappear ... The transcendality inherent in human life is such that we would still reach out towards that mystery that lies outside our control'* (Quoted in Gilbert, 2011).

References

Albom M (2007) *Tuesdays With Morrie: An old man, a young man, and life's greatest lesson.* London: Spear.

Brown G (2007) No way to go. *The Guardian*, 14th November, 2007, p.6.

Canter J (2011) My sister wanted a godless funeral, but still invited God. *The Guardian*, 10th May 2011, p28.

Cassidy S (1988) *Sharing the Darkness: The spirituality of caring.* London: Darton, Longman and Todd.

Cummings J & Bennett V (2012) *Compassion in Practice: Nursing, midwifery and care staff: our vision and strategy.* London: DH.

Day A (2011) *Belief and Social Identity in the Modern World.* Oxford: Oxford University Press.

Department of Health (2008) *End of Life Care Strategy: Promoting high quality care for adults at the end of their life.* London: DH.

Gilbert P (2011) From the cradle – to beyond the grave? *Quality in Ageing and Older Adults* **12** (3).

Greene G (1958/2001) *Our Man in Havana.* London: Vintage.

Hendry M, Pasterfield D, Lewis R, Carter B, Hodgson D & Wilkinson C (2013) Why do we want the right to die?: a systematic review of the international literature on the views of patients, carers and the public on assisted dying. *Palliative Medicine* **27** (1) 13–26.

Humphrys J (2009) My father deserved a better way to die. *The Observer*, 29th March 2009, p35.

Humphrys J & Jarvis S (2009) *The Welcome Visitor.* London: Hodder and Stoughton.

Jenkins S (2012) An atheist's prayer for our churches that keep our soul. *The Guardian*, 21st December 2012, p34.

Parkes M & Gilbert P (2010) God and gurdwaras: the spiritual care programme at the Birmingham and Solihull Mental Health Foundation NHS Trust. *Mental Health, Religion and Culture* **3** (6) 569–583.

Ondaatje M (1992) *The English Patient.* London: Picador.

Simpson J (2012) Remember me this way son. *The Sunday Times,* 1st July 2012, p5.

Spencer N & Weldin H (2012) *Post-religious Britain?: The faith of the faithless.* London: Theos.

Thomas K & Lobo B (Eds) (2011) *Advance Care Planning in End of Life Care.* Oxford: Oxford University Press.

Winston R (2006) *The Story of God.* London: Bantam Books.

Wetherell P (2011) *When You are Dying: A personal exploration of life, suffering and belief.* Malton: Gilead Books.

Woodhead L & Catto R (Ed) (2012) *Religion and Change in Modern Britain.* London: Routledge.

Epilogue

Neil Deuchar

I met Peter Gilbert 10 years ago when I was a medical director in a mental health trust. In a world where the adjective 'clinical' is used in the vernacular to denote an action devoid of emotion, I was struggling to see how to inject compassion and empathy into health care without being excommunicated for heresy.

Peter introduced me to the concept of spirituality and, to cut a long story short, this provided a construct and vocabulary with which I could talk about difficult things without fellow board directors running for the hills. I subsequently became one of a number of lucky people with whom Peter worked in his unwavering and tireless pursuit of spirituality as a cornerstone of good health and social care.

I believe Peter's professional and personal contributions to this agenda have got us to a place it would have been difficult to anticipate just 10 years ago.

This book is one of several incalculably important contributions Peter has made to the cause of spirituality, made poignant because while in the final stages of editing it he was himself diagnosed with motor neurone disease. It is axiomatic of Peter's integrity and commitment that he saw this book through to its fruition despite knowing he himself was going to die. The book itself is made that much more special because we know it was edited with love, devotion and the cruellest, yet somehow most fitting, of insights.